THE STRUCTURAL TRANSFORMATION OF EUROPEAN PRIVATE LAW

This book proposes a new analysis of the transformation of Europe through integration, exactly 30 years after the beginning of transformation scholarship. It consists of a reconstruction of the development and present condition of European integration in relation to private ordering.

Looking at the interface between, on the one hand, the EU constitutional order and, on the other hand, private ordering, the book recounts three major structural transformations over the last six decades.

Delving into the private law areas most exposed to the current modernisation wave – consumer law, internal market, lex mercatoria, digitisation, artificial intelligence, data protection, standardised contracts, finance and political economy, and labour – the book critically explores a reconfiguration of Europe's constitutional structures relative to, and that results from, what to some appears to be an almost irresistible rise of private ordering through a transformed hermeneutics (balancing).

This is a magisterial survey of European law, European private law, and comparative law seen through a pathbreaking comparative methodology labelled 'juridical comparative hermeneutics' within civil law systems and across the civil-common law divide, which offers innovative analytical tools that afford a deep understanding of the evolution of the disciplines.

Volume 115 in the Series Modern Studies in European Law

Modern Studies in European Law

Recent titles in this series:

The Internal Market 2.0
Edited by Sacha Garben and Inge Govaere

New Directions in European Private Law
Edited by Mateja Durovic and Takis Tridimas

Standing to Enforce European Union Law before National Courts
Hilde Ellingsen

The Relative Authority of Judicial and Extra-Judicial Review: The EU Courts, the Boards of Appeal and the Ombudsman
Michal Krajewski

Responsive Human Rights: Vulnerability and the ECtHR
Corina Heri

The Architecture of Fundamental Rights in the European Union
Šejla Imamovic

The EU and its Member States' Joint Participation in International Agreements
Edited by Nicolas Levrat, Yuliya Kaspiarovich, Christine Kaddous and Ramses A Wessel

The UN Convention on the Rights of Persons with Disabilities and the European Union: The Impact on Law and Governance
Carmine Conte

EU Criminal Law, Second Edition
Valsamis Mitsilegas

The EU as a Global Digital Actor: Institutionalising Global Data Protection, Trade, and Cybersecurity
Elaine Fahey

Exporting the European Convention on Human Rights
Maria-Louiza Deftou

Judicial Authority in EU Internal Market Law: Implications for the Balance of Competences and Powers
Vilija Velyvyte

The Changing European Union: A Critical View on the Role of Law and the Courts
Edited by Tamara Capeta, Iris Goldner Lang and Tamara Perisin

The Structural Transformation of European Private Law: A Critique of Juridical Hermeneutics
Leone Niglia

For the complete list of titles in this series see www.bloomsbury.com/uk/series/modern-studies-in-european-law/

The Structural Transformation of European Private Law

A Critique of Juridical Hermeneutics

Leone Niglia

•HART•
OXFORD • LONDON • NEW YORK • NEW DELHI • SYDNEY

HART PUBLISHING

Bloomsbury Publishing Plc

Kemp House, Chawley Park, Cumnor Hill, Oxford, OX2 9PH, UK

1385 Broadway, New York, NY 10018, USA

29 Earlsfort Terrace, Dublin 2, Ireland

HART PUBLISHING, the Hart/Stag logo, BLOOMSBURY and the Diana logo are trademarks of Bloomsbury Publishing Plc

First published in Great Britain 2023

A catalogue record for this book is available from the British Library.

A catalogue record for this book is available from the Library of Congress.

Library of Congress Control Number: 2022946314

ISBN: HB: 978-1-50992-525-4
ePDF: 978-1-50992-527-8
ePub: 978-1-50992-526-1

Typeset by Compuscript Ltd, Shannon

PREFACE

This book proposes a new analysis of the transformation of Europe through integration, exactly 30 years after the beginning of transformation scholarship. It consists of a reconstruction of the development and present condition of European integration in relation to private ordering.

Looking at the interface between, on the one hand, the EU constitutional order and, on the other hand, private ordering, the book recounts three major structural transformations over the last six decades.

After considering the earlier configuration of the EU vis-à-vis the Member State orders in terms of constitutional autonomy, a shift is noted from autonomy towards constitutional absorption. The book recounts the absorption of private ordering's determinations, made stateless, into the body of the EU constitutional material and, coterminously, their heteronomous superimposition on state laws; it also proposes a critique of the current 'third structural transformation' through revisiting the public/private divide.

Delving into the private law areas most exposed to the current modernisation wave – consumer law, internal market, *lex mercatoria*, digitisation, artificial intelligence, data protection, standardised contracts, finance and political economy, labour – the book critically explores a reconfiguration of Europe's constitutional structures relative to, and that results from, what to some appears to be an almost irresistible rise of private ordering through a transformed hermeneutics (balancing).

Through a pathbreaking comparative 'methodology' labelled 'comparative juridical hermeneutics' to the study of the European constitutional and private law constellations, the book critically focuses on the dimension of the private ordering, largely overlooked in conventional transformational literature. It is argued that the dimension of private ordering features as a force that increasingly overshadows and eclipses the EU constitutional order as derived from, and as related to, state orders (Europe's composite constitutional constellation), and the nation-state constitutional order as we have known it since the Weimar Republic.

Through the new comparative approach, the book proposes five intertwined, pathbreaking theses. They are: the coming together, under a new constitutional symbiotic paradigm, of European Union law and of European private law to the point that one cannot understand the former without the latter – and vice versa; the inner relationships between European Union law, European private law and transnational law; the 'taking over' (takeover) of constitutional orders, national and EU, by and through the phenomenal rising of private ordering; the 'totalising' of law under the 'new constitutional symbiotic paradigm'; and bringing to light and denouncing the ongoing phenomenon of the endangering of the tenability of the structure of juridical hermeneutics itself as experienced during the past century as part of the European heritage of law and legal thought and as serving an emancipatory purpose. This emancipatory purpose now increasingly becomes less determinative at the hands of private law actors apparently unconcerned with the poverty of the totalising of the law that they are crafting. In defence of juridical hermeneutics as befitting Europe better than the current structural transformation, the book stresses the unrenounceable role of the hermeneutics of autonomy as embodied in constitutional orders over and above any of law's totalising, at once calling for the responsibility of jurists to counter and reverse the law's totalising trajectory.

Contemporaneously, the book shows that any legal order is hermeneutically embedded, and that this must apply also to the EU legal order, despite the dominant positivistic renditions of EU law that ignore the law's underlying hermeneutical forces; that the transformational scholarship of European Union studies needs to be revised profoundly by taking seriously the phenomenon of private ordering; and that comparativism itself needs to overcome its rigid positioning around conventional material and open up to the challenges of looking at the world through the lenses of 'comparative juridical hermeneutics'.

The third in a trilogy of monographs, the book critically recounts the pathways of European private law as defining a new age reaching beyond that of harmonisation (*The Transformation of Contract in Europe*, 2003) and of codification (*The Struggle for European Private Law. A Critique of Codification*, 2015) towards totalising law around private ordering – at the sacrifice of a range of public interest requirements once cherished but today increasingly rendered constitutionally marginal.

The book is also a companion to two monographic trilogies of essays – *European Private Law* (2006–10) and *European Constitutional Law* (2010–16) – given its recounting, comparatively, of a transformation of the private and constitutional fields, and of their interface.

***

ACKNOWLEDGEMENTS

This book is part of a larger research project undertaken by the author under the auspices of, and with the financial support of (in alphabetical order): the British Academy; the Carnegie Trust for the Universities of Scotland; the European Union Jean Monnet Programme (2021 and 2022 awards); the European Union/Universidad Carlos III de Madrid 'Connecting Excellence' Programme, Universidad Carlos III de Madrid, Instituto Bartolomé de las Casas, Madrid, Spain (EU/FP7 Grant Agreement No 600371, COFUND 2014-51509); the Italian Ministry of Education and Research; the Leverhulme Trust; Sapienza University of Rome (2020–2022 research awards); and the University of Michigan Law School. Thanks also to the European University Institute, the Swiss Institute of Comparative Law, Lausanne, the University of Heidelberg, the University of London and the University of Modena e Reggio Emilia libraries; and the University of Florence, Study Centre for the History of Modern Legal Thought. Parts of this book, in preliminary form, were presented at the University of Cambridge, the Heinrich-Heine University Düsseldorf, Harvard University, the European University Institute, the University of Heidelberg, the London School of Economics and Political Science, the University of Michigan, the University of Modena and Reggio Emilia, the University of Queensland, the University of Salerno, Sapienza University of Rome and Utrecht University. I am grateful to the conveners of those events and to the participants for comments. I am also grateful to many colleagues for the exchanges which have contributed to the shaping of this book; to avoid the risk of omissions, I do not name them here. I hope that in reading this book they will find places where they will see my silent tribute to them. Thanks to Hart Publishing for placing their trust in this project, much honoured as I am for this volume to be one more in the prestigious European law book series, alongside *The Struggle for European Private Law. A Critique of Codification*, 2015.

CONTENTS

TABLE OF CASES AND OPINIONS

I. Court of Justice of the European Union

Advocate Generals' Opinions (CJEU) and Opinions (CJEU)

II. Constitutional Courts (France, Germany, Italy)

III. Canadian, English, French, Italian, United Statesian Courts

IV. International Court of Justice

TABLE OF LEGISLATION

EU

France

UK

Instruments

1

Prologue: Constitutional Ordering vis-à-vis Private Ordering: Of Three Structural Transformations in Europe

I. Europe's Constitutional Constellation: Of Structural Transformations

Over the past six decades, the relationship between Europe's once 'new' legal order[1] and private order(s) has been far from fixed.[2] Indeed, the relationship has been changing over time as a result of the evolution of the jurisprudence of the Court of Justice of the European Union (CJEU) in its interaction with the hermeneutical worlds of private law jurisprudence at the state level.[3] It is submitted in this monograph that the European Union's legal order initially took the form of 'constitutional autonomy'.[4] Through this first structural transformation, 'constitutional

[1] Case 26/62 *Van Gend en Loos* [1963] ECR 1 (on 'new legal order'). On the 'new legal order' as constitutional, see the seminal essays by JHH Weiler, 'The Transformation of Europe' (1991) 100 *Yale Law Journal* 2405 (articulating a narrative of transformation) and E Stein, 'The European Coal and Steel Community: The Beginning of Its Judicial Process' (1955) 55 *Columbia Law Review* 985 (articulating a narrative of a 'beginning').

[2] By 'private ordering' in this book is meant a contingent range of juridical hermeneutical constructs as I identify them selectively (see ch 2 below; and chs 4 and 5 below on order-regimes, on a 'constellation of order-regimes'), including analysing them in constitutional terms (see below at the text corresponding at fn 9; and compare 'the idea of an 'autonomous private law' as deriving 'its normative dignity from its commitment to the transpositive *ordo* of the economy' as quoted and as discussed at n 26 below). 'Outside' Europe, see, eg the judgment of the Supreme Court of Canada *Heller v Uber Technologies*, 2020 SCC 16, [257] (Côté J) ('a focus on inequality of power would undermine *private ordering* and commercial certainty' (emphasis added), quoted in J Gardner, 'Being Conscious of Unconscionability in Modern Times: *Heller v Uber Technologies*' (2021) 84 *MLR* 874, 882).

[3] On juridical hermeneutics, see s IV below.

[4] *Caveat lector:* by 'jurisprudence of constitutional autonomy' in this book is meant not the EU order's 'autonomy' as monistic, as in the conventional, heteronomous readings of the EU order as 'constitutional' through the ritual reference to the classical CJEU judgments, including Case 26/62 *Van Gend en Loos* [1963] ECR 1 and Case 6/64 *Costa Enel* 15 July 1964 (see ch 5 below), but as 'plural autonomy' in the sense of the autonomy of the national private law realms (social state) as recognised and as respected constitutionally by the EU constitutional order for a long time and until the recent changes discussed in this book, as they entail the demise of plural autonomy into the one-sidedness of (market orientated) privatistic order-regimes (see ch 5 below). For the argument that 'autonomy' characterises the relationship between the EU legal order and private ordering, see chs 2 and 5 below.

autonomy' designates the peculiar structural ways in which the EU's legal order has been positioning itself vis-à-vis the plural, state-based private order(s): in the sense of the national private law realms (social state) being, constitutionally speaking, 'recognised' and respected by the EU's legal order.

Since the turn of this century, the relationship between the EU's legal order and the national private law realms has been subjected to a second major constitutional mutation. This mutation is labelled in this book as 'constitutional heteronomy', and it consists of a range of EU determinations in major areas of public life held by the CJEU to prevail over those of national private law.

I then argue that this second structural transformation is, in turn, intertwined with a coextensive third transformation: constitutional absorption. 'Constitutional absorption' consists of the making of a totalising constitutional order (a new constitutional symbiotic paradigm) in the strict service of the arbitrary ways of private ordering, in turn made stateless insofar as private ordering is no longer coupled with, nor conveying the values of, the (social) state.[5]

The triad 'jurisprudence of constitutional autonomy' (chapter two), 'jurisprudence of constitutional heteronomy' (chapter three) and 'jurisprudence of constitutional absorption' (chapter four) makes the European constitutional constellation's mutation over time really intelligible.[6]

***

'Autonomy' is also conventionally referred to in relation to the interface EU law/international law: see, eg Weiler, 'Transformation' (n 1). See also, notably, the Grand Chamber judgment of 3 September 2008, Joined Cases C-402/05 P and Case C-415/05 P *Yassin Abdullah Kadi and Al Barakaat International Foundation v Council of the European Union and Commission of the European Communities* [2008] ECR I-06351, ECLI:EU:C:2008:461. On autonomy according to the CJEU, see also Case 284/16 *Achmea* ECLI:EU:C:2018:158; CJEU Opinion 2/13, EU Accession to ECHR, ECLI:EU:C:2014:2454, 176 (18 December 2014); according to the BVerfG, see BVerfG 89/155 *Maastricht* and BVerfG2 BvE 2/08 *Lisbon*, 30 June 2009; according to the Italian Corte Costituzionale, see It Corte Costituzionale *Frontini* 183/1973; It Corte Costituzionale *Granital* 170/1984.

U Haltern, 'Revolutions, Real Contradictions, and the Method of Resolving Them: The Relationship between the Court of Justice of the European Union and the German Federal Constitutional Court' (2021) 19 *International Journal of Constitutional Law* 208 makes the point at 210, with regard to the Court's holding that Art 267 of the Treaty on the Functioning of the European Union (TFEU) pursues the objective of 'securing uniform interpretation of EU law … thereby serving to ensure its consistency, its full effect and its autonomy' (see Opinion 2/13 above), that: 'While this is an exaggeration – no legal order spread across such a diversity of history, tradition, culture, politics, and economy can be the same everywhere – even relative sameness affords a much firmer legal structure than international law', also referring to S Weatherill, *Law and Values in the European Union* (Oxford, Oxford University Press, 2016). I agree with the comment on the 'much firmness' of the extant EU legal order relative to international law; however, I reconstruct it under the prism of the book's thesis that reads that order (and its 'autonomy') in transformational terms, under the new constitutional symbiotic paradigm that this book recounts, and as contingent on the phenomenon of the transformation of orders that I redescribe it in this book (on 'description', see A Orford, 'In Praise of Description' (2012) 25 *Leiden Journal of International Law* 609) as 'firmly' grounded in jurisprudence.

[5] 'Arbitrary' in the sense of its technicality, through prioritising efficiency whilst excluding non-market normative considerations: see the rest of the book.

[6] See ch 4 (methodology of analysing connected hermeneutical materials – EU law and transnational law).

This three-step structural transformation of Europe's constitutional constellation in relation to private ordering – from autonomy, through the modes of heteronomy and absorption, to total ordering – has been neglected in the literature, in stark contrast to its counterpart, which consists of the 'public-constitutional' dimensions of the story. It is a story yet to be told – of the constitutional law of market integration as it relates to, and is affected by, the major kind of power that is exercised in the form of private ordering through contract, property and finance. And it matters to the construction of the conglomerate of the constitutional orders of the Union and of its constituent states no less than their 'public-constitutional' dimensions that are the object of conventional transformation studies.[7]

The most recent structural transformation of the last two decades or so that this book is bringing to the attention of the reader is, in turn, part of the wider historical process of how private forces can increasingly take control of polities, at the sacrifice of key civic and social liberties. This book contributes to a newer perspective: exploring the terms of a juridical hermeneutics orchestrated by the jurists who have made that 'taking control' legally, and not only politically and economically, possible.[8]

Indeed, it is submitted that today the conditions are being created for the private order to increasingly 'take over' key components of the EU constitutional order and transform the latter into an unrecognisable constitutional thing – a quasi-constitutional order of privatistic relations where exploitation and domination can take place unchecked.[9] It is exactly the dimension of private ordering,

[7] For a genealogy of this argument, see L Niglia, 'The New Transformation of Europe. Arcana Imperii' (2020) 68 *American Journal of Comparative Law* 151. The public–private divide is a contingent way to organise institutions and processes, but possesses no dogmatic impermeability: see L Niglia, *Public v Private* (2022) (on public–private divide); C Joerges, 'A New Type of Conflicts of Law as the Legal Paradigm of the Postnational Constellation' in C Joerges and J Falke (eds), *Karl Polanyi, Globalisation and the Potential of Law in Transnational Markets* (Oxford, Hart Publishing, 2011) 465 et seq. On the literature on the 'public side' of the EU's transformations over the past decades, see the following chapters.

[8] Niglia, 'The New Transformation of Europe' (n 7). The private realms and related interests advantaged as a result include, considering the case studies referred to and commented upon in the remainder of the book (see chs 3 and 4 below): entrepreneurs organising global chains and as such interested in marketing strategies consisting of price/quality combinations that deviate from state law (mandatory or default standards); online operators interested in collecting and using for their purposes data of clients or companies interested in offering services under standardised terms written so as to allocate to clients as many of the contractual risks as possible; businesses interested in lowering wages of workers to the level below that of the host state to which they decide to move their business; and private providers of artificial intelligence manipulating private data for their own benefit or participating in administrative decision-making processes by replacing public interest determinations. As the law undertakes a structural transformation towards accommodating these interests, these private actors will end up seeing their strategies given legal recognition (juridified).

[9] See ch 4 below: in the problem situations considered in this book, 'private ordering' takes on the guise of being 'constitutional' (see ch 5 on private ordering in the sense of 'constitutionalisation'), yet it results at most in being 'quasi-constitutional', since, as I argue in ch 4, private ordering, once made stateless, is lacking, and it is even consciously constructed under the pretence that it can sustain itself without, the constitutionality requirements of both state private law and of European private law (not every constitutionalisation equals or implies constitutionality: see L Niglia, *The Struggle for European*

overlooked in conventional transformational literature, that is becoming the force that overshadows, and works towards annihilating, at once both the EU constitutional order as derived from, and as related to, state constitutional orders and the state constitutional order itself as we have known it since the Weimar Republic.[10]

II. Of European Private Law as European Union Law

We owe much to scholarly efforts to decipher the role and structure of the private law field across states and societies from an interdisciplinary perspective. I refer to writings that have given due attention to the private order in its structural relationship with the historiography and the present condition of, inter alia, the disciplines of comparative law, international law, legal history, philosophy of law and sociology of law.[11] What has attracted less attention and calls for further analysis is the

Private Law. A Critique of Codification (Oxford, Hart Publishing, 2015); L Niglia, 'Of Constitutionality and Private Consumer Law in Europe' (2012) 4 *Journal of European Consumer and Market Law* 223; E Christodoulis, *The Redress of Law: Globalisation, Constitutionalism and Market Capture* (Cambridge, Cambridge University Press, 2021): it is in the process of becoming an artificial (yet powerful) vocabulary if only because it excludes non-market normative considerations altogether, whilst transforming key normative considerations (eg fundamental human rights) in requirements subjected to procedural criteria (see chs 4 and 5) or to criteria that make it constitutionally impossible for them to be acted upon (as in the CJEU judgment C-438/05 *International Transport Workers' Federation and Finnish Seamen's Union v Viking Line ABP and OÜ Viking Line EestiCase* ECLI:EU:C:2007:772, where the right to strike is elevated to the rank of an EU fundamental right yet is made meaningless as a result of a strict interpretation of the proportionality principle that confines it to extreme situations, as opposed to its normal operation under standard national constitutional laws). For the analysis of further judgments see ch 4, where there is also discussion of quasi-constitutionality in relation to exploitation and domination. On established beliefs on 'private ordering' as self-standing, note the paradigmatic statement of one judge in the recent Supreme Court of Canada judgment cited at n 1 above. On 'taking over' as 'totalising' law, see ch 5 below.

[10] See recently PE Gordon and J McCormick (eds), *Weimar Thought: A Contested Legacy* (Princeton, Princeton University Press, 2013); for a reading of the Weimar legacy in relation to integration, see A Menendez ELJ Hermann Heller NOW ELJ 21 2015 285–294 (and special issue).

[11] Enumerated not in order of importance, and only to refer to some of the relevant works, and respectively: as to comparative law see, eg D Kennedy, *The Rise and Fall of Classical Legal Thought* (1998); U Mattei, 'Why the Wind Changed: Intellectual Leadership in Western Law' (1994) 42 *American Journal of Comparative Law* 195; PG Monateri, *Dominus Mundi. Political Sublime and the World Order* (Oxford, Hart Publishing, 2018); R Sacco, *Il Contratto*; R Sacco, 'Legal Formants' (1991) 39 *American Journal of Comparative Law* 1; L Niglia, *The Transformation of Contract in Europe* (The Hague, Kluwer Law International, 2003); Niglia, *The Struggle for European Private Law* (n 9); Niglia, 'The New Transformation of Europe' (n 7). As to international law (and legal history), see M Koskenniemi, 'Sovereignty, Property and Empire: Early Modern English Contexts' (2017) 18 *Theoretical Inquiries in Law* 355; as to legal history, see P Grossi, *Assolutismo Giuridico e Diritto Privato* (Milan, Giuffrè, 1998); P Grossi, *Universalismo e particolarismo nel diritto* (Naples, Editoriale Scientifica, 2011); D Kennedy, 'Three Globalizations of Law and Legal Thought: 1850–2000' in DM Trubek and A Santos (eds), *The New Law and Economic Development: A Critical Appraisal* (Cambridge, Cambridge University Press, 2006) 19; as to European law, see C Joerges, 'The Europeanization of Private Law as a Rationalization Process and as a Contest of Disciplines: An Analysis of the Directive on Unfair Terms in Consumer Contracts' (1995) 3 *European Review of Private Law* 175; F Snyder, 'The Effectiveness of European Community Law: Institutions, Processes, Tools and Techniques' (1993) 56 *MLR* 19; as to sociology of law, see Joerges (ibid) (private law); S Sciarra, *L'Europa e il Lavoro. Solidarieta' e Conflitto in Tempi di Crisi*

role and place of the private law order in relation to EU law, and vice versa, in the transformational terms that this book chooses to explore.[12] Namely, there is indeed an established field named 'European private law', but its orthodox ways are either a positivistic version of EU law and private law,[13] chiefly interested in black letter law analyses, or an entirely comparativist enterprise typically no less positivistic.[14]

(Rome, Laterza, 2013) (labour law); as to philosophy of law, see A Supiot, *Homo Juridicus. Essai sur la Fonction Anthropologique du Droit* (Paris, Editions du Seuil, 2005); A Supiot, 'The Public–Private Relations in the Context of Today's Refeudalization' (2013) 11 *International Journal of Constitutional Law* 129.

[12] In the sense that studies on private law interested in the dynamics of law and transformation draw on the conventional transformation story of the 'public' dimension to integration, at times speculating about the transformation of European private law as a special case relative to the 'public' story that really matters (see, eg H Micklitz, 'The Visible Hand of European Regulatory Private Law' (2009) 28 *Yearbook of European Law* 3): the EU–Member States axis as all that matters for an analysis of the development of integration is not considered in relation to the parameter of private ordering as associated with the state and then as post-state, as in the reading that this book proposes. For an earlier critique, see L Niglia, 'Beyond Enchantment: The Possibility of a New European Private Law (Instalment Two)' (2009) 28 *Yearbook of European Law* 60 (on private law and federalism); L Niglia, 'The Europeanisation of Private Law through Adjudication' (on file with author, 1995: see Niglia 2001); D Caruso, 'The Missing View of the Cathedral: The Private Law Paradigm of European Legal Integration' (1997) 3 *European Law Journal* 3; Joerges, 'The Europeanization of Private Law (n 9). For a critique of the public–private divide, see n 5 above. The method adopted in this book is interdisciplinary and about looking at the dynamics of transformation, that is, it is structural rather than functional-instrumental. On interdisciplinarity and multidisciplinarity in private law, see the remainder of the book; see also M Auer, *Zum Erkenntnissziel Der Rechtstheorie* (Baden-Baden, Nomos, 2018).); D Kennedy, 'Thoughts on Coherence, Social Values and National Tradition in Private Law' in M Hesselink (ed), *The Politics of a European Civil Code* (The Hague, Kluwer Law International, 2006); Niglia, *The Struggle for European Private Law* (n 9). In some writings there is increasing awareness of the key role of private law in EU law through the CJEU case law on the four freedoms (on contract as present in most disputes in the context of which references pertaining to the four freedoms are made to the CJEU, see G Davies, 'Freedom of Contract and the Horizontal Effect of Free Movement Law' in D Leczykiewicz and S Weatherill (eds), *The Involvement of EU Law in Private Law Relationships* (Oxford, Hart Publishing, 2013) 53), yet it has been noticed that 'much research' needs to be done (see, commenting on and agreeing with, Davies, ibid; H Micklitz, 'Thoughts on Martijn W Hesselink's, Justifying Contract in Europe, Political Philosophies of European Contract Law' (2022) 2 *European Review of Public Law* 373, 383–84, also stressing that 'The ECJ has decided more than 100 cases in the field of secondary EU private law, mainly contract law, mainly consumer contract law' (384)), therefore one more knowledge gap that this book addresses in the sense noted in the text.

[13] As to positivism in EU law, the often repeated critical quotation from M Shapiro is still representative of much EU law scholarship across Europe, aside the obvious exceptions. Shapiro described 'the Community as a juristic idea; the written constitution as a sacred text; the professional commentary as the inevitable working out of the correct implications of the constitutional text; and the constitutional court as the disembodied voice of right reason and constitutional theology'. M Shapiro, 'Comparative Law and Comparative Politics' (1980) 53 *Southern California Law Review* 537, 538 (also quoted by JHH Weiler, *The Constitution of Europe; 'Do the New Clothes Have an Emperor?' and Other Essays on European Integration* (Cambridge, Cambridge University Press, 1999) 14–15, who believes that such critical comments 'could be levelled against much of the legal literature on the Community'). The idea that, as a result of the failure of the European codification project, private law would now become more a matter for the Member States to deal with (the nationalist or repatriation thesis) is out of line with the development of the law on the ground, I argue in this book: this book aims to demonstrate the continuous impact of integration on private law in its post-state mode and the impact of this developement for European constitutional integration itself. See ch 3 (on the shift to balancing in EPL scholarship).

[14] See, critically, L Niglia, 'Taking Comparative Law Seriously – Europe's Private Law and the Poverty of the Orthodoxy (Instalment One)' (2006) 54 *American Journal of Comparative Law* 401; Niglia, *The Struggle for European Private Law* (n 9).

I have written elsewhere about this positivistic condition of the European private law discourse in both its private law and comparative law strands. This positivism deprives us of the possibility of understanding much of European law, broadly meant as comprising both EU law and European private law.[15] It is also in striking contrast with pre-Europeanisation scholarship on international law, private law and comparative, theoretical and socio-theoretical aspects of private law, which has moved away from positivistic analyses – as illustrated by the work of various scholars, including Ludwig Raiser and Franz Wieacker.[16] Yet, it seems that today positivism is once again triumphant.

There is therefore an urgent need for advancing a new kind of scholarship that explores European law in its private law context, and vice versa, in terms of the structural transformations of the discourse (hermeneutics) that presides over the architecture of the EU/private orders' relationships.[17] This much needed new kind of scholarship complements conventional transformational scholarship focused on general constitutional aspects – that is, on the relationship between the EU and the Member States' constitutional orders, other than their complex private law dimension. From this vantage point, it is submitted that private law is not just one substantive policy area among those affected by Europeanisation;[18] rather, it is the other structural dimension of the European constitutional constellation's cathedral.[19] For, as this book aims to demonstrate, private law participates in the

[15] See section IV below (on cognitive dissonance).

[16] I am thinking of the following defining books, only as exampla, including diverse approaches: L Raiser, *Die Aufgabe des Privatrechts* (Kronberg/Ts, Athenaeum, 1977); F Wieacker, *Das Sozialmodell der klassischen Privatrechtsgesetzbuecher und die Entwicklung der modernen Gesellschaft* (Karlsruhe, CF Mueller, 1953); F Wieacker, 'Aufstieg, Blüte und Krisis der Kodifikationsidee' in *Festschrift für Gustav Boehmer* (Bonn, Röhrscheid, 1954) 34; F Wieacker, *A History of Private Law in Europe* (Oxford, Clarendon Press, 1995).

[17] On the public law side of transformation, see Weiler, *The Constitution of Europe* (n 13) 2407. By 'structural transformation', I mean transformations of the discoursive structures understood as the changing juridical hermeneutics in their orderly characterisation (that is, the triad of nation-state, EU and private orders, and their relations).

[18] Including as per the understanding of the allocation of competences among the EU and its constituent states, that is, national private laws as encroached upon through market integration/consumer policy protection competence norms (including Arts 114 and 169 TFEU): see ch 4.

[19] On 'cathedral' and law, see Calabresi and Melamed's framework of analysis in G Calabresi and AD Melamed, 'Property Rules, Liability Rules, and Inalienability: One View of the Cathedral' (1972) 85 *Harvard Law Review* 1089, adapted with regard to EU law and private law in Caruso (n 12); for earlier reflections, see Joerges, 'The Europeanization of Private Law (n 9), and the workshop proceedings therein; Niglia, 'The Europeanisation of Private Law' (n 12). In the context of this book's narrative, 'cathedral' is understood in terms of 'order' associated with ('jurisprudence of constitutional autonomy'), and decoupled from ('jurisprudence of constitutional absorption'), the state. Notable exceptions to the lack of analysis of private law transformations in Europe are transformation studies with a focus on private law, that is, a core set of essays and monographs: Joerges (ibid); Caruso (n 12); L Niglia, 'Diritto giurisprudenziale e direttive comunitarie in materia di diritto privato: note critiche' [1998] *Rivista critica di diritto privato* 459; L Niglia, 'The Non-Europeanization of Private Law' (2001) 4 *European Review of Private Law* 575; Niglia, *The Transformation of Contract in Europe* (n 11). These are part of a first wave of writings on the dynamics between the EU order and nation-state private orders. These dynamics are then followed by the new transformation process, through private ordering having

construction over time of the co-evolution of the EU constitutional order and of the Member States' constitutional orders in matters pertaining to so-called horizontal relationships.[20]

III. Of European Union Law as European Private Law

Any market, and market integration, is a contingent product of the law, both public and private.

EU law understood as the constitutional law of market integration – as a body of norms and principles disciplining the four freedoms (negative integration) and harmonisation (positive integration) – includes the body of private law norms and principles aimed at the project of building a pan-European, integrated market. Among these norms and principles are those that conventionalism labels 'European private law'. From this viewpoint, European private law is not just a major component of EU law but, this book argues, its core component. One must therefore write a narrative about the structural interface between, on the one hand, European private law and, on the other hand, the Union's constitutional law as 'ordering' market integration, and their transformations – contributing to a critical line of writings that have made the wider European law scholarship more aware of its complex and multilayered structure.[21]

The objective of this book in adopting this perspective and in proposing a transformational argument is to inaugurate an open debate about EU law, towards overcoming denials and omissions that contribute so much to the untenable conceptual and analytical divide between European private law (EPL) and EU law. The book inaugurates an inclusive and integrated reading of the real condition of EU law in the sense of reading EU law as *also* EPL. From this critical viewpoint, market integration qua Europeanisation does not feature as a monolith because it is a compound of disciplines.

The recognition that Europeanisation is a compound of disciplines comes from certain critical studies of the making and evolution of law in Europe that adopt a legal comparative, historical and philosophical perspective.[22] However, EU constitutional

been made stateless, on which see Niglia 2010; Niglia, *The Struggle for European Private Law* (n 9); Hesselink, *The Politics* (n 12), to which I will return in the remainder of this chapter. On the argument of private law as constitutional private law, see Niglia, *The Struggle for European Private Law* (n 9).

[20] On private law articulated as horizontal relationships in EU law scholarship, see ch 2 below.

[21] Niglia, *The Transformation of Contract in Europe* (n 11); Niglia, *The Struggle for European Private Law* (n 9); Niglia, 'The New Transformation of Europe' (n 7); Micklitz (n 12); see n 12 above. For early works, see Joerges, 'The Europeanization of Private Law (n 9); L Niglia, 'The Europeanisation of Private Law' (n 12); Caruso (n 12); Niglia, 'Diritto giurisprudenziale e direttive comunitarie' (n 19).

[22] See, eg P Grossi, *Assolutismo Giuridico e Diritto Privato* (Milan, Giuffrè, 1998); P Grossi, *Universalismo e particolarismo nel diritto* (Naples, Editoriale Scientifica, 2011); T Herzog, *A Short History of European Law: The Last Two and a Half Millennia* (Cambridge, MA, Harvard University Press, 2019); Niglia, *The Struggle for European Private Law* (n 9).

law studies are an exception not because EPL is not part of that history, for it is, but because of their tendency for reductionist readings of EPL – as encapsulated, for example, in the orthodox treatment of private law in standard presentations of EU law that only reduces EPL to a version of 'top-down' harmonisation, as opposed to recognising the actual operation of EU law as I understand and present it in this book. This is no less true of mainstream market integration law scholarship, that is, the EU law literature that focuses on both negative (qua the four freedoms) and positive aspects of market integration.

Moreover, comparativists who specialise in private law have tended to focus on the black letter law details of EU private law legislation and related nation-state private law, whilst at times neglecting key aspects of the market integration context, including its public law aspects as context, in which private law has been operating for decades – with some notable exceptions.[23]

***

There is urgent need for complementary knowledge, coming from EU law and from comparative law, about the role of the hermeneutics of private law in relation to market-integration building.

Central actors in the building of the law of the internal market are the CJEU and the other European courts. The perspective of the study of the role of the *hermeneutics* of private law in relation to market-integration building is broader and deeper. It comprises both the jurisprudence of the European courts and private law jurisprudence broadly understood to include scholarship and case law applied to the objective of market integration. This book identifies and analyses three sets of hermeneutical narratives located in particular periods of time in which they are prominent, representing idiosyncratic and contentious modalities with which to organise integration.

Under the paradigm of *the jurisprudence of constitutional autonomy* (chapter two), the determination of the CJEU to keep private law at some distance from the Union's legal order is recounted and made intelligible through a close look at what this 'private law' kept at distance consists of. It is submitted that it consists of a hermeneutics of balancing socially orientated determinations, sheltered from market integration by an EU jurisprudence respectful of such determinations. The chapter recounts the self-engineering of an 'autonomous' EU constitutional law relative to 'autonomous' national constitutional order(s),[24] so that juridical hermeneutics as social could flourish and be preserved.

[23] For critical analysis, see Niglia, *The Transformation of Contract in Europe* (n 11); Niglia, *The Struggle for European Private Law* (n 9). See also ch 3.

[24] On balancing in comparative studies, see, among others, TA Aleinikoff, 'Constitutional Law in the Age of Balancing,' (1987) 96 *Yale Law Journal* 943; J Bomhoff, *Balancing Constitutional Rights: The Origins and Meanings of Postwar Legal Discourse*, Cambridge Studies in Constitutional Law (Cambridge, Cambridge University Press, 2013); and, with a focus on EU law, see the analysis of balancing in L Niglia, 'Eclipse of the Constitution' (2016) 22 *European Law Journal* 132; 'Taking Private Law

In the discussion regarding the paradigm of *the jurisprudence of constitutional heteronomy* (chapter three), the shift towards the determination of the CJEU to superimpose a range of EU private law norms on Member States' jurisdictions, and the resulting position of national private laws, is recounted. It is submitted that EPL takes on the characterisation of a heteronomously imposed law of economised balancing in conditions in which the autonomy of EU constitutional law correspondingly recedes. Here, the juridical hermeneutics hardly remains unaltered as one can argue that it collapses in economic-orientated language.

The chapter on 'constitutional absorption' (chapter four) looks critically into the jurisprudence of constitutional heteronomy, as discussed in chapter three as being intertwined with, and belonging to, a deeper transformation that, it is argued, has been changing EU law itself. This transformation pertains to a major reconstitution by absorption of the relationships between Europe's constitutional order and private ordering.

Chapter five then critically considers the totalising of law as a result of the jurisprudence of constitutional absorption understood as new juridical discourse[25] whose effect is that market forces gain constitutional legitimation through 'taking over' the already constituted (in constitutional-composite mode) integration order.[26]

Rights Seriously – Of Balancing and the Jurisprudence of the Court of Justice of the European Union' in L Niglia (ed), 'Symposium "Balancing in European Law"' (2013–14) 16 *CYELS* 394. Intersecting Catherine Valcke's arguments (C Valcke, 'Book Review' [2014] *American Journal of Comparative Law* 809: commenting on Jacco Bomhoff's book on 'balancing' in private law as not just an 'analytical process', that is, a 'technique amenable to cognitive appropriation' by any 'legal actor so inclined', but 'balancing' seen as a defining 'form of legal argument, which accordingly boasts an intensely discursive … dimension'; see also, for German and US views on balancing as not just an analytical process but emphasising discoursive aspects, the contributions of N Reich, 'Balancing in Private Law and the Imperatives of the Public Interest' in R Brownsword, H Micklitz, L Niglia and S Weatherill (eds), *The Foundations of European Private Law* (Oxford, Hart Publishing, 2011) 221 and D Kennedy, 'A Transnational Genealogy of Proportionality in Private Law' in Brownsword et al (ibid) 185), this book considers and maps the discursive structures (hermeneutical) as structuring 'form', as they underlie and make intelligible the choice of an interpretation by legal actors. At the same time, the book explores 'balancing' as a key discursive dimension of private law as 'transnational', whilst balancing in constitutional law studies is seen as constructed 'locally – by time- and space-specific groups of actors, as against particular sets of cultural referents' (Valcke, ibid).

[25] 'New' in the limited sense of being proposed towards making intelligible the state of integration and not in the further sense of having begun now, given that it is a discourse with a long history which I recount elsewhere: see Niglia, 'The New Transformation of Europe' (n 7).

[26] See ch 5 and n 7 above. On 'order' as conceived of in ordo-liberalist thought, see ch 4 below (German Federal Constitutional Court, judgment of the Second Senate of 5 May 2020, 2 BvR 859/15, 2 BvR 1651/15, 2 BvR 2006/15, 2 BvR 980/16: 'PSPP'). Note also Joerges, 'A New Type of Conflicts' (n 7) 469 et seq, commenting inter alia on the German case through a reading of the work of KW Noerr, *Die Republik der Wirtschaft. Recht, Wirtschaft und Staat in der geschichte Westdeutschlands*, Teil I (Tübingen, Mohr/Siebeck, 1999), but considering the German case 'not a real *Sonderweg*' and therefore pointing to the Europeaness of 'the idea of an autonomous private law which derived its normative dignity from its commitment to the transpositive *ordo* of the economy, and which was to provide the ideational infrastructure for the new republic and its "social market economy"'. On private order's 'transposition' understood as relatedness between, on the one hand, private laws in France, Germany, Italy and the UK, and, on the other hand, social constitutionalism as both national and as European, see also Niglia, *The Transformation of Contract in Europe* (n 11); Niglia, *The Struggle for European*

IV. Between Comparative Law and European Union Law

With a view to putting forward the chief argument about the structural transformations of the EU and its order in relation to private law, this book redeploys the substantive and methodological tools that denote the literature regarding the public side of the EU's transformations over the past decades[27] and applies them to the area of private law, alongside the conventional focus on the public side of the EU's transformations. Autonomy, heteronomy and absorption, and the underlying focus on the dynamics of change, are among the tools adapted to the object of study of this book.

Moreover, this framework for analysis is seen as integrated with the background conception of composite constitutionalism as discussed in my essay 'Eclipse of the Constitution':[28] from autonomy to heteronomy and absorption is seen as a process that entails the undoing of composite constitutionalism.

The book equally employs and rearranges, complementarily and innovatively, certain methodological tools derived from comparative law. Broadly speaking, they are the tools developed in relation to the comparative study of forms and structures of legal reasoning and techniques as part of the area of 'comparative jurisprudence'.[29] However, by comparative jurisprudence, I mean more than just 'ideas' or 'reasoning': here, comparative jurisprudence indicates a conglomeration of legal hermeneutical structures and their effects in terms of the relations of orders.[30] I look at hermeneutical material as a factor of construction, of relational transformation, of orders. It is at the level of these relations that stands the study of the interdisciplinary intersection between EU law and legal comparative studies

Private Law (n 9). On anarchy and arbitrariness as characterising the rising new private constitutional order, as opposed to the composite character of private ordering in the time of the jurisprudence of constitutional autonomy as I redescribe it in ch 2, see chs 4 and 5. On 'constitutional-composite', see the remainder of this chapter. On 'compounds of market forces', see chs 4 and 5 below on order-regimes.

[27] See the respective seminal works of M Cappelletti, M Seccombe and JHH Weiler, *Integration through Law* (Boston, MA, Walter de Gruyter, 1986) 3, 4; Weiler, 'Transformation' (n 1); Stein (n 1). On global transformations and the law, see also Kennedy, 'Three Globalizations' (n 11) 19. On 'global lawyering' and contemporary private law, see ch 4.

[28] Niglia, 'Eclipse of the Constitution' (n 24).

[29] See W Ewald, 'Comparative Jurisprudence (I): What Was It Like to Try a Rat?' (1995) 143 *University of Pennsylvania Law Review* 1889; JQ Whitman, 'A Simple Story' (2006) 4 *Rechtsgeschichte* 206. Comparative jurisprudence is about 'the way that legal actors *reason on the inside*' (emphasis added) (Ewald, ibid); see also M Lasser, 'Judicial (Self-)Portraits: Judicial Discourses in the French Legal System' (1995) 104 *Yale Law Journal* 1325.

[30] On this methodological approach as transformative comparative jurisprudence, see Niglia, *The Transformation of Contract in Europe* (n 11); Niglia, *The Struggle for European Private Law* (n 9); Niglia, 'The New Transformation of Europe' (n 7). Transformative comparative jurisprudence can be found at times when orders keep their own (alleged) 'identity' (by tradition, as jurisdiction: see L Niglia, 'Comparative Jurisprudence', unpublished manuscript on file with author, 2023) and at times when orders' relations become blurred and are characterised by a process of 'replacement': for this argument, see ch 5 below.

as a body of knowledge that, once combined, allows the meaning of those relations to be captured.

Fundamentally, in this book I am proposing a new reading of comparative jurisprudence as designating an approach to the study of orders and their transformations as seen through the prism of hermeneutics – through law's (juridical) hermeneutics.[31] I will label this approach by the term '*comparative (juridical) hermeneutics*'.[32]

By comparative (juridical) hermeneutics, I mean the comparative analysis not just of norms, facts, ideas or function,[33] but of the legal actors' uses of the technique

[31] On hermeneutics, see HG Gadamer, *Wahrheit und Methode. Grundzüge einer philosophischen Hermeneutik* (Tübingen, JCK Mohr, 1990); HG Gadamer, *Gesammelte Werke* (Tübingen, Mohr/Siebeck, 10 vols, 1985–97); M Heiddeger, *Collected Works, vol 63, Ontology – the Hermeneutics of Facticity* (John van Buren trs, Bloomington, Indiana University Press, 1999, first published in 1988; 1923 lectures); F Schleiermacher, *Zur Philosophie* (1938). On hermeneutics and law, see Gadamer, *Wahrheit und Methode* (ibid); E Betti, *General Theory of Interpretation* (*Teoria Generale dell'Interpretazione*) 1st edn (Milan, Giuffré, 1955). See also J Esser, *Vorverständniss und Methodenwhal in der Rechtsfindung* (Athenäum Fischer Taschenbuch Verlag, 1970, 1972); and note the statement by J Habermas, 'Reply to Symposium Participants', quoted at n 38 below. On hermeneutics and comparative law, see P Legrand, 'Jameses at Play: A Tractation on the Comparison of Laws' (2017) 65(suppl 1) *American Journal of Comparative Law* 1; S Glanert and F Girard (eds), *Law's Hermeneutics: Other Investigations* (London, Routledge, 2017); S Glanert, 'Method' in PG Monateri (ed), *Methods of Comparative Law* (Cheltenham, Edward Elgar, 2012) 61 et seq; Ewald (n 27) on 'comparative jurisprudence'; Niglia, *The Struggle for European Private Law* (n 9); Niglia, 'Comparative Jurisprudence' (n 30) on hermeneutical struggles. Comparative hermeneutics is related to hermeneutical struggles: see the remainder of the book. Nothing of the hermeneutical perspective, as adopted in philosophical writings, is represented as being the end of the story in that this perspective is in itself part of a *Wirkungsgeschichte* that requires to be investigated and understood – considering that Gadamer, *Wahrheit und Methode* (ibid) refers to 'historically-effected consciousness' ('*wirkungsgeschichtliches Bewußtsein*') as a mode of being that is sensitive to its own historical situatedness. On this situatedness in the context of my arguments for a comparative hermeneutics, see below at fn 3.

[32] See n 31. I am using the work method and methodology advisedly in that, on the one hand, in this way I can refer to, and address, the methodologies of comparative law and of EU law as they manifest themselves in the notions and conceptions that I analyse and criticise in this book whilst, on the other hand, I am conscious of the argument that hermeneutics (and law's hermeneutics) cannot just be, and/or cannot and must not be, 'methodical' insofar as, in Gadamer's words, 'man anders versteht' (one understands differently: Gadamer, *Wahrheit und Methode* (n 31); see discussion in terms of law's hermeneutics in P Legrand Kischel, 'Comparative Law: Fortschrift ohne Fortschrift' [2020] *Journal of Contract Law* 292, 318–21): by which I mean that our understanding of the contingency of the law as considered in this book is embedded in the hermeneutical struggles and their inter-orderly characterisation (in the sense of *wirkungsgeschichtliches Bewußtsein*: see n 29) as I discuss them in the rest of the book in terms of a law's hermeneutics of orderings and their structural transformations (relations of orders). From this vantage point, in this book method and methodology are always meant to indicate 'method' and 'methodology', that is, they are meant to be structurally qualified in the sense just noted. Compare H Patrick Glenn, 'Against Method?' in M Adams and D Heirbaut (eds), *The Method and Culture of Comparative Law: Essays in Honour of Mark Van Hoecke* (Oxford, Hart Publishing, 2014) 17 ('There is no comparative method').

[33] On comparative positivistic analysis of norms across legal 'systems', see the critical review of Legrand, 'A Tractation on the Comparison of Laws' (n 31); L Niglia, 'Taking Comparative Law Seriously – Europe's Private Law and the Poverty of the Orthodoxy' (2006) 54 *American Journal of Comparative Law* 401; on comparativism and the factual, see R Sacco, 'Legal Formants' (1991) 39 *American Journal of Comparative Law* 1; on comparativism and ideas, see comparative jurisprudence in Ewald (n 27); on function, see KE Zweigert and H Kotz, *An Introduction to Comparative Law* (T Weir trs, Oxford, Clarendon Press, 1998).

of 'balancing'[34] in European law and in national private laws as the contingent hermeneutical material giving rise to structural transformations of orders and of relations among orders. This is an examination that requires comparing in parallel both European law and national laws – the European legal order and national orders.

The focus is on the comparative analysis of the hermeneutics of *balancing* as a technique deployed by both judges and scholars.[35] The book thus adopts the approach, labelled comparative juridical hermeneutics – already applied previously in a different guise[36] – qua the study of the preconditions upon which legal interpretation is premised and predicated in the contexts under scrutiny.[37]

This methodological approach, in turn, entails taking into account perspectives orientated to 'projects', in the sense of the conscious reflecting of a form of life, as Jürgen Habermas phrases it;[38] correspondingly, it also entails both awareness of the hermeneutical struggles that characterise our time and the responsibility that comes with participating in them, that is, in neutralising them or in making them explicit.[39]

***

As to European law, this is the first monograph to address the issue of balancing as a defining feature of contemporary European law – insofar as adopting a post-positivistic approach to the law of the EU rather than the more conventional

[34] What I mean by 'balancing' in this book is spelled out in the next chapters. In writing about the hermeneutics of balancing, this book contributes to the literature on balancing in the areas of comparative private law, comparative constitutional law, European law and legal theory – it proposes a genealogy of 'balancing' (understood as privatistic technique playing, it is argued, a constitutional role). On the related, broader notion of legal consciousness, see Kennedy, 'Three Globalizations' (n 11) 19–73. On European law and balancing, see n 41 below.

[35] On discourse in private law understood, comparatively, as both judicial and scholarly, see Niglia, *The Struggle for European Private Law* (n 9).

[36] In the sense that the new theory connotes previous work of the author, including Niglia, *The Struggle for European Private Law* (n 9); Niglia, 'The New Transformation of Europe' (n 7).

[37] Gadamer, *Wahrheit und Methode* (n 31). The book aims, inter alia, at contributing to the challenge of filling a gap identified by J Basedow, H Fleischer and R Zimmermann, *Legislators, Judges and Professors* (Tübingen, Mohr/Siebeck, 2016) VII, insofar as comparative hermeneutics as proposed here is about comparatively focusing on methodology itself: 'What is … largely lacking is the comparative study of legal methodology itself, ie of the way in which lawyers apply, develop, find, argue, communicate, and do research about, the law: a study of comparative legal methodology rather than a methodology of comparative law'. I refer to 'method' and 'methodology' in the sense clarified above at n 32.

[38] Note J Habermas, 'Reply to Symposium Participants' in M Rosenfeld and A Arato (eds), *Habermas on Law and Democracy* (Berkeley, CA, University of California Press, 1998) 381–452: 'The court's judgment is then itself a value judgment that more or less adequately reflects a form of life articulating itself in the framework of a concrete order of values.'

[39] See Niglia, *The Struggle for European Private Law* (n 1); see also ch 5. On the hermeneutical meaning of 'balancing', see the rest of the chapter and of the book.

focus on specific judicial decisions, as they deploy balancing, without looking at the broader state, and transformation of juridical hermeneutics.[40]

Looked at from a comparative perspective, balancing in the EU context features the institutional 'response' to conflicts of interests as they characterise the EU, and the Member State, polities, through institutionalising decisions about where reason lies in conflicts, which, in turn, depends on complex factors, from ideological to political to economic to societal – conflicts that this book considers in the juridical terms of the role that balancing plays in dealing with them. In dealing with conflicts, actors deploy technical rules (balancing) whilst neutralising and depoliticising them.[41]

[40] To EU law scholars interested in proportionality understood as principle ex Art 5 TUE, and as a general principle of EU law, as well as relevant in the CJEU case law on fundamental rights (T Tridimas, *The General Principles of EU Law* (Oxford, Oxford University Press, 2007); see also P Mengozzi, 'The Judicial Protection of Individual Rights and the Principle of Proportionality after Lisbon' in L Niglia (ed), 'Symposium "Balancing in European Law"' (2013–14) 16 *Cambridge Yearbook of European Legal Studies* 335; L Niglia, 'Taking Private Law Rights Seriously – Of Balancing and the Jurisprudence of the Court of Justice of the European Union' in L Niglia (ed), 'Symposium "Balancing in European Law"' (2013–14) 16 *Cambridge Yearbook of European Legal Studies* 394; A Rosas, 'Balancing Fundamental Rights in EU Law' in L Niglia (ed), 'Symposium "Balancing in European Law"' (2013–14) 16 *Cambridge Yearbook of European Legal Studies* 348; T Tridimas, 'Fundamental Rights, General Principles of EU Law, and the Charter' in L Niglia (ed), 'Symposium "Balancing in European Law"' (2013–14) 16 *Cambridge Yearbook of European Legal Studies* 362), it will become evident throughout this book that the notion of proportionality as balancing (referred to in standard literature as a third-stage assessment of proportionality – following suitability and necessity) is analysed genealogically, that is, as developed in the case law of the CJEU in relation to private law from social (see ch 2 below) to economised (see chs 3–5) in terms of redefining relations among the EU and the nation state orders; and that balancing is considered not just as a third-stage assessment of proportionality, but as it matters beyond the scope of application of the principle of proportionality (see ch 5). This is an analysis that must be read alongside conventional accounts of balancing as part of the principle of proportionality in EU law towards contributing further to our understanding of proportionality in EU law, and of balancing in general, by looking into the technique of balancing as situated (in the sense of situatedness as noted at n 31).

[41] See chs 4 and 5. On the anatomy of the underlying hermeneutical struggles as they give rise to discrete, never natural and always contingent, never fixed and always dynamic, formations labelled 'orders', see the rest of the book. On judicial conflicts and their effects on the relations among orders, see the rest of the book; also note, recently, BVerfG Order of 15 April 2021, 2 BvR 547/21 (unsuccessful application for preliminary injunction against promulgation of the domestic act ratifying the EU Own Resources Decision (Council Decision (EU, Euratom) 2020/2053 of 14 December 2020 on the system of own resources of the European Union and repealing Decision 2014/335/EU, Euratom [2020] OJ L424/1) on the national 'constitutional order' in collision with EU law, and on 'restoring' the constitutional order (*Verfassungsordnung*) in case of ultra vires) at para 111: 'Stellt der Senat einen Ultra-vires-Akt fest oder sollte er entgegen der summarischen Prüfung im vorliegenden Beschluss eine Berührung der Verfassungsidentität durch den Eigenmittelbeschluss 2020 bejahen, müssten Bundesregierung, Bundestag und Bundesrat die ihnen zu Gebote stehenden Maßnahmen ergreifen, um die Verfassungsordnung wiederherzustellen.'). For a restatement of the point of view of 'the unity of the EU legal order', see the communiqué of the Court of Justice of the European Union (press release No 58/2020 of 8 May 2020, https://curia.europa.eu/jcms/upload/docs/application/pdf/2020-05/cp200058en.pdf) in the shadow of three judgments of the CJEU to which reference is made (Case C-446/98 *Fazenda Pública* ECLI:EU:C:2000:691, para 49; Case C-314/85 *Foto-Frost* ECLI:EU:C:1987:452, paras 15 and 17; Case C-212/04 *Adeneler and Others* ECLI:EU:C:2006:443, para 122): 'The Directorate for Communication of the Court of Justice received many enquiries concerning the judgment delivered by the German Constitutional Court on 5 May 2020 regarding the European Central Bank's PSPP programme. The departments of the institution never comment on a

This is no denial of the role of external factors, from economics to politics. However, this monograph's choice is to focus on the juridical terms of the resolution of conflicts as part of broader struggles. The book is about comparing hermeneutical (balancing) material and its trespassing across polity boundaries through the modes of autonomy (chapter two), heteronomy (chapter three) and absorption (chapter four). Each chapter is a case study of the ways of coexistence of laws as orders, which respectively can be analysed through the looking glass of, and taking the form of, autonomy, heteronomy and absorption. As the ways of balancing mutate (from being social orientated to being technocratic-efficiency orientated), so do the relationships among orders (from autonomy to heteronomy and absorption).

In analysing the patterns of *interdependence* across the EU's and the Member States' orders, the book also refers back to, and develops further, comparative scholarship that has adopted the methodological study of legal transformation and legal change – illustrations being the theories of legal irritants; of interdependence versus closure; of hegemony versus anti-hegemony;[42] and of juridical interdependence, hegemony and federalisation in relation to European private law.[43]

Adopting this methodological framework allows analysis of the deep structures and related cleavages pertaining to the complex of interests that underly the EU and of the Member States' constitutional orders. This is a perspective that the comparativist can and should entertain, considering particularities and universalities as interrelated: entailing both 'micro-comparativism' and 'macro-comparativism' at the same time.[44]

judgment of a national court. In general, it is recalled that the Court of Justice has consistently held that a judgment in which the Court gives a preliminary ruling is binding on the national court for the purposes of the decision to be given in the main proceedings. In order to ensure that EU law is applied uniformly, the Court of Justice alone – which was created for that purpose by the Member States – has jurisdiction to rule that an act of an EU institution is contrary to EU law. Divergences between courts of the Member States as to the validity of such acts would indeed be liable to place in jeopardy *the unity of the EU legal order* and to detract from legal certainty. Like other authorities of the Member States, national courts are required to ensure that EU law takes full effect. That is the only way of ensuring the equality of Member States in the Union they created. The institution will refrain from communicating further on the matter' (emphasis added).

[42] See respectively G Teubner, 'Legal Irritants: Good Faith in British Law or How Unifying Law Ends Up in New Divergencies' (1998) 61 *MLR* 1, 11; HP Glenn, *The Cosmopolitan State* (Oxford, Oxford University Press, 2013); and, on hegemony, critically, see U Mattei, 'A Theory of Imperial Law: A Study on US Hegemony and the Latin Resistance' (2003) 3(2) *Global Jurist* 202; Monateri, *Dominus Mundi* (n 11) 166 et seq (on hegemony as 'control of the imagination' at 172); Niglia, 'The New Transformation of Europe' (n 7); Niglia, *The Transformation of Contract in Europe* (n 11). In the broader comparative law area of law and legal change, see the distinct positions of A Watson, *The Making of the Civil Law* (Cambridge, MA, Harvard University Press, 1981); P Legrand, 'Against a European Civil Code' (1997) 60 *MLR* 44; Legrand, 'A Tractation on the Comparison of Laws' (n 31); Niglia, *The Transformation of Contract in Europe* (n 11); Niglia, *The Struggle for European Private Law* (n 9).

[43] See Niglia, 'Comparative Jurisprudence' (n 30); Niglia, 'The New Transformation of Europe' (n 7); L Niglia, 'Beyond Enchantment: The Possibility of a New European Private Law' (2009) 28 *Yearbook of European Law* 60. See also ch 5 (on interdependence, taking over, totalising, 'entwinments').

[44] See below the 'microcomparativist' focus on the following private law norms, institutions and practices: right of cancellation, unfair terms and standard form contracts, *lex mercatoria*, digital contracting, labour law (right to strike), labour law (rights of employees in case of transfer of businesses), data

The methodological perspective adopted here, it should be stressed, is one that goes against the grain of the dominant positivist position, both in EU legal studies and in comparative and private law studies. For, where there is transformation (diachrony), the positivist sees only static (synchronic) categories (such as system, codification), resulting in a lack of awareness of, and engagement with, the living law: an obfuscation that hinders real knowledge whilst equally depoliticising, in the sense of unrecognising and neutralising, the struggles over the law that define our age.[45]

protection, fundamental rights and the constitutionalisation of private law, fundamental rights and private law, balancing, general principles of law (EU), general principles of law (civil law), *culpa in contrahendo*, *aufklärungsrichtiges Verhalten* and transparency in digitisation.

[45] See above and ch 4 below on 'cognitive dissonance' (see, critically, Weiler, 'Transformation' (n 1) 2435). Adopting the comparative hermeneutical methodology means acting in dissonance (vis-à-vis 'cognitive dissonance') by both intercepting and representing that dissonance, while at the same time criticising it in the light of the framework for analysis proposed in this book.

2

Autonomy

I. Introduction

By 'jurisprudence of constitutional autonomy' in this chapter is meant the contingent European constitutional law engineered by the Court of Justice of the European Union (CJEU, the Court) through the key doctrinal fabric of the interpretative obligation.

The interpretative obligation is a doctrinal construction that, in its interface with the (state) private order(s), is designed to a principled respect of the autonomy of private law discourse as nationally constituted.

'Autonomy', in turn, designates a constitutional framework of coexistence of orders, national and EU, each with its own 'autonomous' constitutional character. This is because the CJEU-designed 'rules of the game' structure the EU constitutional order dialectically vis-à-vis the 'other orders' (the Member States' orders), that is, in the threefold logic of mutual learning, mutual respect and co-evolutionary normativisation (co-normativisation).[1] Deep down, autonomy entails a composite constitutionalist framework whereby the EU and the national order(s) stand side by side as constitutional co-normativising orders, rather than in a heteronomous logic of superordination/subordination.[2]

From this vantage point, one can say that the jurisprudence of constitutional autonomy is a design for a hermeneutically 'co-authored' private law that emerges

[1] See section IV below (on mutual learning, mutual respect and co-evolutionary normativisation as structures of the jurisprudence of constitutional autonomy). 'Normativisation' indicates the process of making law as explained in the rest of this chapter. On the notion of 'autonomy', see ch 1 above. For a critique of the conventional argument whereby plurality would just be a phenomenon contingent on the crisis of EU law and its order, against the portrait of a European integration process that would have previously consisted of 'unity' (monism), see L Niglia, 'Eclipse of the Constitution' (2016) 22 *European Law Journal* 132; ch 4 below (explaining pluralisation today in terms of plural regimes working on the basis of 'privatistic balancing', against the backdrop of pluralism as characterising constitutional autonomy yesterday as I discuss it in this chapter). On pluralism and private law, see L Niglia (ed), *Pluralism and European Private Law* (Oxford, Hart Publishing, 2013). Also, contrast, on the one hand, classical international law, where the plural consists of a number of (state) entities each authoring their own world, each enforcing international law at their own whim, and, on the other hand, the intertwining of 'constitutional Europe' and of 'nation-state constitutionalism'. On international law versus European constitutional law, see JHH Weiler, *The Constitution of Europe; 'Do the New Clothes Have an Emperor?' and Other Essays on European Integration* (Cambridge, Cambridge University Press, 1999).

[2] On composite constitutionalism in Europe, see Niglia, 'Eclipse of the Constitution' (n 1).

out of both market integration and nation state legal bodies of knowledge, that is, respectively, national private laws and European private law *sensu stricto* (applied to the EU activities).

At the same time, the jurisprudence of constitutional autonomy is a design for a double-engagement, plural-normative, in that it hermeneutically rests on the cooperation between, on the one hand, European and national courts and, on the other hand, European private law and national private law scholarship – weaving norms and principles meant to adapt to, and participate in, the project of market integration to the extent that they deem it 'possible' under the constraints of national private law.

Accordingly, a first structural transformation of the hermeneutics of private law as 'Europeanisation',[3] that is, the creation of a private law discourse directed at building market integration, developed in the form of, and within the boundaries of, the CJEU-designed 'jurisprudence of constitutional autonomy'. In section IV I shall explain that it equally consisted of hermeneutical material that could then generate structural changes in the relations of orders.

***

In this chapter I consider a constitutional process that started some 50 years ago and that lasted until the changes that I recount in the following chapters. It is a process that can be succinctly recounted as follows.

At a certain point in time after the establishment of the European Communities (now Union) with the Paris and Rome Treaties of the 1950s, starting from around the 1970s scholars, judges, legislators and policymakers envisaged a new kind of private law aimed at building an integrated market and no longer entirely associated with the nation-state, as had been the case as a result of the nationalisation of private laws during the modern codification age.[4] Ever since, scholars have been speculating about a pan-European private law, defending either a decodified scheme or a codified scheme, or a mixture of both, open to the 'outside world' in the sense of nation-state legal material being adapted for the objective of market integration.[5] The Lando Principles (the Principles of European Contract Law) are among the most widely known results of this process, albeit representative of a codified mentality.[6]

[3] On the character of the hermeneutics of private law pre-existing Europeanisation, see L Niglia, *The Transformation of Contract in Europe* (The Hague, Kluwer Law International, 2003); L Niglia, *The Struggle for European Private Law. A Critique of Codification* (Oxford, Hart Publishing, 2015).

[4] On the modern codification age, see Niglia, *The Struggle for European Private Law* (n 3). On the ties of European private law with national private law, see the rest of this chapter; on these ties as ever more rescinded as a result of the work of European private law scholarship see ch 3.

[5] Niglia, *The Struggle for European Private Law* (n 3) (on 'decodification' in relation to the Europeanisation of private law).

[6] Niglia, *The Struggle for European Private Law* (n 3).

However, through a careful line of decisions of the CJEU, in dialogue with the national courts and communities of interpreters and inaugurating the so-called 'interpretative obligation' or 'indirect effect',[7] private law at large (national) remained sheltered from market integration so that its social core (the ways in which social values are embedded in private law) could be exposed to it, though to a limited extent, that is, under a reasoning conditional on the possibility of the conforming interpretation that, as such, enabled a substantial degree of respect of national private laws.

In this mode of Europeanisation as engineered by the CJEU, the hermeneutics of private law has resulted in being the 'negative', in the sense of remaining, constitutionally (as a relationship between the EU constitutional order and the private order(s)), 'outside' of market integration. Yet this was only apparently so, considering that the hermeneutics of private law has been playing a positive role in enabling the sustainability of the extraordinary phenomenon of the marketisation process by sheltering the nation state from much of its potential to bring about deep conflicts with, and the erosion of, national private law cultures and traditions.[8] This chapter makes this argument in explaining the complex phenomenon labelled here as 'jurisprudence of constitutional autonomy'.

Below, I first reconstruct the CJEU jurisprudence of constitutional autonomy as a major constitutional tool for hetero-directing private law to the building of the internal market (section II); then I look at the construction in private law circles of a private law hetero-directed at building market integration through the reception of, adaptation to, and participation in, the CJEU jurisprudence of constitutional autonomy (section III); finally, in the third step of the argument, I undertake an analysis of the relationship between the EU's constitutional order and the private law order as a result of the making and development of the jurisprudence of constitutional autonomy and its impact and reception at the level of the private (state) order (section IV).[9]

[7] Case C-91/92 *Faccini Dori* [1994] ECR I-3325, ECLI:EU:C:1994:292; see also the rest of this chapter.

[8] On these conflicts, see the classical writings by C Joerges, 'The Europeanization of Private Law as a Rationalization Process and as a Contest of Disciplines: An Analysis of the Directive on Unfair Terms in Consumer Contracts' (1995) 3 *European Review of Private Law* 175; D Caruso, 'The Missing View of the Cathedral: The Private Law Paradigm of European Legal Integration' (1997) 3 *European Law Journal* 3; L Niglia, 'Diritto giurisprudenziale e direttive comunitarie in materia di diritto privato: note critiche' [1998] *Rivista critica di diritto privato* 459; L Niglia, 'The Non-Europeanization of Private Law' (2001) 4 *European Review of Private Law* 575; L Niglia, 'Taking Comparative Law Seriously – Europe's Private Law and the Poverty of the Orthodoxy (Instalment One)' (2006) 54 *American Journal of Comparative Law* 401; L Niglia, 'Of Harmonisation and Fragmentation – The Problem of Legal Transplants and the Europeanisation of Private Law (Instalment Three)' (2010) 2 *Maastricht Journal of European and Comparative Law* 116; Niglia, *The Struggle for European Private Law* (n 3); L Niglia, 'The New Transformation of Europe. Arcana Imperii' (2020) 68 *American Journal of Comparative Law* 151. On cultural aspects underpinning European private law in comparative perspective, see P Legrand, 'Jameses at Play: A Tractation on the Comparison of Laws' (2017) 65 (suppl 1) *American Journal of Comparative Law* 1.

[9] And see also chs 3–5.

II. The Making of the Jurisprudence of Constitutional Autonomy

The CJEU's jurisprudence of constitutional autonomy was fully developed in a time frame that goes from the mid-1980s until around the turn of the century, before a new transformation took place over the last two decades or so.

When cases that were about labour law and contract law as affected by certain EU directives (respectively *Von Colson*, *Faccini Dori*) reached the CJEU,[10] the Court decided not to further 'constitutionalise' private law in the sense of making it subject to EU law through direct effect. Instead, the Court chose to leave it entirely to the autonomous determinations of the hermeneutics of private law(s) to settle the relevant disputes in the light of EU law, that is, in the light of the relevant directive, according to the canon of the interpretative obligation, whilst respecting those determinations.

A concrete 'margin of appreciation' (after 'margin of discretion' in *Von Colson*)[11] or, as one might call it, constitutional respect for the national realms – has been granted as a result to national private law communities, with the consequence that the EU Member States could ultimately remain constitutionally in control of the law.

Reliance on the appreciation of Member States is known in other areas of EU law, such as the Member States' own determinations as to the meaning of 'public morality' under Article 36 TFEU according to their national understanding of it, as respected by the CJEU,[12] so that it is the determinations of the Member States that become the applicable and applied European law.

However, here 'margin of appreciation' designates a phenomenon of deeper constitutional depth, as I will detail in the rest of this chapter (through analysing the triad of mutual learning, mutual respect and co-evolutionary normativisation). Moreover, and in turn, this 'constitutional respect' arrangement was part of the broader settlement of a 'composite constitutionalism' consisting of the

[10] Respectively CJEU, 10 April 1984, Case 14/83 *Von Colson v Land Nordrhein-Westfalen* [1984] ECR 1891 and *Faccini Dori* (n 7). At the time, the CJEU consciously chose to differentiate between primary norms such as the principle of equal pay (direct effect) and directive norms (indirect effect): on the relationship between the EU constitutional order and the nation-state private order(s) through EU primary legislation, with regard to the principle of non-discrimination in horizontal relations, see, notably, the judgment of the Court in *Defrenne* [1976] ECR 455, ECLI:EU:C:1976:56, paras 38–39: 'It is not possible to sustain any objection that the application by national courts of the principle of equal pay would amount to modifying independent agreements concluded privately or in the sphere of industrial relations such as individual contracts and collective labour agreements. In fact, since article 119 is mandatory in nature, the prohibition on discrimination between men and women applies not only to the action of public authorities, but also extends to all agreements which are intended to regulate paid labour collectively, as well as to contracts between individuals.' For subsequent case law, see the following chapters. See also Niglia, 'Of Harmonisation and Fragmentation' (n 8); Niglia, 'Eclipse of the Constitution' (n 1).

[11] See Case 14/83 *Von Colson*.

[12] See Art 36 TFEU (on condition of not entailing arbitrary discrimination nor a disguised obstacle to trade).

co-evolutionary characterisation of EU constitutional law and national constitutional laws.[13] National courts have participated in the construction of this jurisprudence in dialogue with the CJEU.[14]

Such orientation to 'constitutional respect' concretised the principle whereby only a conforming interpretation of national private law vis-à-vis EU law (the relevant directive in the concrete dispute in the context of which the preliminary reference originates) would generate (juridically) and legitimate (constitutionally), hermeneutically, the incorporation of the directive's dictates into the body of national law – as distinct from, and in parallel to, the process of transposition of directives through national legislation. The range of possible interpretations of the singular directive was conceptualised so as to align with, and be conditional upon, the extent to which national private law could be reinterpreted in its light.[15] In other words, unlike those areas where constitutional transformation proper manifests itself through the doctrine of direct effect, no 'hardening of law' has taken place here: rather, here is an opening of EU law to the internal (that is to say, national) hermeneutical private law determinations.[16]

Namely, more than two decades after *Van Gend* and a full decade after *Van Duyn*,[17] the CJEU chose not to extend its direct effect doctrine to cases of unimplemented or incorrectly implemented directives that individuals rely upon against other individuals. A new path was opened up as the Court ruled out the possibility of invoking a directive against individuals, thus effectively confining its direct effect only to claims against the state. *Van Duyn*'s *effet utile* rationale would have made it compelling for the Court to allow a horizontal effect (a direct effect applied at private qua horizontal relationships), whatever the type of European rule at stake (primary or secondary).[18] In the words of the Court:

> It would be incompatible with the binding effect attributed to a directive by Art 189 to exclude, in principle, the possibility that the obligation which it imposes may be invoked

[13] For this argument, see Niglia, 'Eclipse of the Constitution' (n 1) (composite constitutionalism in Europe as entailing a contingent kind of constitutional respect for the private law determinations as made nationally).

[14] See section III below.

[15] See the rest of the chapter.

[16] 'Hardening' of the law indicates a law that constitutionalises around entitlements and rights according to internal (autonomous) EU law constitutional parameters and, as a result, to the degree to which national law is subjected to it, whilst here I am referring to the degree to which national law is respected in its determinations as adopted in the light of the relevant EU (directives) norms (under indirect effect). I refer here to the *hermeneutical* determinations of private law, considering that, as a result of the constitutional respect for national laws, it is the hermeneutics of private law that is preserved whilst, with the turn to constitutional heteronomy discussed in ch 3, then being subjected to, and made instrumental to, the EU law determinations. This then entails a new configuration of private law at odds with traditional hermeneutical structures, as I also explain in ch 4.

[17] Case 26/62 *Van Gend en Loos* [1963] ECR 1 (direct effect of treaty rules); Case 41/74 *Van Duyn v Home Office* [1974] ECR 1337 (direct effect of directives). For further discussion, see L Niglia, 'Form and Substance in European Constitutional Law: The Social Character of Indirect Effect' (2010) 16 *European Law Journal* 439.

[18] *Van Duyn* (n 17) para 2.

> by those concerned. In particular, where the Community authorities have, by directives, imposed on Member States the obligation to pursue a particular course of conduct, the useful effect of such an act would be weakened if individuals were prevented from relying on it before the national courts and if the latter were prevented from taking into consideration as an element of Community law.

Instead, the Court chose not to act 'coherently' at all. It held that the justification for direct effect is based not on *effet utile*, but on the 'estoppel argument'. That is, the state may not rely, as against individuals, upon its own failure to implement a directive faithfully and timeously (in the sense of not to take advantage of that failure).[19] Therefore, the Court concluded, 'direct effect' cannot apply to horizontal claims.[20]

In a parallel line of cases, started with *Von Colson* and *Kolpinghuis*,[21] the Court constructively identified what would become known as 'indirect effect' doctrine. It positively commanded the domestic courts to follow this new doctrine in cases of horizontal claims: in such cases, courts are not required to adjudicate under direct effect, as per Marshall, but only indirectly to rely on the relevant directive in the following way:

> [T]he Member States' obligation arising from a directive to achieve the result envisaged by the directive and their duty under Article 5 of the Treaty to take all appropriate measures, whether general or particular, to ensure the fulfillment of that obligation, is binding on all the authorities of Member States including, for matters within their jurisdictions, the courts. It follows that, in applying the national law and in particular the provisions of a national law specifically introduced in order to implement directive no. 76/207, national courts are required to interpret their national law in the light of the wording and the purpose of the directive in order to achieve the result referred to in the third paragraph of Article 189 … It is for the national court to interpret and apply the legislation adopted for the implementation of the directive in conformity with the requirements of Community law, insofar as it is given discretion to do so under national law.

In order to really understand the emergence of the then new doctrine of 'conformity', one must look at the following background dynamics.

In the mid-1980s, a number of cases reached the courts in which challenges to democratically shaped, nationally grounded, collective choices were at stake in the socially sensitive field of labour law. At the time, labour law was understood as an articulation of private order disciplined under state constitutional law. One landmark judgment (*Von Colson*) exemplifies the line of cases in which workers' rights to equal treatment of various kinds, such as access to work, age or sex discrimination, were at stake.

[19] Case 148/78 *Public Ministero v Tullio Ratti* [1979] ECR 1629; see also Case 152/84 *Marshall* [1986] ECR 723; *Faccini Dori* (n 7).

[20] See eg J Coppel, 'Rights, Duties and the End of Marshall' (1994) 57 *MLR* 859, 859–64.

[21] *Von Colson* (n 10); Case 80/86 *Kolpinghuis Nijmegen BV* [1987] ECR 3969.

In *Von Colson*,[22] two workers, Sabine Von Colson and Elisabeth Kamann, claimed to have been refused employment on discriminatory grounds of sex regarding access to employment prohibited under Council Directive 76/207/EEC (Equal Treatment Directive).[23] The Court excluded that the relevant directive provides for compensation in kind, that is, for the imposition on the employer of the obligation to conclude a contract of employment with the candidate discriminated against (paragraph 19). It then added, in paragraph 23, that:

> although … full implementation of the directive does not require any specific form of sanction for unlawful discrimination, it does entail that that sanction be such as to guarantee real and effective judicial protection … it must also have a real deterrent effect on the employer … It follows that where a Member State chooses to penalise the breach of the prohibition of discrimination by the award of compensation, that compensation must in any event be adequate in relation to the damage sustained.

As nominal compensation (limited to expenses incurred in submitting the job application) 'would not satisfy the requirements of an effective transposition of the directive' (paragraph 25), as provided for under paragraph 611A of the Bürgerliches Gesetzbuch (BGB), the Court went on to hold that as

> [t]he German government maintained … that that provision did not necessarily exclude the application of the general rules regarding compensation … [i]t is for the national court alone to rule on that question concerning the interpretation of its national law.

At this point, the court was officialising an interpretative obligation, at the discretion of domestic courts, by straightforward reliance on one submission of the German government whereby

> it is possible for the German courts to work out, on the basis of private national law and in conformity with the substance of the directive, adequate solutions to satisfy both the principle of equal treatment and the interests of all the parties.

Here, the national courts are requested to try and interpret the general rules on compensation with a view to adequately compensating the workers.

The interpretative obligation that originated in this very submission of the German government centred on concerns for the autonomy of domestic law. It was a blanket acceptance of such submission before the courts. For the Court did not demand that the principle of equal treatment be superimposed upon domestic law, thus siding with the interests of the claimants and playing down those of the employer, but required domestic courts to balance the interests of all the parties involved. This is a balancing that rests on, and is conditional on, hermeneutically exploring the possibility, 'on the basis of private national law' and

[22] Judgment of 10 April 1984 in *Von Colson* (n 10); see also Case C-334/92 *Wagner-Miret* [1993] ECR I-6911, paras 20 et seq; Case C-131/97 *Carbonari v Universita degli Studi di Bologna* [1999] ECR I-1103, paras 48 et seq; Joined Cases C-397/01 to C-403/01 *Pfeiffer and others* [2004] ECR I-8835.

[23] [1976] OJ L39/40.

'in conformity with the substance of the directive', of 'adequate solutions' with a view 'to satisfy[ing]' 'both the principle of equal treatment and the interests of all the parties'. In other words, the European Court of Justice (ECJ) converted the German submission into a rule of construction binding on domestic courts and solely understood to be about leaving it to 'the national courts alone' to make their determinations on the balancing of the interests at stake.

In subsequent cases in which workers have claimed the application of social policy directives vis-à-vis private employers or the state,[24] the Court has retained this minimalist understanding of the interpretative obligation as a devise aimed at leaving it to the national courts alone to make the ultimate determination of the interests at stake in the dispute. Indeed, at the core of these cases is an interface between, on the one hand, fragments of domestic social laws being challenged by the likes of Sabine Von Colson and, on the other, the interpretative obligation intended to be a tool to protect those laws by leaving it to the national judiciary to make a decision as to the appropriate balance between the claimants' concerns and national welfare policies.

As the Court developed this interpretative doctrinal construct further, the issue of the extent to which national law would enable a conforming interpretation has given rise to judgments in which the Court itself has indicated the 'correct' interpretation, sometimes favourable and sometimes against conformity. For example, sometimes the Court has come to the conclusion that domestic law cannot be interpreted by domestic courts in conformity with the relevant directive at all, due to the mere consideration that domestic social policy is different from the relevant directive's norms. *Wagner-Miret*[25] is a representative case of a court explicitly defending this position. *Wagner-Miret* was a case about compensation for unpaid salaries in case of insolvency of the employer, with Spanish legislation prior to the relevant directive (Council Directive 80/987/EEC,[26] protecting employees in case of insolvency of the employer) excluding compensation for managers as opposed to general workers. Here one finds an explicit defence of the Spanish policy to exclude compensation for higher management staff on the basis

[24] As I have argued elsewhere, the hands-off approach of the ECJ/CJEU appears to be consistent throughout its case law, whether concerning vertical (such as *Von Colson* and *Wagner-Miret*) or horizontal claims (such as *Pfeiffer*) – including claims decided with no reference at all to indirect effect in cases in which the Court has equally defended the autonomy of domestic laws in matters of social policy (*cf* Case C-411/05 *F Palacios de la Villa v Cortefiel Servicios SA* [2007] ECR I-8531, paras 69–71: 'it is … for the competent authorities of the Member States to find the right balance between the different interests involved' on the basis of 'political, economic, social … and/or budgetary considerations and having regard to the actual situation in the labour market in a particular Member State', for example in relation to choices regarding the prolonging of people's working life or, conversely, the provision of early retirement.' The Court then confirmed that the Member States enjoy 'broad discretion in matters of social policy' in the remarkable Case C-388/07 *The Incorporated Trustees of the National Council on Ageing v Secretary of State* [2009] ECR I-1569, para 65, before turning to its new jurisprudence of heteronomy, which I discuss in the rest of the chapter (see also Niglia, 'Eclipse of the Constitution' (n 1)).

[25] *Wagner-Miret* (n 22) paras 20 et seq.

[26] [1980] OJ L283/23. See *Wagner-Miret* (n 22).

of the straightforward consideration that Spanish legislation prior to the directive explicitly excluded it (paragraph 22).

Sometimes the Court has instead focused on the Union law side of the equation, suggesting ways for the domestic courts to 'rationalise' domestic social law in the light of the relevant directive. This happened in *Habermann*,[27] a case regarding the termination of a contract of employment under German special legislation prohibiting assignment of women who are pregnant to night-time work. Here the Court held that to apply the Equal Treatment Directive would lead not to 'excessive protectionism' of mother workers with bad consequences for the rest of the workers, as per one submission before the Court, but to effective protection of the worker and therefore better implementation of the very policy underlying domestic legislation:

> In the circumstances, to acknowledge that the contract may be held to be invalid or may be avoided because of the temporary inability of the pregnant employee to perform the night-time work for which she has been engaged would be contrary to the objective of protecting such persons pursued by Article 2(3) of the directive, and would deprive that provision of its effectiveness.
>
> Accordingly, termination of a contract for an indefinite period on grounds of the woman's pregnancy, whether by annulment or avoidance, cannot be justified by the fact that she is temporarily prevented, by a statutory prohibition imposed because of pregnancy, from performing night-time work.[28]

And yet, in its case law, the Court recalls that it is up to domestic courts 'as far as possible' to interpret national legislation in conformity with the relevant directive, thus adopting its usual hands-off approach that leaves to domestic courts the power to make their own determinations in balancing the interests at stake. One more case that falls in line with the *Habermann* approach is *Pfeiffer*.[29]

In *Pfeiffer*, the Court praised the relevant directive's requirements and yet, once more, left it to the domestic courts to decide the way they think most appropriate in the circumstances. Thus, the Court considered the 48 working hours' weekly limit contained in Council Directive 93/104/EC to be a key social right, but made its operation conditional on whether the national courts could implement that right by way of conforming interpretation – even for a highly regarded right such as the right to rest (at paragraph 99). It should be noted that, in this sense, *Pfeiffer* is similar to *Von Colson*. For here, the Court equally left it to the national courts to decide ultimately on the issue – despite the fact that it was strongly held that any sanction needs to be adequate (that is to say, effective and deterrent) and, specifically, that a nominal regime of damages fails to be adequate.[30]

[27] Case C-421/92 *Habermann-Beltermann v Arbeiterwohlfart* [1994] ECR I-1657, paras 17 et seq.
[28] ibid paras 24–25.
[29] *Pfeiffer* (n 22).
[30] *Von Colson* (n 10) para 28.

After the introduction of the new doctrine, the Court not only confirmed it in labour law disputes, but broadened its scope to cover another socially sensitive field – that of private consumer law.[31] *Faccini Dori*[32] is the landmark judgment that exemplifies the line of cases in which indirect effect has been applied in consumer private law disputes. As usual, here the Court acted out of majoritarian concerns, that is, the strongly held belief among political actors that Union private law consumer rules via directives should be enacted to facilitate the internal market, but on condition of not endangering the autonomy of states in regulating private law matters of relevance to consumer policy.[33] This equilibrium was then put at risk by the introduction of majority voting. As a result of the introduction of the new system of voting, various directives could be approved that would bluntly overstep those limitations, thanks to the strong bargaining position in which the Commission found itself vis-à-vis the Member States.[34]

Ever since *Faccini Dori*, the Court has been applying 'indirect effect' in both labour and consumer law disputes,[35] thus ultimately empowering judges to defend domestic social policies, in reaction to the Commission-led project of harmonisation via directives that, starting from the late 1980s and in the light of the deregulatory policies enshrined in the Single European Act,[36] has become highly sceptical of, and indeed interested in dismantling, the system of domestic interventionism in the social sphere.[37]

* * *

Looking at the interpretative obligation, or indirect effect, case law of the CJEU from the perspective of national law, what has been disputed in scholarship is the extent

[31] See Niglia, *The Struggle for European Private Law* (n 3); H Micklitz, *The Politics of Judicial Co-operation in the EU* (Cambridge, Cambridge University Press, 2005) 30 ('distributive and substantive justice … form the core of private consumer law').

[32] *Faccini Dori* (n 7).

[33] S Weatherill, 'The Constitutional Competence of the EU to Deliver Social Justice' (2006) 2 *European Review of Contract Law* 136, 143.

[34] Niglia, *The Transformation of Contract in Europe* (n 3) 93 et seq; L Niglia, '"The Rules Dilemma" – The Court of Justice and the Dilemma of the Regulation of Standard Form Contracts in Europe' (2006) 13 *Columbia Journal of European Law* 124. As I have noted elsewhere (Niglia, 'Form and Substance in European Constitutional Law' (n 17)), consider also P Beaumont and S Weatherill, *EU Law* (Harmondsworth, Penguin, 1999) (interpreting *Faccini Dori* as a reaction to the Maastricht-Urteil of the German Federal Constitutional Court, that is, as a sign of a more cautious judicial approach to the issue of 'competences').

[35] *Pfeiffer* (n 22). The defence of domestic policies vital to national sovereignty, such as those in the area of labour and consumer law, as central to the construction of 'indirect effect' explains why the Court has employed the same doctrine in relation to another range of disputes – those in which individual freedoms protected under the principle of legality in criminal matters are at stake – with a view to defending one more area vital to state sovereignty: that of criminal law. For the Court holds that the application of 'indirect effect' cannot result in the imposition or aggravation of criminal liability on an individual: *cf* the discussion in P Craig and G de Búrca, *EU Law. Text, Cases and Materials*, 4th edn (Oxford, Oxford University Press, 2007) ch 8 (where there is relevant case law).

[36] Niglia, *The Transformation of Contract in Europe* (n 3) 93 et seq (in relation to private consumer law); S Giubboni, *Social Rights and Market Freedom in the European Constitution. A Labour Law Perspective* (Cambridge, Cambridge University Press, 2006) 56 et seq (in relation to labour law).

[37] See ch 3 below.

to which domestic techniques of interpretation are amenable to, and are required to, accommodate the requirement of a 'conforming interpretation'.

Some argue that indirect effect is a heuristic tool that obliges national courts to use any domestic technique of interpretation in a way that achieves the objective of conformity in any case.[38]

Others argue that domestic techniques of interpretation should be used so as to do only what is 'possible' under the constraints of national methods of interpretation.[39] The latter is a position that, in contrast to the former, admits of the possibility that no domestic techniques of interpretation are available for the job of conforming interpretation, and that, in such a case, the relevant directive's rule would not be applicable per 'indirect effect'.

A middle-of-the-ground thesis has also been suggested. According to this understanding, judges are supposed to strive for interpretative conformity, at the cost of sacrificing interpretive methods recognised by national law, only to the extent that the will of the national legislature to transpose the directive correctly can be proven to exist.[40]

This overall debate and its conflicting positions have been perceived as evidencing a kind of internal 'weakness' of the interpretative obligation doctrine, insofar as it is not capable of ensuring the full effectiveness of the relevant directives in horizontal relationships. According to this perception, the CJEU has been 'wrong' in not adopting direct effect in horizontal relationships. Also, there has always been controversy as to the 'correct interpretation' of the interpretative obligation with regard to the extent to which, and as to whether, it could entail a duty to interpret consistently even in situations in which adapting a conforming interpretation would entail a *contra legem* interpretation of national law.[41] However, a

[38] *cf* eg W Brechmann, *Die Richtlinienkonforme Auslegung: Zugleich ein Beitrag zur Dogmatik der EG-Richtlinie* (Munich, CH Beck, 1994): a view thus reconstructed and labelled 'absolute primacy' by M Amstuz, 'In-Between Worlds: Marleasing and the Emergence of Interlegality in Legal Reasoning' (2005) 11 *European Law Journal* 766, 770 et seq.

[39] See the rest of this chapter for the development of this position as articulated, inter alia, in the works of, eg Craig and de Búrca (n 35) 290; C-W Canaris, 'Die richtlinienkonforme Auslegung und Rechtsfortbildung im System der juristischen Methodenlehre' in H Koziol and P Rummel (eds), *Im Dienste der Gerechtigkeit: Festschrift für Franz Bydlinski* (Berlin, Springer, 2002) 60; M Zuleeg, *Auslegung europäischen Privatrechts und angeglichenen Rechts* (Baden-Baden, Nomos, 1999) 163 et seq. See further the literature cited in Amstuz (n 38) 772, on which I have drawn for this reconstruction of the German side of the debate in Niglia, 'Form and Substance in European Constitutional Law' (n 17).

[40] S Grundmann, *Europäisches Schuldvertragsrecht: Das europäische Recht der Unternehmensgeschäfte* (Berlin, de Gruyter, 1999) 116 et seq (a view labelled as 'limited primacy' by Amstuz (n 38)). For more discussion, see L Niglia, 'Conforming Interpretation' [2022] *European Review of Private Law* 635.

[41] See eg the Opinion of the Advocate General Ruiz-Jarabo Colomer in *Pfeiffer* (n 22) http://curia.europa.eu/juris/document/document_print.jsf;jsessionid=D2C3F75944C3C23BF118D2A877BA78DD?docid=49085&text=&dir=&doclang=EN&part=1&occ=first&mode=DOC&pageIndex=0&cid=16750632 and the discussion surrounding the judgment Case C-106/89 *Marleasing* [1990] ECR I-4135. For criticism of the scholarship that considers the interpretative obligation negatively for not being capable of enabling the full effectiveness of the relevant directives compared to the 'better' available doctrine of direct effect, see Niglia, 'Form and Substance in European Constitutional Law' (n 17) (such scholarship being too biased towards a centralised and hierarchical interpretation of the meaning

look at the wider constitutional context that this chapter proposes enables a better understanding of the doctrine of the interpretative obligation.

Upon a closer reading of the above-noted case law, one can see how the interpretation emphasising the aspect of the 'extent of possibility' captures in full the deep structure of the position of the CJEU. In fact, a *contra legem* interpretation is not required according to a comprehensive reading of the decisions of the Court.[42] This is also evident in the judgment *Pfeiffer*, where the Court has reinterpreted the judgment *Marleasing* as not commanding a *contra legem* interpretation.[43] Note paragraphs 115 and 116 of the *Pfeiffer* decision:

> Although the principle that national law must be interpreted in conformity with Community law concerns chiefly domestic provisions enacted in order to implement the directive in question, it does not entail an interpretation merely of those provisions but requires the national court to consider national law as a whole in order to assess to what extent it may be applied so as not to produce a result contrary to that sought by the directive. In that context, if the application of interpretative methods recognised by national law enables, in certain circumstances, a provision of domestic law to be construed in such a way as to avoid conflict with another rule of domestic law or the scope of that provision to be restricted to that end by applying it only insofar as it is compatible with the rule concerned, the national court is bound to use those methods in order to achieve the result sought by the directive.

***

Consideration of the most recent case law of the CJEU, over the last decade or so, allows one to capture the meaning of the interpretative obligation better, by looking at what has been lost of it and what it has become in recent times, that is, a proxy for the doctrine of direct effect mechanically applied to horizontal relationships.

Let me analyse this case law for the purpose of describing better the interpretative obligation whilst leaving it to chapter three to deal with the heteronomous aspects of the new jurisprudence.

By considering the case law of the last decade, one can see what has been negated and left behind relative to the above-noted jurisprudence. This comparative contrast helps us understand better the features of the jurisprudence of constitutional autonomy through the interpretative obligation. The radical element of the top-down regimentation of interpretation through the interpretative obligation, as in the *Marleasing* judgment[44] interpretative position whereby a consistent interpretation should go as far as being *contra legem*, has always been out there and ready made for blocking off the approach towards an open rendition of the

of EU constitutional law); see also Niglia, 'Eclipse of the Constitution' (n 1) (on composite constitutionalism in Europe). See also Niglia, 'Conforming Interpretation' (n 40).

[42] Craig and de Búrca (n 35) 290.

[43] See respectively *Pfeiffer* (n 22) paras 87 et seq; *Marleasing* (n 41).

[44] *Marleasing* (n 41).

interpretative obligation:[45] that radical element emerges now as the one that in the end appears to win the day, ultimately prevailing over the once established position.

Namely, over the last decade, the interpretative obligation has taken on a new substance. It has been radically transformed into its constitutional reverse, that is, an obligation placed on national courts to interpret national law so as to make it enforce European law (the relevant directives), notwithstanding any of the limitations that might be derived under national law, which the judge is bluntly requested to ignore in order to comply with the pre-eminent objective of achieving effectiveness in any case. I will first look at the recent case of *OPR-Finance*.[46]

The dispute concerned a revolving credit agreement concluded between GK and OPR-Finance by means of 'distance communication', with GK failing to repay a due credit instalment, and in relation to which OPR-Finance neither stated nor proved that 'before concluding the credit agreement in question, it had assessed the borrower's creditworthiness'.[47] At the same time, 'GK did not raise an objection of nullity of the agreement on that ground', considering the circumstance that 'Under Paragraph 87(1) of Law No 257/2016 on consumer credit, nullity of the credit agreement is a penalty that is applicable only if an objection to that effect has been raised by the consumer' – the preliminary reference having been brought before the CJEU in consideration of the fact that 'The referring court takes the view that such a rule undermines consumer protection, as guaranteed by Directive 2008/48'.[48]

As far as EU law is concerned, the applicable directive, Directive 2008/48, in its Articles 8 and 23, provides for the nullity of the credit agreement in the case of a lack of assessment of 'the consumer's creditworthiness on the basis of sufficient information, where appropriate, obtained from the consumer and, where necessary, on the basis of a consultation of the relevant database'. Nullity, in turn, entails that the consumer will have to repay only the principal sum and not interests.[49] That is, in the words of the Court:

> In the present case, according to the information contained in the request for a preliminary ruling, a failure to comply with the creditors pre-contractual obligation to assess the borrowers creditworthiness imposed by Paragraph 86 of Law No 257/2016 on consumer credit is penalised, in accordance with Paragraph 87 of that law, by the nullity of the credit agreement, linked with an obligation on the consumer to return only the principal sum to the creditor at a time appropriate to the consumers financial capacity, *on condition that that consumer raises that objection of nullity within a limitation period of three years from the conclusion of the agreement.* Thus, in the event that the penalty provided for by that law is applied, namely the nullity of the credit agreement, the creditor loses its rights to payment of the agreed interest and costs. (emphasis added)

[45] In the sense of blocking off the opening of EU law to the internal (that is to say, national) hermeneutical private law determinations.

[46] Case 679/18 *OPR-Finance s.r.o. v GK* 5 March 2020.

[47] ibid para 12.

[48] ibid para 13.

[49] ibid para 29.

However, this being the matter referred to the CJEU:

> [A]ccording to the information contained in the request for a preliminary ruling, *the national court is, according to established Czech legal practice, prohibited from applying, of its own motion, the penalty of nullity* of the credit agreement linked with an obligation to return the principal sum, provided for in the event of failure of the creditor to comply with the pre-contractual obligation to assess the consumers creditworthiness. (emphasis added)[50]

The Court then decided the issue through an explicit reference to the interpretative obligation applied along the following lines of reasoning:

> As regards that prohibition, it must be borne in mind that, as the Court has consistently held, when national courts apply domestic law, they are bound to interpret it, so far as possible, in the light of the wording and the purpose of Directive 2008/48 in order to achieve the result sought by that directive and consequently comply with the third paragraph of Article 288 TFEU. This obligation to interpret national law in conformity with EU law is inherent in the system of the TFEU Treaty, since it permits national courts, for the matters within their jurisdiction, to ensure the full effectiveness of EU law when they determine the disputes before them (judgment of 21 April 2016, *Radlinger and Radlingerová*, C-377/14, ECLI:EU:C:2016:283, paragraph 79).
>
> Moreover, the Court has ruled on numerous occasions that the principle that national law must be interpreted in conformity with European Union law requires national courts to do whatever lies within their jurisdiction, taking the whole body of domestic law into consideration and applying the interpretative methods recognised by domestic law, with a view to ensuring that the directive in question is fully effective and to achieving an outcome consistent with the objective pursued by it (see, to that effect, judgment of 24 January 2012, *Dominguez*, C-282/10, ECLI:EU:C:2012:33, paragraph 27 and the case-law cited).
>
> It should be added that national courts, including those giving judgment at final instance, *must change their established case-law, where necessary, if it is based on an interpretation of national law that is incompatible with the objectives of a directive* (see, to that effect, judgment of 5 September 2019, *Pohotovosť*, C-331/18, ECLI:EU:C:2019:665, paragraph 56 and the case-law cited).
>
> It follows that the referring court cannot, in the main proceedings, validly claim that it is impossible for it to interpret the provisions of national law at issue in a manner that is compatible with EU law, for the sole reason that those provisions have been interpreted, by the Czech courts, in a way that is not compatible with EU law. Thus, it is for the referring court to ensure that Directive 2008/48 is given full effect, and if necessary to disapply, on its own authority, the interpretation adopted by the Czech courts, since that interpretation is not compatible with EU law (see, by analogy, judgment of 8 November 2016, *Ognyanov*, C-554/14, ECLI:EU:C:2016:835, paragraphs 69 and 70 and the case-law cited). (emphasis added)[51]

[50] ibid para 40.
[51] ibid paras 41–44.

In other words, here is a Copernican-like revolutionary step of the CJEU interpretative obligation jurisprudence, considering that, in case of an internally established case law whereby national law is interpreted in ways that are incompatible with the objectives of a directive, the national courts are placed under an obligation *to change their own established case law* with a view to making it compatible with the relevant directive's objectives.

The interpretative obligation remains a tool of 'indirect effect' only to the minimal extent that national law must be interpreted in the light of the relevant directive as opposed to the previous maximal extent of any such interpretation being made conditional on the possibility of the conforming interpretation. This is an articulation of the doctrine of 'direct effect' by other means.

Note the remarkable requirement 'if necessary, to disapply, on its own authority, the interpretation adopted by the Czech courts' insofar as it is not consistent with the directive'. Here is a turning upside down of the core hermeneutical structure of the interpretative obligation and of its substantive meaning. Rather than making determinations depend on the extent of possibility of interpretation, the interpretative obligation turns into an instrument for the mere effectiveness of EU law. Rather than the authority of the national courts as traceable to their own understanding of the law, here is an articulation of authority meant to be about just implementing the commands based on EU law. And interpretations of national law are targeted and 'disapplied' through the deployment of the long-established institute of disapplication outside the realm of direct effect and within the realm of the interpretative obligation.[52]

***

This transformation of the interpretative obligation into a direct effect tool, as manifested by the obligation placed on the national courts to change their own national law, effectively entails a neutralisation of the interpretative obligation as developed until the new jurisprudence epitomised by the *OPR-Finance* judgment.[53]

It is only part of a line of cases in which the CJEU has started gradually to shift away from the paradigm of constitutional autonomy, based on the pillar of the interpretative obligation, towards an absolutisation of European law understood as 'incorporating' (by constitutional absorption) national law – given that any interpretation of national law conflicting with EU law must be disapplied and set aside.

[52] As a result of the CJEU's *OPR-Finance* decision, the consumer is protected from paying fees and interest on the instalments for cases where the bank fails to comply with the obligation to assess creditworthiness, notwithstanding the consumer's failure to raise the objection of the said failure within three months. In other words, the CJEU is firmly implementing the balancing provided for by the directive consisting of the bank's own assessment of the creditworthiness of any potential borrowers towards enabling 'informed choice' regardless of the formal system of rights and duties (including procedural) provided for under national law. Therefore, at work is not protection of the consumer under national law, but 'protection' based on market circumstances: for a genealogy of market circumstances in European (and private) law, see Niglia, *The Transformation of Contract in Europe* (n 3).

[53] See CJEU *OPR-Finance* (n 46).

The above-noted *OPR-Finance* judgment is one step in this process, itself preceded by two major decisions, *Dominguez* and *Radlinger and Radlingerová*, which are worthy of attention in order to capture the graduality of, and the firmness of, the CJEU in shifting away from the traditional jurisprudence on the interpretative obligation whilst adopting instead a transformed kind of interpretative obligation akin to direct effect.

First is the Grand Chamber decision *Dominguez* of 2012.[54] This is a kind of intermediate decision in which the Court both confirms the previous case law on the interpretative obligation and breaks new boundaries towards the position then established in the *OPR-Finance* judgment. After the premise:

> Since Article 7(1) of Directive 2003/88 fulfils the conditions required to produce a direct effect, it should also be noted that the CICOA, one of the two respondents in the main proceedings and Ms Dominguez's employer, is a body operating in the field of social security.

Recalling the 'estoppel principle', the Court held that:

> It is true that the Court has consistently held that a directive cannot of itself impose obligations on an individual and cannot therefore be relied on as such against an individual (see, inter alia, Case C-91/92 *Faccini Dori* [1994] ECR I-3325, paragraph 20; Case C-192/94 *El Corte Inglés* [1996] ECR I-1281, paragraph 15; *Pfeiffer and Others*, paragraph 108; and *Kücükdeveci*, paragraph 46).
>
> It should also be recalled however that, where a person is able to rely on a directive not as against an individual but as against the State he may do so regardless of the capacity in which the latter is acting, whether as employer or as public authority. In either case it is necessary to prevent the State from taking advantage of its own failure to comply with European Union law (see, inter alia, Case 152/84 *Marshall* [1986] ECR 723, paragraph 49; Case C-188/89 *Foster and Others* [1990] ECR I-3313, paragraph 17; and Case C-343/98 *Collino and Chiappero* [2000] ECR I-6659, paragraph 22).
>
> Thus the entities against which the provisions of a directive that are capable of having direct effect may be relied upon include a body, whatever its legal form, which has been made responsible, pursuant to a measure adopted by the State, for providing a public service under the control of the State and has for that purpose special powers beyond those which result from the normal rules applicable in relations between individuals (see, inter alia, *Foster and Others*, paragraph 20; *Collino and Chiappero*, paragraph 23; and Case C-356/05 *Farrell* [2007] ECR I-3067, paragraph 40).
>
> It is therefore for the national court to determine whether Article 7(1) of Directive 2003/88 may be relied upon against the CICOA.

However, the Court then chose to exercise caution:

> If that is the case, as Article 7 of Directive 2003/88 fulfils the conditions required to produce a direct effect, the consequence would be that the national court would have to disregard any conflicting national provision.

[54] Case 282/12 *Maribel Dominguez v Centre informatique du Centre Ouest Atlantique and Préfet de la région Centre* ECLI:EU:C:2011:559. See also Case 282/12 *Maribel Dominguez* in ch 3.

> If that is not the case, it should be borne in mind that even a clear, precise and unconditional provision of a directive seeking to confer rights or impose obligations on individuals cannot of itself apply in proceedings exclusively between private parties (see *Pfeiffer and Others*, paragraph 109).
>
> In such a situation, the party injured as a result of domestic law not being in conformity with European Union law can none the less rely on the judgment in Joined Cases C-6/90 and C-9/90 *Francovich and Others* [1991] ECR I-5357 in order to obtain, if appropriate, compensation for the loss sustained.
>
> The answer to the second question is therefore that it is for the national court to determine, taking the whole body of domestic law into consideration, in particular Article L. 223-4 of the Code du travail, and applying the interpretative methods recognised by domestic law, with a view to ensuring that Article 7 of Directive 2003/88 is fully effective and achieving an outcome consistent with the objective pursued by it, whether it can find an interpretation of that law that allows the absence of the worker due to an accident on the journey to or from work to be treated as being equivalent to one of the situations covered by that article of the Code du travail.
>
> If such an interpretation is not possible, it is for the national court to determine whether, in the light of the legal nature of the respondents in the main proceedings, the direct effect of Article 7(1) of Directive 2003/88 may be relied upon against them.
>
> If the national court is unable to achieve the objective laid down in Article 7 of Directive 2003/88, the party injured as a result of domestic law not being in conformity with European Union law can none the less rely on the judgment in Francovich and Others in order to obtain, if appropriate, compensation for the loss sustained.

The Court stressed the point that at stake was a claim against a body that might be held to be statist (a vertical claim) and yet, under the so-called 'estoppel principle', it nevertheless applied the doctrine of the interpretative obligation, thus reconstructing it not as autonomous from, and radically alternative to, the line of case law on direct effect but as if becoming part of it. 'Applying the interpretative methods recognised by domestic law' with a view to 'achieving an outcome consistent with the objective pursued by' the directive (ie conformity) is prioritised over the use of direct effect by the national courts given the verticality of the claim against a body that might be held to be statist (were the national court to believe that that body is to be assimilated to the state because the company is a social security entity).

This effectively deconstructs the proper domain of the interpretative obligation as autonomous and a radically alternative doctrine relative to direct effect. It makes the interpretative obligation just one more step of the classical direct effect reasoning apparatus: according to this decision, once a vertical claim against a state body fails due to a lack of the possibility of a conformity in interpretation, there would then be scope for assessing whether the relevant norms have direct effect and, should the relevant norms in turn not be held to be characterised by direct effect, reliance on state liability would be available as a further remedy.

This is a line of argument that is then carried to its extreme consequences, that is, to the obliteration of indirect effect understood as articulation of the jurisprudence of constitutional autonomy, in the judgment of *Radlinger and Radlingerová*.

The second step of the path of the jurisprudence under consideration, leading to the above-noted *OPR-Finance* judgment, can be seen in the CJEU judgment of 21 April 2016 in C-377/14 *Radlinger and Radlingerová*[55] – a judgment that furthers the alteration of (that is, the transformation of) the doctrine of the interpretative obligation by developing further the Court's approach adopted in *Dominguez*. Specifically:

> By its third question, the national court, after having noted that the dispute in the main proceedings concerns two individuals, asks, in essence, whether the relevant provisions of Directives 93/13 and 2008/48 have direct effect.
>
> In that connection, it must be recalled that, under the third paragraph of Article 288 TFEU, the directive, while binding, as to the result to be achieved, upon each Member State to which it is addressed, leaves to the national authorities the choice of form and methods. Thus, *a directive cannot of itself impose obligations on an individual and cannot therefore be relied on as such against an individual* (judgment of 24 January 2012 in *Dominguez*, C-282/10, ECLI:EU:C:2012:33, paragraph 37 and the case-law cited). *Nonetheless the obligation on a Member State to take all the measures necessary to achieve the result prescribed by a directive is a binding obligation imposed by the third paragraph of Article 288 TFEU and by the directive itself. That duty to take all appropriate measures, whether general or particular, is binding on all the authorities of Member States including, for matters within their jurisdiction, the courts* (judgment of 24 June 2008 in *Commune de Mesquer*, C-188/07, ECLI:EU:C:2008:359, point 83 and the case-law cited).
>
> In the present case, firstly, the obligation to examine ex officio the unfairness of certain terms and the presence of mandatory information in a credit agreement constitutes a procedural rule placed not on an individual but on the courts (see, by analogy, judgments of 10 September 2014 in *Kušionová*, C-34/13, ECLI:EU:C:2014:2189, paragraph 67, and 18 February 2016 in *Finanmadrid EFC*, C-49/14, ECLI:EU:C:2016:98, point 35 and the case-law cited).
>
> Secondly, as is apparent from the wording of Article 23 of Directive 2008/48, the Member States' authorities must ensure, when transposing and implementing the directive, that effective, proportionate and dissuasive penalties are implemented.

Moreover, it must be borne in mind,

> *as the Court has consistently held, that when national courts apply domestic law, they are bound to interpret it, so far as possible, in the light of the wording and the purpose of Directive 2008/48 in order to achieve the result sought by the directive and consequently comply with the third paragraph of Article 288 TFEU. This obligation to interpret national law in conformity with EU law is inherent in the system of the FEU Treaty, since it permits national courts, for the matters within their jurisdiction, to ensure the full effectiveness of EU law when they determine the disputes before them* (see, by analogy, judgment of 24 January 2012 in *Dominguez*, C-282/10, ECLI:EU:C:2012:33, paragraph 24 and the case-law cited). It is therefore unnecessary to answer the third question. (emphasis added)[56]

[55] Judgment of 21 April 2016, Case C-377/14 *Radlinger and Radlingerová* ECLI:EU:C:2016:283.
[56] ibid.

The response is caught in the language of the principle of effectiveness. Here, one question had been put to the Court:

> Do the provisions of the directives applied above have direct effect and is their direct application precluded by the fact that the initiation of an incidental action by the court ex officio (or, from the point of view of national law, the inadmissible review of a claim on the basis of an ineffective contestation by the debtor-consumer) encroaches on the horizontal relationship between the consumer and the supplier of goods or services?

It is a question about horizontality as precluding direct effect that is not really answered other than through reliance on an altered rendition of the interpretative obligation as imposing an obligation 'not on individuals', but on 'the courts', that is, as if removing the fact that previously the Court had been consistently holding that it is exactly for the purpose of sheltering individuals from obligations descending from the directives that the courts, under indirect effect, have been held to be subjected to an obligation to interpret in conformity to the extent that this is possible. Here, instead, the court sees national courts as addressees of the Article 288 TFEU obligation to enforce the directive whilst sacrificing the purpose of sheltering individuals from the substantive obligations provided for in the relevant directive. This the Court does through simply automatically demanding that the national court apply the interpretative obligation doctrine through reference to *Dominguez*, as a means of ensuring the effectiveness of EU law.

Disregarding even any reference to the so-called estoppel principle, which *Dominguez* did, here the Court mistakes a dispute about horizontal relationships for one about vertical relationships insofar as applying to the former a modified version of the conventional set of doctrines associated with the latter. The interpretative obligation as a result becomes a mere tool for ensuring the outright effectiveness of EU law. This amounts to a true obliteration of the structure and function of the doctrine of interpretative obligation,[57] considering that the Court chooses to obliterate its traditional meaning through only formalistic arguments, that is, the argument from its holding regarding 'inherence' 'in the system of the TFEU Treaty' and arguments from 'analogy'. These formalistic arguments are, in turn, adopted with a view to setting aside exactly those dimensions of the traditional structure of the interpretative obligation formula whose objective is to protect individuals from the substantive obligations contained in the relevant directive. 'It is therefore unnecessary to answer the third question', the Court apodictically holds.

Here, the Court re-embraces the naked *Van Duyn*-like policy, consisting of a kind of fundamentalisation of EU rights as contained in directives, which the Court will then soon dress up again in the doctrinal garb of the interpretative obligation, but reread as a direct effect tool: this being the output of the 2020

[57] Compare Case C-237/02 *Freiburger Kommunalbauten GmbH Baugesellschaft and Co KG v Ludger Hofstetter and Ulrike Hofstetter* [2004] ECR I-3403: see ch 3 (also obliterating the doctrine of interpretative obligation not by changing it but by omitting mentioning it); Case C-341/05 *Laval un Partneri Ltd v Svenska Byggnadsarbetareförbundet* ECLI:EU:C:2007:809 (on the Directive on Posted Workers).

decision in *OPR-Finance*, noted above, where a further step is accomplished – that of making all the more clearer that the interpretative obligation would entail the obligation to 'change the established case-law' if inconsistent with EU law.

III. The Jurisprudence of Constitutional Autonomy Through the Lenses of National Private Laws

This section considers the jurisprudence of constitutional autonomy from the bottom up, that is, from the viewpoint of the constitutional, hermeneutical praxis of national private laws.

Through the jurisprudence of constitutional autonomy, and specifically its concretisation through the interpretative obligation, that developed until its structural transformation over the last 10 years into a proxy for direct effect,[58] the Court of Justice has chosen to shelter from the reach of market integration a world of determinations based on 'balancing' as articulated under national law. That is, the balancing of normative considerations as undertaken in national private law circles (judges, lawyers) in relation to issues such as the right of cancellation (eg *Faccini Dori*) or labour rights (eg *Von Colson*) are not meant to be encroached upon by EU law norms (the directives) unless it is *possible*, under national law, to achieve conformity.[59] It is an 'outside-inside' space that the interpretative obligation has given rise to, consisting of the legal actors operating under the triad of mutual learning, mutual respect and co-evolutionary normativisation (co-normativisation) as I reconstruct it in section IV.

Here, determinations based on balancing are a contingent phenomenon, that is, the phenomenon of the relevant legal actors' work – the constitutional praxis of judges deciding disputes, and the related scholarly commentaries – of balancing the interests at stake in contracts or property or tort liability relations with a 'social' orientation (social balancing).[60]

By social orientation of such balancing is meant determinations aimed at (embeddedness in) societal expectations, as interpreted and defended by the legal actors, in terms of interdependence and solidarity, according to the imperative of the protection of weak contractual parties.[61]

Such determinations are, in turn, *constitutionally* entrenched, as opposed to allegedly descending from natural law, or characterised as outrightly non-secular/religious law or as merely about and deriving from economic criteria of legitimation.[62] At the same time, they are also determinations which are 'statist'

[58] On this transformation, see ch 3 and above at section II.

[59] See above at section II.

[60] On further actors in the context of transformation, see ch 4.

[61] On interdependence and solidarity in private law, see Niglia, *The Struggle for European Private Law* (n 3) (with relevant references).

[62] For more discussion of the interface between sociality and private law, see Niglia, *The Struggle for European Private Law* (n 3).

in the sense that their articulation of the private law discourse is part of the *state* constitutional order. In other words, balancing here is both societal-social constitutional and state-social constitutional at once. This is what can be labelled *social-constitutional balancing*.

***

Market integration confronts a variety of policy preferences and institutional sensitivities incorporated in national jurisdictions. Such policy and institutional variety is also connotative of the European private law field. Here, the relevant actors (judges, scholars, legislators) work towards balancing the interests at stake in contracts or property relations (balancing). Distinct types of capitalism ('varieties of capitalism', more or less liberal, more or less interventionist) correlate with the contingent patterns of balancing as they characterise the national legal traditions of private law.[63] Yet, as developed nationally for a long period of time until the recent new transformation detailed in the following chapters, such balancing patterns have all been 'social' (social balancing) due to their close link with (embeddedness in) societal expectations as interpreted and defended by the legal actors operating in a paradigm of welfare state constitutional systems. This paradigm is characterised by the traits of interdependence and solidarity standards,[64] and is also 'statist' in the sense of intending private law to be part of the state constitutional order (balancing as societal and state-constitutional at once).[65] This structural alignment of balancing as plural/societal and as statist at once indicates that the phenomenon under scrutiny is a contingent kind of Europeanisation that targets, whilst being respectful of, long-established forms of social-constitutional balancing.[66]

Diachronically, Europeanisation has been organised according to the paradigm of constitutional autonomy in two complementary ways, then set aside in a new jurisprudence that I consider in the chapters that follow.[67]

[63] G Teubner, 'Legal Irritants: Good Faith in British Law or How Unifying Law Ends Up in New Divergencies' (1998) 61 *MLR* 1; Niglia, *The Struggle for European Private Law* (n 3); on varieties of capitalism, see J Hien and C Joerges (eds), *Responses of European Economic Cultures to Europe's Crisis Politics: The Example of German–Italian Discrepancies* (Florence, European University Institute, 2018); PF Kjaer, *The Law of Political Economy. Transformation in the Function of Law* (Cambridge, Cambridge University Press, 2020).

[64] See the rest of this chapter.

[65] Integration can be organised in ways that enable such plural chains of balancing (constitutional autonomy) or in ways that are about closure towards them and even about suppressing them, as in the modes of constitutional heteronomy and of constitutional absorption, as I shall explain in the rest of this book: see chs 3–5.

[66] On disalignments, that is, on balancing decoupled from both state constitutionalism and the plural-societal at the same time as a result of 'absorption', see chs 3 and 4 below.

[67] On the synchronic relevance of the constitutional autonomy paradigm in the context of the present interpretative-discursive struggles, see ch 4 (the paradigm of constitutional autonomy as remaining a reference point in terms of contradictory element and/or 'resistance paradigm': see ch 5). Also see ch 4 on the CJEU deployment of the interpretative obligation recently, which corresponds to the new current transformations.

First, in the conventional sense of positive integration, European harmonisation measures in the area of private law have shown for a long period of time respect for the diverse policy and institutional varieties through the conventional forms of 'limited harmonisation', as with the EU directives based on 'minimum harmonisation', such as the Unfair Terms Directive (1993).[68]

Second, and correspondingly, the case law of the CJEU on the indirect effect (interpretative obligation) of the directives that has developed since *Von Colson* has been equally directed at implementing a limited, discrete kind of harmonisation. Consider, if read from the viewpoint of the interpretative obligation, the choice not to establish European constitution-based entitlements to strict rights to withdraw from contracts in *Faccini Dori*; or the choice to not encroach upon the autonomy of labour agreements.[69] Such are choices that consist of the reverse side of respecting the ways in which these issues are dealt with under balancing as practised within the nation-state orders – that is, I am arguing in this section, 'social balancing'.

This interface between, on the one hand, the settlement of disputes between private parties as they arise under the aegis of European law and, on the other hand, the national ways of balancing in private law as the determinant for the resolution of those disputes independently of European law is a key point of comparison in assessing the possibility or otherwise of interpretative conformity. It is also an interface that works in at least three senses, which I detail below. Each of the three senses shows the central role played by private law in the paradigm of constitutional autonomy, and vice versa – not unlike national constitutional systems whenever (structurally and functionally) the relationships between, on the one hand, constitutional norms and principles and, on the other hand, private law norms and principles are arranged under a scheme of interpretative obligation rather than the superimposition of the former over the latter, arrangements that have been commented upon in the literature that focuses on German law[70] and

[68] Council Directive 93/13/EEC of 5 April 1993 on unfair terms in consumer contracts [1993] OJ L95/29 (The Unfair Terms Directive 1993).

[69] CJEU Judgment of the Court of 21 September 1999, Case C-67/96 *Albany International BV v Stichting Bedrijfspensioenfonds Textielindustrie* [1999] ECR I-05751: see discussion in Niglia, 'Eclipse of the Constitution' (n 1).

[70] Compare, in Germany, the deployment of the doctrine of conforming interpretation, the so-called *gemeinschaftsrechtskonforme Auslegung*, as mediating between constitutional and private law materials. On the *gemeinschaftsrechtskonforme Auslegung – obligation d'interprétation conforme – interpretive obligation – obbligo di interpretazione conforme*, see, eg C Herresthal, 'Die richtlinienkonforme und die verfassungskonforme Auslegung, Privatrecht' [2014] *Jus* 289; Canaris, 'Die richtlinienkonforme Auslegung und Rechtsfortbildung im System der juristischen Methodenlehre' (n 39) 47, 81 et seq; P Müller-Graff, in Horn/Baur/Stern, 40 Jahre Röm. Verträge (1998) 107 et seq; L Niglia, 'Ai confini tra diritto privato e legislazione comunitaria. La teorica dell'obbligo interpretativo' (2001) 1 *Rivista Trimestrale di Diritto e Procedura Civile* 65; L Niglia, 'Diritto giurisprudenziale e direttive comunitarie in materia di diritto privato: note critiche' [1998] *Rivista critica di diritto privato* 459; Niglia, 'Form and Substance in European Constitutional Law' (n 17).

on other jurisdictions,[71] as well as in writings on both EU law and civil law.[72] The three senses, which I now consider, are: (i) constitutional hybridity; (ii) constitutional pluralism; and (iii) diffuse constitutional change.[73]

A. Constitutional Hybridity

Through the construction of the interpretative obligation – with its restraining approach that mirrors that of the EU legislature whenever choosing to issue

[71] Compare, in Italy, the relevance of the argument from constitutional conformity in the area of Italian constitutional law and constitutional adjudication: see, eg the discussion in G Azzariti (ed), *Interpretazione Costituzionale* (Turin, Giappichelli, 2007); G Zagrebelsky, 'La giustizia costituzionale nel 2003' [2004] *Giurisprudenza Costituzionale*; see, notably, Corte costituzionale judgment n 356 of 1996, holding that the question of unconstitutionality raised before the Constitutional Court is inadmissible, because there are various arguments and precedents supporting the possibility of interpreting the current legislation in conformity with the constitution ('inammissibilità della questione di costituzionalità sollevatale in quanto il giudice ha omesso di ricercare – o ha ricercato in modo inadeguato – l'interpretazione conforme a Costituzione') and that:'in principle, legislation is not considered unconstitutional because it is possible to interpret it *as difforming from* the constitution but because it is impossible to interpret it in conformity with the constitution ("In linea di principio, le leggi non si dichiarano costituzionalmente illegittime perchè e' possibile darne interpretazioni incostituzionali (e qualche giudice ritenga di darne), ma perchè e' impossibile darne interpretazioni costituzionali" and adding: "argomenti e precedenti giurisprudenziali non mancano a dimostrazione che il risultato al quale il giudice rimettente mira e ch'egli considera dovuto per ragioni costituzionali – la perdurante vigenza della norma del 1962 – può essere raggiunto sulla base dell'interpretazione delle norme vigenti, senza involgere la questione di legittimità costituzionale delle norme del 1992")' (emphasis added; G Zagrebelski as *redattore* of the judgment).

[72] For a treatment of the interpretative obligation with attention to both EU law and the civil law, see, eg Brechmann (n 38); Canaris, 'Die richtlinienkonforme Auslegung und Rechtsfortbildung im System der juristischen Methodenlehre' (n 39), 60; C-W Canaris, 'Grundrechte und Privatrecht' (1984) 184 *Archiv für die civilistische Praxis* 201; S Grundmann, *Die Auslegung des Gemeinschaftsrechts durch den Europäischen Gerichtshof: Zugleich eine rechtsvergleichhende Studie zur Auslegung im Völkerrecht und im Gemeinschaftsrecht* (Konstanz, Hartung-Gorre Verlag, 1996); H Heinrichs, 'Umsetzung der EG-Richtilinie ber mißbräuchliche Klauseln in Verbraucherverträchen durch Auslegung' [1995] *Neue Juristische Wochenschrift*; Niglia, 'Ai confini tra diritto privato e legislazione comunitaria' (ibid); Niglia, 'Diritto giurisprudenziale e direttive comunitarie' (ibid); Niglia, 'Form and Substance in European Constitutional Law' (n 17); Zuleeg (n 39) 163; H Heinrichs, 'Die Entwicklung des Rechts der Allgemeinen Geschaftsbedingungen im Jahre 1998' [1999] *Neue Juristische Wochenschrift* 1596, 1603; H Roth, 'EG-Richtlinien und Buegerliches Recht' [1999] *Juristen Zeitung* 529, 535. On the role of fundamental rights as protected under national constitutional laws, see C-W Canaris, 'Drittwirkung der gemeinschftsrechtichen Grundfreiheite' (2002) S [29]–67 *Umwelt, Wirtschaft und Recht* 31; G Brüggemeier, A Colombi Ciacchi and G Comandé, *Fundamental Rights and Private Law in the European Union*, vols I and II (Cambridge, Cambridge University Press, 2010); D Leczykiewicz and S Weatherill (eds), *The Involvement of EU Law in Private Law Relationships* (Oxford, Oxford University Press, 2013); K Lenaerts and J Gutierrez-Fons, 'The Constitutional Allocation of Powers and General Principles of EU Law' [2010] *CML Rev* 1629; H Micklitz and N Reich, *Europäisches Verbraucherrecht* (Baden-Baden, Nomos, 2003) 49 et seq and 95 et seq (on the impact of the European *Marköffnung*); S Perner, *Grundfreiheiten, Grundrechte-Charta und Privatrecht* (Tübingen, Mohr Siebeck, 2013) 84; see also the contributions by S Perner, P Lewish, P-W Müller-Graf and LK Binder in F Leidenmühler (ed), *Grundfreiheiten – Grundrechte – Europäisches Haftungsrecht* (Vienna, Verlag Österreich, 2012); R Brownsword, H-W Micklitz, L Niglia and S Weatherill (eds), *The Foundations of European Private Law* (Oxford, Hart Publishing, 2011).

[73] Each of the three show the central role played by private law in the paradigm of constitutional autonomy.

minimum rather than maximum harmonisation directives[74] – the Court has been setting out an 'outer limit' for European law, which is constitutionally relevant in the sense that,[75] where it is not possible to interpret national law in the light of the relevant directive, the law of market integration will end up being constituted by the autonomous (social balancing) determinations of the state's private law actors. However, where an interpretation in conformity is held to be possible, such 'outer limits' will consist of hybrid norms. This is true in one major respect, namely: the mechanism of the interpretative obligation is organised in a way that it produces a variety of private law (contractual, tort or proprietary) regimes, depending on the assessment of conformity or otherwise of national laws with EU law (the directives). This, in turn, produces a juridical pluralism that participates in the ongoing constitution of market integration made dependent on the extent of the interpretative possibility of any 'hybridisation' (interpretative) between, on the one hand, the directives' norms and, on the other hand, national private law norms and principles. To give one illustration: product liability as regulated under the relevant directive is bound to admit or not the risk development defence, as provided for by the directive, depending on the extent of conformity, with the consequence that any such hybridity (where possible) will give rise to a range of norms and principles 'common' in the plural sense of being part of the living law, rather than norms and principles common only because hypostasised as part of an artificially codified construct. Out of such hybridisation patterns emerges a living law that is constitutional in character insofar as it is embedded in the constitutionality of national private laws[76] and, specifically, the balancing determinations emerging out of the national private law communities.

A cascade of norms and principles constituted by the hybridised interface of the EU directives with national private law jurisprudence have been developing as couplings – that is, constructs entailing both EU and national normative dimensions – as a result of the judges engaging experimentally with both. These couplings are contingent on the modalities of the jurisprudential (EU–nation) encounters through the interpretative obligation – modalities which define the material substance of the 'outer limit' – considering that each dispute may give rise to a hybridised norm or to the restatement of national private law. In other words, they are engagements that are founded upon a mutually recognised relationship of autonomy.

[74] For a full discussion of minimum harmonization, see Niglia, *The Transformation of Contract in Europe* (n 3) (even minimum harmonisation has been interpreted as characterised by concerns for supremacy; therefore, what really matters is to look at the implementation and enforcement ways of the relevant directive). On the unfair terms directive, see ibid. See also ch 3 on recent consumer private law directives' proposals.

[75] On limits of EU constitutional law relative to national constitutional laws, see L Niglia, 'Beyond Enchantment: The Possibility of a New European Private Law (Instalment Two)' (2009) 28 *Yearbook of European Law* 60.

[76] See Niglia, *The Struggle for European Private Law* (n 3). On product liability see L Niglia,' A" European" Tort Law? Comparative Thoughts on an" Essentially Contested" Private Law Institution' in P Gilliker (ed), *Research Handbook on European Tort Law* (Cheltenham, Edward Elgar, 2017) 321.

At work are jurisprudential encounters across the EU and the national constitutional orders rather than within each of them. This is because it is not abstract legislation (the directives, a code)[77] but the actual living jurisprudence that determines if at all, or to what extent, abstract, artificial norms from the EU gain effectiveness at the level of the nation-state orders.[78] Effectiveness becomes a variation on the theme of constitutional relations among orders, rather than hypostasised as value in and by itself. Correspondingly, there is no 'primacy' of the work of one legislative or judicial institution (the European legislator or the CJEU) over another (the national legislature or the national courts) in that the law develops out of patterns of mutual learning, mutual respect and co-evolutionary normativisation, as I shall discuss them in the rest of this chapter.[79]

B. Constitutional Pluralism (Osmosis)

Two paths unfold from the above-noted mechanisms that point to constantly recreating the hermeneutics of European private law according to the interpretative obligation. They are: (i) nation-state private law norms and principles are reinvented around the artificial norms of the directives – this is a successful conforming interpretation; or (ii) lacking the possibility of a conforming interpretation, the national private law norms and principles are judged not to be capable of a conforming interpretation that is recognised as relevant in the EU legal order, that is, as applicable to disputes arising under the relevant directive. As a result of this double recognition through the two paths, constitutional autonomy generates an osmosis across the EU and the national private law norms and principles whilst admitting of the constitutionality of a pluralism of norms and principles.

With its principled 'recognition by respect' of national private laws, whether through reinvention or through preservation, the 'autonomous' law of the EU ends up by mirroring the nation state (reinvented or preserved) private law norms and principles constituting the irreducibly different national law regimes both in case of a successful conforming interpretation and whenever it is recognised that no conformity is possible under the interpretative obligation. This I label 'incorporation by respect', in striking contrast to the paradigm of constitutional absorption, which is about hierarchical *annexation* of nation-state private law by means of EU law, as I will argue in chapter four. It is part of the legacy of dogmatic thinking through supremacy and direct effect to not have acknowledged, at the level of EU scholarship – as opposed to the broader scholarly and judicial discourse qua the living law as construed and presented in this chapter – that, as a result

[77] Niglia, *The Struggle for European Private Law* (n 3) (critically, on code and on directives).

[78] On 'effectiveness' in EU law, see the seminal work of F Snyder, 'The Effectiveness of European Community Law: Institutions, Processes, Tools and Techniques' (1993) 56 *MLR* 19.

[79] See Niglia, 'Conforming Interpretation' (n 40).

of any unsuccessful attempt at interpretation through conformity, the national private law norms will apply not only as a matter of national constitutional law, but, equally, as a matter of EU law (through 'recognition').

C. Diffuse Constitutional Change

Looking at the above-considered two features of hybridity and pluralism from the viewpoint of national private law jurisdictions, one can say that national private law actors have also been actively involved in changing their own norms and principles towards accommodating market integration, to the extent that this has been possible for them, rather than passively assisting in the development of, and the mechanical application of, the CJEU's jurisprudence.

At the level of analysis that this chapter adopts, one encounters the phenomenon of the construction, in nation-state private law circles,[80] of a kind of private law directed at building market integration through the reception of, adaptation to, and participation in, the jurisprudence of constitutional autonomy.

Whenever conformity has been 'possible', private law actors have adapted their own national private laws from strict norms on formation of contract to incorporating the right of cancellation, from liability at fault to strict liability, and the like. Such adaptation has taken place in line with social balancing standards as practised at the level of the nation-state, while preventing (as they were required to under the doctrine of the interpretative obligation) any kind of conformity that would entail a disruption and/or a rupture within the body of norms and principles in existence before the relevant directives – had these been applied regardless of the requirement of conformity and under the 'direct effect' logic. In other words, the interpretative obligation creates an environment (hermeneutical) of dialogue and of participation from below – law as 'diffuse', one might say, as opposed to centralised and artificially so had EU norms been applied apodictically without the prism of the interpretive requirement under consideration.[81]

This mirrors the working of national constitutional systems whenever they entertain forms of conforming interpretation – insofar as entailing that ordinary judges act as if they were constitutional judges exercising a diffuse control of constitutionality.

Also, the conventional argument, whereby circumscribing the obligation to disapply conflicting national norms only in relation to EU norms embodying direct effect is premised on preventing the phenomenon of a diffuse control of legality (under EU law), cannot apply to the interpretative obligation in the light

[80] For transnational private law circles and European private law, see Niglia, *The Transformation of Contract in Europe* (n 3): Niglia, 'Taking Comparative Law Seriously' (n 8); Niglia, 'The New Transformation' (n 8); ch 4 below.

[81] To contrast the culture of the orthodox discourse of the common rules (private law), see the critique in Niglia, 'Taking Comparative Law Seriously' (n 8).

of the reading proposed in this chapter, considering that, under the interpretative obligation, a kind of diffuse constitutional review takes place in that the ultimate decision-makers on conformity are all national courts, including ordinary judges. To paraphrase the Italian Constitutional Court, one can say that in horizontal relationships, in principle, European norms (directives) cannot be invoked by individuals against other individuals both because it is possible to interpret national private law as differing from them and because it is impossible to interpret national private law in conformity with them.[82]

This characterisation of the interpretative obligation as entailing dialogue and participation from below can be evidenced from essays of leading national private law scholars who have captured the gist of the interpretative obligation in the light of their own national traditions regarding the corresponding use of the technique of conforming interpretation:[83] an illustration is Canaris' statement that in Germany recourse is made to general clauses of private law because, by doing so, it becomes easier to interpret private law in conformity with the Basic Law (Grundgesetz).[84]

IV. The Jurisprudence of Constitutional Autonomy as Orders' Coexistence

The above-considered (hermeneutical) praxis of the interpretative obligation has its own implications in terms of the relationships among constitutional orders in Europe. It is a praxis that was the determinant of, and an articulation of, composite constitutionalism as this structured the relationships between the EU constitutional order and the Member States' constitutional orders before the turn of the century's transformation that I consider in chapters three and four.[85]

The perspective adopted here enables a renewed understanding of the orders' relations that contrasts starkly with conventional readings, whereby a regimented logic of superordination/subordination would inform the entirety of the EU–Member States relationships. Equally, the dogmatic rendition of EU law fails to acknowledge, and hides from view, the true position of the 'new legal order' (under the paradigm of the jurisprudence of constitutional autonomy) in its interface with the private orders as coupled with, and mediated by, state institutional structures.

The interpretative obligation praxis has given rise to a condition of 'constitutional coexistence and co-evolution' of the European constitutional order and

[82] See above at section II and earlier in this section.

[83] See, eg C-W Canaris, 'Die richtlinienkonforme Auslegung und Rechtsfortbildung' in FS Bydlinski, *Ausführlich zur Auslegung des Gemeinschaftsrechts durch den EuGH zuletzt Müller/Christensen*, Juristische Methodik, Bd II (Berlin, Europarecht, 2003).

[84] ibid.

[85] Niglia, 'Eclipse of the Constitution' (n 1).

of the nation-state (and) private orders. The encroachment of the 'new legal order' over the nation-state private orders cannot be made intelligible in terms of imposition, but of coexistence and co-evolution side by side. The dogmatics about primacy and direct effect have made interpreters blind to this phenomenon of (state) private law as autonomous constitutional ordering being respected by the EU constitutional order's determinations,[86] preferring instead to treat private law as if it were passively subjected to the 'normal' public-constitutional law requirements of supremacy and of direct effect – through lamenting the 'failure' of the interpretative obligation to not be able to match the gift of its counterpart, direct effect, in ensuring the effectiveness of rights provided for under EU law (by directives).[87] Yet this dogmatic negation of the plural character of the orders' relationships should not obscure the actual development on the ground, as evidenced by the interpretative obligation praxis as recounted in this chapter. It is a dogmatic negation built on the view of the interpretative obligation[88] as if it were somehow of lesser value than the allegedly 'high doctrines' of supremacy and direct effect, assumed to be somehow 'perfect' renditions of an idealised, comprehensive European Union constitutional law – a view which entails failing to appreciate and to take into account the living constitutionalism embedded in, and embedding (through the interpretative obligation), the private order.

By constitutional coexistence therefore I mean the complementary structural relations characterising at once the triad of orders and their relations (the EU/European order, the state-constitutional order, the private order), that is, indirect constitutionalisation (mutual respect), constitutional osmosis (mutual learning) and constitutional co-normativisation.[89]

[86] I must stress again here the different take that this book adopts in relation to the notion of 'autonomy' – not looking at the EU constitutional order as complete and self-standing, but as the product of the 'jurisprudence of constitutional autonomy' as discussed in this chapter: see ch 1.

[87] For this criticism, see Niglia, 'Form and Substance in European Constitutional Law' (n 17) (scholarship depicting negatively the lack of direct effect in horizontal relationships entailed in directives, in turn projecting the objective of aligning vertical and horizontal relationships under the doctrine of direct effect as the only allegedly 'optimal' resolution to the question concerning the application of EU secondary legislation, ie the directives, to horizontal relationships). For the critique of this conventional dogmatic position in relation to the conventional rendition of EU transformation, see Niglia, 'Of Harmonisation and Fragmentation' (n 8); Niglia, 'Eclipse of the Constitution' (n 1).

[88] See discussion above.

[89] Bearing in mind that, in the age of the jurisprudence of constitutional autonomy, the private order is at once with the state-constitutional order as part of the European constellation of orders before the coming of the decoupling of private ordering from the state in the age of constitutional heteronomy and absorption, as I argue in chs 3 and 4. On non-state private ordering, see ch 4. On pluralism and European private law, see Niglia, *Pluralism and European Private Law* (n 1); V Mak, *Legal Pluralism in European Private Law* (Oxford, Oxford University Press, 2020); S Grundmann, 'Pluralistische Privatrechtstheorie. Prolegomena zu einer pluralistisch gesellschaftswissenschaftlichen Rechtstheorie als normativem Desiderat ("normativer Pluralismus")' (2022) 86 *Rabels Zeitschrift* 364.

A. Mutual Respect qua Indirect Constitutionalisation (Conditional Reasoning)

A requirement of conditional reasoning is entailed in the praxis of the interpretative obligation whereby reasoning towards implementing European law (the Directives) is made possible only through the working out of conformity at the level of national private law. As a result of this, European law through its directives becomes the 'law of the nation-state land' only on the condition that a conforming kind of reasoning is possible,[90] as in the combined reading of the paradigmatic judgments *Faccini Dori*[91] and *Von Colson*.[92] This is in striking contrast to the apodictic logic of European law as based on direct effect (and as the supreme law of the land), and ultimately as superimposition and imposition of European norms over nation-state orders, as in the classical 'new legal order' scholarly vocabulary. Only 'indirectly' can European law become the constitutional law of the national land whenever a conforming interpretation is possible.[93] Constitutionalisation under indirect effect is conditional on these reasoning premises.

From this viewpoint, in contrast with the conventional apodictic position that looks at European law 'inwardly', it should be stressed that the interpretative obligation is but the reception of a model existing within national jurisdictions and transferred to the European Union level. It is the model of the 'indirect constitutionalisation of private law'.[94] This reception makes intelligible the framework adopted by the CJEU and its legal brethren. Under national law considered independently of European law, national constitutional law gets to rule over private law disputes, as long as private law can be held to be consistent with the national constitutional charter (under doctrines such as that of the *interpretazione costituzionalmente orientata*); similarly, the European constitutional order's norms apply to horizontal relationships as long as national private law can be held to be consistent with European law under the framework of the interpretative obligation doctrine (the directives).[95]

Relatedly, under 'indirect constitutionalisation', no constitutional conflicts between the EU constitutional order and the national constitutional order are bound to unfold. Any such constitutional conflicts are prevented insofar as, in the face of any incompatibility of a directive norm with private law materials

[90] Compare Weiler (n 1) (discussing instances of European law as becoming law of the national land).

[91] *Faccini Dori* (n 7).

[92] See nn 7 and 10 above.

[93] 'Indirect effect' is normally understood by conventional EU scholarship to entail the achievement of direct effect by interpretation, but here it means that, constitutionally, it is nation-state private law that preserves the autonomy of national private laws according to the parameters of the interpretative obligation, an autonomy that is ultimately constitutional and therefore 'indirectly constitutional'.

[94] On constitutionalisation of private law, see Niglia, *The Struggle for European Private Law* (n 3).

[95] See L Niglia, 'Tra Europa e diritto privato. La questione del bilanciamento secondo il diritto civile comparato' (2018) 1 *EDP* 159.

(lacking the conditions for the possibility of a conforming interpretation), there is no requirement for adopting an interpretation that, over and above national private law systems' interpretative constraints, would aim to achieve unbounded conformity.[96]

B. Mutual Learning qua Osmosis

The interpretative obligation praxis, as developed until its structural transformation over the last decade, constitutes not only an 'indirect' means of the constitutionalisation of national orders, but also entails what can be labelled a praxis of orders' osmosis through 'mutual learning' across orders. Any successful conforming interpretation, and even any dialogues towards ascertaining the extent of possibility of a conforming interpretation and eventually ending up with a negative result (non-conformity), involve mutual learning for the following reason: in case of a positive result of conformity, the relevant private law norms happen to be incorporated in the EU order whilst European law norms and principles contained in the directives happen to be reconstructed in the light of the relevant private law norms – with the important consideration that the European law norms and principles contained in the directives are only artificial until they are embedded in the structures of national private laws, which give them 'life' as private law norms. Examples include the cancellation rights in relation to the formation of contract doctrine: the clash between rules on the formation of contracts and the right of cancellation, and their subsequent acquired interdependence, with the former rights becoming relevant in terms of private law through the conforming reading. From this viewpoint, the hermeneutics of both the CJEU and of national private law actors are equally ordained insofar as they are part of an inter-order jurisgenerative learning process with (European) private law being redetermined as a result.[97]

In case of a negative result – that is, in case of a lack of conformity – dialogues about the extent of 'possible' interpretations of conformity that may end up with a

[96] This means, inter alia, preventing any attempt at transplanting in situations in which 'contexts, at the receiving end of the legal transplants, are fundamentally at odds with the rules-to-be-transplanted': see Niglia, 'Of Harmonisation and Fragmentation' (n 8) 119 and 127. See also S Ferreri and LA DiMatteo, 'Terminology Matters: Dangers of Superficial Transplantation' (2019) 37 *Boston University International Law Journal* 35 (referring to Niglia, 'Of Harmonisation and Fragmentation' (n 8) 57, and reinterpreting one quotation in terms of 'transplanted terms', that is: 'the transplanted terms are meaningless in "situations in which contexts, at the receiving end of the legal transplants, are fundamentally at odds with the rules-to-be-transplanted"'). On achieving conformity unboundedly, see above and ch 4.

[97] On jurisgenerative constitutionalism, compare PS Berman, 'Jurisgenerative Constitutionalism: Procedural Principles for Managing Global Legal Pluralism' (2013) 20 *Indiana Journal of Global Legal Studies*, drawing on RM Cover, 'The Supreme Court, 1982 Term – Foreword: Nomos and Narrative (1983) 97 *Harvard Law Review* 4, 53.

negative result signify a praxis that legal actors choose to embark on by embracing the interpretative obligation, that produces jurisgenerative 'rereadings' of private laws – including reflexive critical understandings of each jurisdiction's own laws in relation to the challenges of confronting the transnationalisation (Europeanisation) of law. One example is the interpretation of Advocate General Mengozzi regarding the possibility of adapting through interpretation the relevant directive in the judgment in *Laval* towards a hermeneutics of dialogue aimed at conformity, rather than the outright imposition of European norms (in the *Laval* case, 'general principles of law'), as in the decision then adopted instead by the CJEU; equally, the debates on certain Unfair Terms Directive's norms as resisted in German legal circles,[98] and on the Directive on Product Liability's norms as resisted in national legal circles,[99] go towards instantiating such rereadings through dialogue.[100]

One aspect of this dual process is co-learning, in that, in 'co-normativising' (a point that I address below), the private law actors learn from each other's laws through a change of the hermeneutics of private law insofar as the balancing of normative considerations enshrined in national private law opens up to the knowledge of the EU system, however artificial, with a view to considering a broader balancing that might include (if national legal actors so wish) the normative considerations related to market integration.[101]

[98] Niglia, *The Transformation of Contract in Europe* (n 3).

[99] Niglia, 'A "European" Tort Law?' (n 76).

[100] On *Laval* (n 57), as commented on in the text, see Niglia, 'Eclipse of the Constitution' (n 1).

[101] On 'learning capacity' in relation to private law, see Study Group on Social Justice in European Private Law, 'Social Justice in European Contract Law: A Manifesto' (2004) 10 *European Law Journal* 653, 672 (discussing the 'learning capacity' of private law and specifically arguing that 'In evaluating the legitimacy of uniform laws it is important to recognise that the risk exists that, in the long run, the elimination of national diversity in contract law will deprive the law of a learning capacity to achieve superior outcomes in terms of efficiency or efficacy'). See also J Smits, 'Private Law and Fundamental Rights: A Sceptical View' in T Barkhuysen and S Lindenbergh (eds), *Constitutionalisation of Private Law* (Leiden, Martinus Nijhoff, 2006) 15 ('Private law can be interpreted in the light of fundamental rights, but can in the end *not* be absorbed by these rights: the private law rules remain decisive for deciding the case. A different view would be counterproductive as the existing knowledge about the best way to solve an issue would be discarded. What would be the use of replacing the existing private law on protection of property rights by new rules based on the constitutional protection of this right?'); Niglia, *The Struggle for European Private Law* (n 3). An illustration of how private law's learning capacity matters in contexts of Europeanisation is the *Schulte* saga (Case C-350/03 *Schulte* [2005] ECJ I-9215), where *culpa in contrahendo*, as a doctrinal construct, has been deployed in the German courtrooms for the purpose of achieving the objective of protecting the consumer, as I discuss in the remainder of the chapter. One more illustration is the *Courage* saga in relation to the English principle whereby unlawful contracts cannot give rise to compensation in the context of an argument put forward by a common law scholar, which mirrors the civilian lawyers' criticism of the direct application of constitutional law in the private sphere: see H Collins, *The European Civil Code: The Way Forward* (Cambridge, Cambridge University Press, 2007) 55 (lack of fit of the decision in *Courage*, in allowing compensation for damages for the party to an unlawful contract, with 'the existing framework of private law rights and duties' in England that prohibits doing that with good reasons; there is no indication of how to conceptually implement the decision, whether via compensation for breach of contract, in tort or via unjustified enrichment – Case C-453/99 *Courage Ltd v Bernard Crehan* [2001] ECR I-6297).

C. Co-normativisation

Through mutual learning, (re)normativisation is bound to emerge among the legal actors involved in the praxis of the interpretative obligation. By (re)normativisation, I mean a declination of juridical hermeneutics understood as 'project orientated'[102] as embedded at both the EU and at the national level at once, as opposed to 'hetero-normativisation', understood as the imposition of the EU artificial private law norms upon the national constitutional orders.[103] The scholarly debate on the methodological premises regarding the 'possibilities' for conformity (including the premise of a clear wording of the national norms or *klare Wortlaut*, or the premise of the argument of the national norm being in need of a gap-filling interpretation then entertained through a conforming interpretation with EU law)[104] are evidence that the legal communities of interpreters have been engaging in 're-normativising' private law, that is, in renovating it by confronting the exogenous legal material coming from the EU and incorporating it (if possible) in the body of national private laws.[105]

The CJEU's exercise of its institutional task of interpreting the directives' norms is an act of normativisation in itself and yet it is made conditional on the national legal actors' own autonomous determinations, which depend on the requirements of their own tradition of law. Under the interpretative obligation, the law comes to be designed not as belonging to one order or another exclusively, but as the product of both – and concurrently so, through the normatively inspired cooperation of the insiders (that is, the legal actors that participate in the process) in the mode of 'co-evolutionary normativisation'.[106]

[102] See ch 1 above.

[103] See ch 3 (recounting hetero-normativisation in the form of the hermeneutics of balancing and specifically of economised balancing, having divested balancing of its deep hermeneutical character of multi-normativisation understood as not reducible to only being instrumental to the monologics of economisation).

[104] On the key relevance of the wording of the texts of national laws in the context of the application of the doctrine of the interpretative obligation, according to German scholarship, see, eg B Heiderhoff, *Europäisches Privatrecht* (Heidelberg, CF Mueller Verlag, 2012) 121: 'Die richtlinienkonforme Rechtsfortbildung ist also nach überzeugender Ansicht immer dann möglich, wenn nicht der klare Wortlaut des Gesetzes sie verbietet'; in the case-law, see BGH v. 29 April 2003, XI ZR 201/02, NJOZ 2003, 1811, 1814. Teleological methodologies used with a view to interpreting in conformity can take various forms, from arguing for the filling of a gap in the implementing legislation to making recourse to the directive seen as a measure for interpreting the implementing legislation in the sense of remedying inconsistencies (see, eg the discussion in C-W Canaris, 'Gemeinsamkeiten zwischen verfassungs- und richtlinienkonformer Rechtsfindung' in H Bauer, D Czybulka and W Kahl, *Wirtschaft im offenen Verfassungsstaat, FS für Reiner Schmidt* (Munich, Verlag CH Beck, 2006) s 53; see also S Grundmann, 'Richtlinienkonforme Auslegung im Bereich des Privatrechts – insbesondere: der Kanon der nationalen Auslegungsmethoden als Grenze?' [1996] *Zeitschrift für Europäisches Privatrecht* 399).

[105] On 'possibility' in terms of the *contra legem* requirement, see Niglia, 'Conforming Interpretation' (n 40).

[106] For a paradigmatic rebuttal of this position, see, critically, ch 4.

The *Schulte* saga illustrates these complex traits of the praxis of co-normativisation insofar as it consists of a hermeneutics of texts (directives, codes, constitutions, judicial decisions, scholarly writings) and of doctrines grounded in balancing determinations that target the relevant conflicts.[107] That is, the legal actors deploy this hermeneutics in their dealing with an underlying set of conflicts arising out of the relevant disputes, regarding (in *Schulte*) whether the cancellation of a contract (the litigants having invoked the right of cancellation based on the Doorstep Directive) should also entail releasing the consumer from their obligation linked to the property assets, with a view to really providing the consumer with effective protection otherwise not afforded; and providing for such protection by redeploying the autonomous ways in which the national legal actors have been hermeneutically dealing with similar conflicts and their resolutions independently of European law. Let me explain.

Overall, the German courts complied with the main body of the CJEU *Schulte* decision,[108] insofar as they implemented the CJEU decision through not releasing the consumer from the obligations linked to the property assets – the cancellation of the contract having been held to apply to the credit agreement but not to the property arrangements, which would remain as binding on the consumer.[109] To some, however, this sounded like not affording any real protection at all, and could even be making the consumer worse off overall compared to a hypothetical non-application of the right to cancellation. Many lower courts were convinced that the consumer should be liberated from the whole range of linked obligations, including those related to property. Having failed to find the support of the CJEU on the point when referring to the matter in *Schulte*, they clung to the only passage of the judgment that lends itself to be interpreted as remedying what they felt constituted its overall harshness, that is, the requirement to 'ensure that their legislation protects consumers who have been unable to avoid exposure to such risks by adopting suitable measures to allow them to avoid bearing the consequences of the materialisation of those risks'.[110]

[107] *Schulte* (n 101). For further case law, see Niglia, *The Struggle for European Private Law* (n 3). For further illustrations, see Federal Court of Justice Judgment of 26 November 2008 in *Quelle*, VIII ZR 200/05, BGHZ 179 (*cf* also Case C-404/06 *Quelle AG v Bundesverband der Verbraucherzentralen und Verbraucherverbände* ECLI:EU:C:2008:23) and Federal Court of Justice Judgment of 21 December 2011, VIII ZR 70/08, BGHZ 192 as commented on by TMJ Möllers, 'The Principle of Directive-Compliant Development of the Law and the *Contra Legem* Limit' (2020) 16 *European Review of Contract Law* 465. See also Niglia, 'Conforming Interpretation' (n 40). See further discussion of the *Schulte* saga in N Reich, 'Balancing in Private Law and the Imperatives of the Public Interest' in Brownsword et al (n 72); see also Niglia, *The Struggle for European Private Law* (n 3).

[108] *Schulte* (n 101). Note Reich (n 107) 230 et seq, according to whom the subsequent BGH case law allowed 'a claim in compensation by the consumer if he can prove that he has been deceived about his rights by the developer, and that the bank should have known of this behaviour; the bank may also be held liable under a theory of *culpa in contrahendo* for not having informed the consumer of his right of withdrawal' in the judgments BGHZ 169, 109; BGH – XI ZR 104/08 of 29 June 2010, *VuR* 2010, 382 (bank responsible for misrepresentations vis-à-vis the intermediary concerning the amount of the commission).

[109] Reich (n 107) 227.

[110] *Schulte* (n 101) para 101.

Such risks pertain to the loss of rental income and property value incurred due to not having been made aware of and knowing their right of cancellation under the directive.[111] By clinging to alternative 'suitable measures', the domestic courts (and the scholars discussing the decisions) engaged in the practice of co-normativisation as 'conforming interpretation', a tool notably developed as part of the 'indirect model' of constitutionalisation of private law, broadly understood, and consisting of its twofold reliance on doctrinal material and on fundamental human rights as protected under the Basic Law. Echoing the ethos of protecting fundamental human rights in private law relations by reinterpreting doctrinal material (paragraph 242 BGB) in their light, as decided in the *Bürgschaft* decision of the Bundesverfassungsgericht (BVerfG) saga (Article 2 of the Basic Law), the lower courts have been attempting to provide for a level of protection equivalent to placing the consumer in the same position as if he had been liberated from the property obligations altogether.[112] Specifically, placing compensatory obligations on the stronger contractual party indicates the willingness of the lower courts to counter the logic of 'private autonomy' as defended in certain judgments of the Bundesgerichtshof (BGH) – with the BGH clinging to a formalistic interpretation of autonomy whereby private parties should be left free to underwrite risky transactions, somehow returning to pre-1993 interpretations as rejected by the *Bürgschaft* decision of the German Constitutional Court (BVerfG).

It should be noted that the placing of compensatory obligations on the stronger contractual party is, for the German community of interpreters, practicable and credible only on the condition that the code-based private law doctrinal material lends itself to be rearranged accordingly in conformity with the relevant directive. This explains the reference to doctrines such as *culpa in contrahendo* or *aufklärungsrichtiges Verhalten* for the purpose of compensating the consumer in relation to the risks consequential to having to comply with property-related obligations as per the above-noted core passage of the CJEU's *Schulte* decision.[113] In each case in which such engagement has taken place in the context of the *Schulte* saga, domestic courts (including the BGH) have been re-editing their own traditional system of constitutionalisation that relies on the technique of rearranging doctrinal material to resolve disputes that involve constitutional rights with a view to reinterpreting private law in conformity with the Basic Law.[114]

[111] ibid 234.

[112] Obviously, one may speculate on the 'actual meaning' of the CJEU decision, but I only aim to offer an illustration. The BGH has restored protection of the consumer, albeit in a contested judicial environment in which lower courts have acted at variance with the BGH, sometimes going in a direction antithetical to that of the BGH on the point of how to implement the requirement of 'suitable measures': for discussion, see Reich (n 107); see also n 108.

[113] For discussion, see Reich (n 107) 235. For counter-tendencies towards the imposition of European law on private law traditions, framing a new paradigm, see chs 3 and 4.

[114] For a description of this kind of consciousness see ibid.

From the *Schulte* saga emerges a kind of 'constitutional coexistence' of legal actors through co-normativisation that has been far from 'static'. Changes have been taking place as a result of this 'encounter by respect', meaning a private law hermeneutics that is no longer exclusionary (nation-state) but shared – as dialogical coexistence. Constitutional coexistence has also worked not in the sense of inhibiting conflicts, but as transforming them into opportunities for redetermining decisions on allocation of resources through, rather than at the sacrifice of, the epistemic requirements of national private law jurisprudence. The impact of the Doorstep Directive right of cancellation across various subfields of private law, from consumer to financial to sale contracts, is indicative of how an apparently unassuming private law norm has been re-elaborated further to become a cornerstone of new interpretative practices in the private law area, including new conceptions of private autonomy and of contract law, towards a market-functional kind of protection of contractual parties.[115] As a result, according to the 'constitutional autonomy' paradigm of relations among orders, the constitutional order of Europe and that of private ordering stand in a composite, dynamic constitutional relationship.

V. Conclusion

Following the establishment of the once 'new legal order', the jurisprudence of constitutional autonomy characterised the constitutional condition of Europe for a number of decades until the turn of the century. At this turning point, which I consider in the following chapters, almost everything that constituted constitutional autonomy changed, whilst, it should be stressed, constitutional autonomy has remained a hermeneutical reference point never entirely given up or annihilated, that is, it is a discoursive basis for participating in the ongoing struggles over the law in Europe, as I explain in chapter four.

The following chapter considers the ways in which balancing has been incorporated in EU law by the judges of the CJEU and by scholars once more, yet this time through absolutising it in the mode of economisation – in lieu of it being, under the paradigm of constitutional autonomy, the reverse side of national jurisdictional modes of (social) balancing in the mode of co-normativisation.

[115] See, eg ch 3 on the argument from shifting the moment of formation of contract to the expiration of the period for exercising the right of cancellation not only as a matter of reconceptualisation of general categories regarding the codified notion of contract (N Jansen and R Zimmermann, 'Recasting the *Acquis Communautaire*? A Critical Evaluation of the Principles of the Existing EC Contract Law' [2008] *MLR* 505; Niglia, *The Transformation of Contract in Europe* (n 3)), but also across a variety of types of contract, from finance to mortgages. As to Italy, see L Niglia, 'Tra Europa e diritto privato. La questione del bilanciamento secondo il diritto civile comparato' (2018) 1 *EDP* 159 (with relevant literature); as to Germany, see the above-noted *Schulte* saga (n 101). On 'opportunities', see more in Niglia, *The Transformation of Contract in Europe* (n 3) (on legal change through Europeanisation as taking place at the same time at the EU and national levels).

This move consists of a new 'internalisation' characterised by selectivity, in that it is about drawing on societal claims only in the sense that economised claims get recognition. At the same time, one sees the turning upside down of the once 'constitutionality' as open to the plurality of societal claims and to the nation-state (integration as 'composite'). Chapter three details the making of a shift towards closure vis-à-vis the plurality of societal claims whilst selectively opening only to economised claims; and, equally, chapter three considers the shift towards a kind of market integration meant to be 'total' as a result of a mode of balancing reduced to facilitating economised objectives of market optimisation. The cathedral of 'social' law has been under attack ever since, I argue in chapters three and four. Law turns into mere technique devoid of the mechanics of law's mediation as embedded in social balancing.

Chapter four will look deeper at the more recent transformations of balancing and at their effects on market integration and its law – as closure towards societal claims other than economised and as totalising market integration.[116] Here, counterforces will also be considered towards mapping the new wave of hermeneutical struggles that characterise Europe's realm in the face of the increasing process of law's regimentation around privatistic relations of unequal power.

[116] It is not only by a 'code' that law can be thought of as total (Niglia, *The Struggle for European Private Law* (n 3)), but also by jurisprudence (ibid).

3

Heteronomy

I. Introduction

This chapter considers the second structural transformation, as 'Europeanisation', of the hermeneutics of private law: the making of a contingent judicial and scholarly private law discourse hetero-directed at building market integration. By hetero-directed is meant the effect of repositioning the EU constitutional order vis-à-vis the national (private) constitutional orders away from indirect constitutionalisation, constitutional osmosis (mutual learning) and constitutional co-normativisation.

The first structural transformation, considered in the previous chapter, consisted of the making and development of the 'jurisprudence of constitutional autonomy' as the pre-eminent Europeanisation phenomenon until the turn of the century. This chapter considers a second structural transformation that has been taking place over the last 20 years in the form of 'constitutional heteronomy'.

By 'jurisprudence of constitutional heteronomy' is meant the move of the Court of Justice of the European Union (CJEU, the Court) away from the policy of integrating markets through constitutional respect for the autonomy of national legal systems and their private laws, in the mode of the jurisprudence of constitutional autonomy, towards designing self-contained EU privatistic norms to be applied to national realms, through setting aside the interpretative obligation. This move correlates with, and results from, a structural transformation of the hermeneutics of European private law as decoupled from the nation state and as becoming an 'exogenous', self-contained, normativising body revolving around economised balancing. In parallel, scholarly writings have been developing a supportive hermeneutics that both makes possible and reinforces, in terms of efficacy and effectiveness, the move of the CJEU towards the heteronomous imposition of self-contained economised balancing determinations.

In this chapter I describe this process in the terms of the triad of direct constitutionalisation, impermeability and hetero-normativisation – replacing, and as dialectically opposed to, respectively, the relational modes of indirect constitutionalisation, constitutional osmosis and co-normativisation. Once more, hermeneutical material generates a new set of structural changes in the relations of the European constellation's orders (from composite to heteronomous).[1]

[1] On hermeneutics and orders' relations' transformations, see chs 1 and 2 above. On hermeneutics as change (transformations), see the methodology in ch 1 above.

This chapter reconstructs the traits of the jurisprudence of constitutional heteronomy by looking at the jurisprudence of the CJEU (section II) and at the broader scholarly landscape (section III), whilst the following chapter critically notes that this jurisprudence is, on close inspection, intertwined with a third transformation, labelled *constitutional absorption*, in that it must be understood as direct constitutionalisation, impermeability and hetero-normativisation whilst at the same time being about establishing a form of 'total (constitutional) law'.

II. A Heteronomous Judicial Hermeneutical Transformation

A turning point in the making of the jurisprudence of constitutional heteronomy consisted of two major decisions of the CJEU, each entailing the reversal of the interpretative obligation. I am referring to the judgments *OPR-Finance* and *Freiburger*.[2]

A. The Reversal of the Interpretative Obligation

The interpretative obligation is the doctrine, engineered by the CJEU, that presides over the relationship between the EU constitutional order and national legal orders in matters of horizontal effects (private law). Over the last decade, the jurisprudence of the CJEU on the interpretative obligation has undertaken a major transformation.

Let me recall the key moments of the making of this new jurisprudence,[3] considered in the previous chapter, before commenting on its characterisation in terms of constitutional heteronomy.[4]

In the Grand Chamber judgment of *Dominguez* in 2012, the Court incorporated the interpretative obligation in the body of the direct effect doctrinal framework by applying a requirement of conformity (the doctrine of indirect effect through the interpretative obligation) to a question concerning a claim against a body that may be held to be an organ of the state – up until *Dominguez*, typically governed by the estoppel rationale under the doctrine of direct effect.[5] Thus, in *Dominguez*, the

[2] Case 679/18 *OPR-Finance s.r.o. v GK* ECLI:EU:C:2020:167; Case C-237/02 *Freiburger Kommunalbauten GmbH Baugesellschaft and Co KG v Ludger Hofstetter and Ulrike Hofstetter* [2004] ECR I-3403.

[3] See ch 2 above.

[4] See section B below.

[5] See ch 2 above; the Court holds that the relevant body may be held to be private or public without differentiating its reasoning (the application of the doctrine of indirect effect through the interpretative) depending on the nature of the relevant body: Case 282/12 *Maribel Dominguez v Centre informatique du Centre Ouest Atlantique and Préfet de la région Centre* ECLI:EU:C:2011:559.

Court required the national courts first to entertain the conformity interpretation and then to consider whether the relevant directive could be held to provide for 'direct effect' norms. This is a double reversal of the interpretative obligation in the sense that, first, the interpretative obligation is eradicated from its proper place as engineered by the CJEU in a long line of jurisprudence and rather generalised to enter the realm of vertical relationships (state–individuals) and, second, it must be applied in the first instance and before considering the application of the directive under direct effect.[6]

In the judgment of *Radlinger* of 2016, the Court took this approach one step further:[7] the Court chose not to address or discuss the key question of whether or not the relevant directive is invoked horizontally in the dispute at stake, that is, applying indirect effect only in contexts of horizontal claims, according to the once established case law on the matter. Instead, the Court chose to automatically demand the national court to apply the interpretative obligation doctrine as a means of ensuring the effectiveness of EU law and regardless of any limitations that might arise under national law vis-à-vis the conforming interpretation – limitations that, in turn, preside over the requirement of sheltering individuals from any obligations contained in the directives. The Court made reference to the previous decision in *Dominguez*, but without distinguishing the *Dominguez* decision, in relation to claims against the 'state' (broadly interpreted), so as to justify why it would be justified to introduce an altered version of the interpretative obligation that bluntly imposes on individuals the directive's obligations without the mediation of the architecture of national law.

In the 2020 judgment of *OPR-Finance*, the CJEU then applied the interpretative obligation to horizontal relationships by going as far as limiting the application of the *contra legem* principle.[8] In this way, the Court chose to shift away from the kernel of the interpretative obligation according to its previous jurisprudence, that is, whether national interpretative materials allow changing national law or otherwise, rather than just implementing change whatever the interpretative contingencies. For, requesting that national judges make a change in interpretation towards ensuring the effectiveness of European law, whatever the contingency of the interpretative materials available, means establishing an unprecedented rule of superordination among orders that places private law in a position of subordination vis-à-vis European law, rather than the 'constitutional respect' of private law that characterises the core of the pre-existing traditional doctrine of the interpretative obligation.

[6] Note how this 'reversal' is one more example of what I consider to be a rearrangement of EU constitutional principles for the purpose of heteronomisation, with ensuring the effectiveness of EU law becoming the overarching concern of the CJEU at the expense of the varieties of other EU constitutional principles that may counter effectiveness: for further examples, see ch 4.

[7] Case C-377/14 *Radlinger and Radlingerová* ECLI:EU:C:2016:283.

[8] On *contra legem*, see L Niglia, 'Conforming Interpretation' [2022] *European Review of Private Law*; see also Case Pfeiffer (n 22).

To capture further the importance of this shift, one should note that it entails a reconfiguration of European law around the blending of the interpretative obligation with effectiveness, and of the authority of national law as autonomous with the prioritisation of the conception of the 'authority' of EU constitutional law above national law, as mere instruments for ensuring the effectiveness of EU law and its order.[9] The Court shows that it is concerned about ensuring the effectiveness of EU law through an amended version of the interpretative obligation,[10] which is now applied in relation to framework decisions as well as directives. In the judgment *Popławski* of 2019,[11] the Court holds that national courts should not disapply provisions of national law incompatible with the relevant framework decision (whose provisions lack direct effect) but ensure the effectiveness of EU law through deploying the interpretative obligation as a mere instrument of effectiveness – as a result complementing in this dispute the established mechanism of supremacy/direct effect/disapplication built up in a line of cases including *Van Gend*, *Costa Enel*, *Ratti*, *Marshall* and *Symmenthal*, in order to simply see national courts as enforcers of the EU decisions through the shortcut of the interpretative obligation deployed as a proxy for effectiveness:[12]

> In the light of the foregoing, the answer to the first question is that the principle of the primacy of EU law must be interpreted as meaning that it does not require a national court to disapply a provision of national law which is incompatible with the provisions of a framework decision, such as the framework decisions at issue in the main proceedings, the legal effects of which are preserved in accordance with Article 9 of Protocol (No 36) on transitional provisions, annexed to the treaties, since those provisions do not have direct effect. The authorities of the Member States, including the courts, are nevertheless required to interpret their national law, to the greatest extent possible, in conformity with EU law, which enables them to ensure an outcome that is compatible with the objective pursued by the framework decision concerned.[13]

[9] On legitimation and authority, see L Niglia, *The Struggle for European Private Law. A Critique of Codification* (Oxford, Hart Publishing, 2015).

[10] See ch 4 (on changing EU constitutional law through altering conventional EU constitutional doctrines and principles).

[11] Case C-573/17 *Popławski* ECLI:EU:C:2019:530.

[12] See respectively the line of CJEU jurisprudence: Case 26/62 *Van Gend en Loos* [1963] ECR 1; Case 6/64 *Costa Enel* 15 July 1964; Case 148/78 *Public Ministero v Tullio Ratti* [1979] ECR 1629; Case 152/84 *Marshall* [1986] ECR 723; *Symmenthal* [1978] ECR 629.

[13] Note also that the Court concedes that 'the principle of conforming interpretation cannot serve as the basis for an interpretation of national law *contra legem*' (judgment of 29 June 2017, Case C-579/15 *Popławski* ECLI:EU:C:2017:503, para 33 and the case law cited), yet it now qualifies it in the sense of imposing an obligation to interpret domestic law in conformity with EU law that 'requires national courts to change established case law, where necessary' (see also judgment of 8 November 2016, Case C-554/14 *Ognyanov* ECLI:EU:C:2016:835, para 66). In other words, according to previous case law, as noted in the above, the obligation to interpret national law in conformity with EU law entails that it may not be 'possible' to achieve a result compatible with that envisaged by the framework decision concerned; yet now, *contra legem* is ultimately turned from preserving national law (L Niglia, 'Form and Substance in European Constitutional Law: The Social Character of Indirect Effect' (2010) 16 *European Law Journal* 439) into preserving European law in a move that repositions the whole doctrine of the interpretative obligation far away from its previous constitutional realm proper, that is, the jurisprudence of constitutional autonomy.

Consider also that, in the judgment *Popławski* of 2017,[14] the Court refers back to the argument for a 'necessary change' of the established case law, where the established case-law is incompatible with the objectives of an EU framework decision, effectively delegating to the national courts the task of rebalancing national law so as to make it conform with EU law under a normative requirement made absolute, that is, the requirement of ensuring the efficacy and effectiveness of EU law:

> However, the fact remains that the principle that national law must be interpreted in conformity with EU law requires national courts to do whatever lies within their jurisdiction, taking the whole body of domestic law into consideration and applying the interpretative methods recognised by it, with a view to ensuring that the framework decision in question is fully effective and to achieving an outcome consistent with the objective pursued by it (judgment of 5 September 2012, *Lopes Da Silva Jorge*, C-42/11, ECLI:EU:C:2012:517, paragraph 56 and the case-law cited).
>
> In that connection, the Court has already held that the obligation to interpret domestic law in conformity with EU law requires national courts to change established case-law, where necessary, if it is based on an interpretation of domestic law that is incompatible with the objectives of a framework decision (judgment of 8 November 2016, *Ognyanov*, C-554/14, ECLI:EU:C:2016:835, paragraph 67 and the case-law cited).

***

Freiburger,[15] a judgment of 2004, is another landmark decision in this regard that complements and anticipates the above jurisprudence, given that it brings the materials revolving around the interpretative obligation to an extreme hermeneutical position, obliterating the doctrine of the interpretative obligation altogether – 'suspending' the interpretative obligation insofar as the national court is placed under the obligation to implement balancing, regardless of considerations concerning direct effect or indirect effect, which are not articulated in the judgment.[16]

The Court only refers to the substantive issue of the balancing of the interests involved, offering an interpretation of the Unfair Terms Directive whereby it is required, under EU law, to balance the quality of a contractual term with the price and/or a guarantee – and specifically setting the disadvantage of the lower quality

[14] Case C-579/15 *Popławski* (n 13).

[15] Case C-237/02 *Freiburger Kommunalbauten GmbH Baugesellschaft and Co KG v Ludger Hofstetter and Ulrike Hofstetter* [2004] ECR I-3403; for a full discussion of this case, see the rest of this chapter and ch 4 below.

[16] An interpretation that I have proposed in a line of writings to which I refer the reader for further discussion concerning other relevant aspects of the judgment: L Niglia, '"The Rules Dilemma" – The Court of Justice and the Dilemma of the Regulation of Standard Form Contracts in Europe' (2006) 13 *Columbia Journal of European Law* 124; L Niglia, 'Of Harmonisation and Fragmentation – The Problem of Legal Transplants and the Europeanisation of Private Law (Instalment Three)' (2010) 2 *Maastricht Journal of European and Comparative Law* 116; Niglia, *The Struggle for European Private Law* (n 9).

of the term against the 'advantage' of a lower price and/or of a guarantee 'protecting' the consumer nevertheless. Here, the interpretative obligation is neutralised outright, and not just 'internally', as in the parallel line of cases noted above, where it is made reference to and deployed albeit with diminished bite (compared to the previous jurisprudence of the CJEU on the matter).

Freiburger shows how the Court's overall strategy consists of both obliterating the interpretative obligation and conjuring up an economised balancing test as contemporaneous operations aimed at redesigning European constitutional law around market order requirements of efficiency.[17] This strategy overlaps with a wider movement towards a new kind of balancing (economised) which the rest of this chapter considers, looking at scholarly discourse and signifying the hermeneutical transformation that underlies the restructuring of inter-order relations to which I now turn. Constitutional heteronomy is substantively (discursively) determined, in the same way as constitutional autonomy.

B. Of Constitutional Heteronomy: Restructuring Inter-orderly Effects

The turn of jurisprudence away from the interpretative obligation as it had been previously constructed to a new configuration of it, keeping it only in name, consists of turning away from the previous structures of the jurisprudence of constitutional autonomy in three respects, each giving rise to the new paradigm of the heteronomous jurisprudence – from indirect constitutionalisation to direct constitutionalisation, from constitutional osmosis (mutual learning) to constitutional closure (impermeability) and from constitutional co-normativisation to constitutional hetero-normativisation.

(i) From Indirect to Heteronomous qua Direct Constitutionalisation Through Unconditional Reasoning

First is a shift entailed in the transformation of the interpretative obligation (and implied in the suspension of the interpretative obligation in *Freiburger*): it is the shift from conditional reasoning[18] to what one might call unconditional reasoning.

Through its directives, European law becomes the law of the nation-state land no longer on the condition that a conforming kind of reasoning is possible, as in the paradigmatic cases of *Faccini Dori*[19] and *Von Colson*,[20] but heteronomously,

[17] For 'disciplination' based on market balancing order, see ch 4.

[18] See ch 2 above.

[19] Case C-91/92 *Faccini Dori* [1994] ECR I-3325, ECLI:EU:C:1994:292.

[20] *Von Colson* (n 10).

that is, in line with the now extended apodictic logic of direct effect (*Dominguez*,[21] *Radlinger* and *OPR-Finance*[22]), that is, through the imposition of EU law (directives) norms over and above nation-state orders, as in the classical 'new legal order' scholarly vocabulary now made ever more powerful (from the viewpoint of the CJEU).[23]

In turn, this move obstructs and even makes redundant the internal interpretative chains, based on the reception of EU law through the interpretative obligation as applied to national laws, as in the above-noted *Schulte* saga[24] and as they also exist within national jurisdictions independently of European law under the so-called 'indirect constitutionalisation of private law'.[25] By 'indirect constitutionalisation of private law' I mean the impact of constitutional norms and principles in the private law realm through the working out of private law doctrinal structures whenever interpreted, and on the condition of being open to being interpreted so as to accommodate the constitutional commands.[26] Reasoning regarding the directives in the above-mentioned judgments now becomes entirely about the unconditional imposition of artificial EU law norms and principles as embedded in the directives themselves (and in framework decisions).

This trend towards heteronomy is in line with case law and scholarship on the constitutionalisation of European private law through fundamental rights[27] as one more step on the march towards an even greater centralisation and hierarchisation of constitutional relations among orders in Europe by means of unconditional reasoning – as constructed by the CJEU in recent years in other areas, such as the free movement of services, establishment and workers.[28]

This trajectory seems to show little awareness of, and no sensitivity towards, the 'loss' in terms of the legitimation of EU constitutional law that results from the heteronomous turn, as I have argued in 'Eclipse of the Constitution'.[29] Constitutional reasoning here becomes flattened around hierarchical structures that, in turn, rest on artificial material made out of 'general principles of law' defined abstractedly – a phenomenon that I have labelled elsewhere with the oxymoron of 'hierarchical balancing'.[30] I will return in section III to this emerging new structure of balancing that reaches beyond, and aims to cancel out, the conventional hermeneutics of social balancing.

Equally, the model decision of *Freiburger* introduces a thematisation of European constitutional law that follows reasoning patterns based on the objective

[21] Above n 5.
[22] Above nn 2 and 7.
[23] See *Van Gend* (n 12).
[24] See ch 2 above.
[25] ibid.
[26] See, in Germany, the writings of Canaris, above. For further discussion, see Niglia, 'Conforming Interpretation' (n 8).
[27] See discussion in Niglia, *The Struggle for European Private Law* (n 9).
[28] L Niglia, 'Eclipse of the Constitution' (2016) 22 *European Law Journal* 132.
[29] ibid.
[30] ibid.

of efficiency optimisation, which is, in turn, superimposed unconditionally upon national legal orders – insofar as in *Freiburger* the CJEU suspends the interpretative obligation applicable *ex hypothesi*. This mirrors a pattern followed by the CJEU in transforming the interpretative obligation from within (through the decisions in *Dominguez*, *Radlinger* and *OPR-Finance*) – replacing the existing interpretative obligation with another conception of it orientated to just enhancing effectiveness; the Court alters the interpretative obligation radically rather than just suspending it, that is, it replaces it altogether with a transformed interpretative obligation which carries the same name but is a distinct new doctrine. In both cases, heteronomous constitutionalisation takes place, given that horizontal relations end up being ruled by the 'new' version of the interpretative obligation doctrine.[31]

(ii) From Constitutional Osmosis to Constitutional Closure (Impermeability) Through Unlearning

Alongside the process of heteronomous constitutionalisation through unconditional reasoning, one must register the contemporaneous process of a shift away from mutual learning through engagement with the hermeneutical materials of private laws.[32]

The model decisions of *Freiburger* (suspension of the interpretative obligation) and *OPR-Finance* (transformation from within of the interpretative obligation) both fail to recognise any of the legal material coming from the national jurisdictions. Specifically, the principle of contemporary performance *ex hypothesi* is applicable to the dispute, as, equally, it is the case of the argument from nullity conditional on it having been raised by the consumer. Both decisions represent a refusal to open up to any learning as deriving from the ground level of the national legal systems of private law.

This is because, through embracing unconditional reasoning, legal actors are supposed no longer to, and no longer be required to, cling on to national traditions of private law so as to 'learn' from them, with a view to attempting to transpose this learning into the body of EU law norms and principles to the extent that this is possible – as in the learning mechanism underlying the interpretative obligation.[33]

This entails a constitutional closure of the EU order and its law, and, correspondingly, a closure of national law seen as not capable of having its own autonomous voice but as only seen as obliged to passively adapt to the determinations of the EU order. This is so in the following two senses.

[31] See also ch 4.

[32] See ch 2 above.

[33] ibid. The transposition of learning from a higher level (above national legal traditions) as defended by certain proponents of EPL common norms and principles is far from what the interpretative obligation entails – a transposition of knowledges from national legal traditions into EU law. For this criticism, see L Niglia, 'Taking Comparative Law Seriously – Europe's Private Law and the Poverty of the Orthodoxy (Instalment One)' (2006) 54 *American Journal of Comparative Law* 401.

Whenever the interpretative obligation gives rise to the positive result of a conforming interpretation of national law in the light of the relevant directive, mutual learning entails the reformulation of the national norms and their incorporation into the European law norms and principles contained in the directives – thus transforming the latter and embedding them in the structures of national private laws, thereby giving them life as new private law norms. As this mechanism leading to a conforming interpretation has now been abandoned by the new jurisprudence of the Court, the hermeneutics of the CJEU and of national private law actors are no longer part of an equally ordained, jurisgenerative, process of private law redetermination. Rather, the jurisprudence of the Court takes precedence in that it is ultimately imposed upon national laws. Here, 'unlearning', the opposite to mutual learning, takes place.

Whenever the interpretative obligation gives rise to the negative result of a lack of a conforming interpretation of national law in the light of the relevant directive, it nevertheless enables dialogues about possibilities of conformity as instantiation of the coexistence praxis – insofar as they produce both rereadings of private laws and reflexive critical understandings of each jurisdiction's own laws in relation to the challenges of confronting the transnationalisation of law. Such instantiation is now barred by the setting aside of the interpretative obligation in the new jurisprudence of the Court – this being another articulation of 'unlearning'.

This double implication, in turn, entails the barring of any kind of cooperative work towards mutual understanding as conceived of under the paradigm of constitutional autonomy.

(iii) From Constitutional Co-normativisation to Constitutional Hetero-normativisation Through Disciplining

There is a third aspect that needs to be looked at – the shift from cooperation qua 'co-evolutionary normativisation'[34] to hetero-normativisation qua 'disciplinary'.[35]

The model decision of *Freiburger* entails the disciplining of national legal actors so that they adapt to the requirements of EU law whilst depriving them of the co-normativising tool of the interpretative obligation. EU law is constructed by the Court as requiring them to undertake balancing acts according to certain defined parameters of economisation. Balancing is conceived of by the Court as imposing an obligation on the part of the national courts to weigh the relative costs and benefits to the advantage of the efficient solution of enabling the seller to offer combinations of terms that may also sacrifice contractual protection (as traditionally understood) by offering a lower price and/or a guarantee for the case of failure to perform. The Court prescribes a disciplinary regime about consumer contracts

[34] See ch 2 above.

[35] On the further aspect of disciplining as 'disciplination' (discipline and private ordering), see ch 4.

that challenges and that ultimately aims at replacing the national private orders' own requirements.[36] As a result, normativisation is no longer co-evolutionary in the sense that it is no longer the EU and the national actors that co-determine the content of the law.

The same can be said for the new conception of the interpretative obligation insofar as it is now seen as a mere instrument of effectiveness, as this conception transpires from the above-noted judgments of the Court, entailing as it does a restricted kind of balancing that subordinates every other normative consideration to the requirement of effectiveness.

The Court creates a 'hermeneutical space' within which legal actors can and are supposed to enact their own interpretation of the law which is narrower than the hermeneutical 'space' that previously (under the jurisprudence of constitutional autonomy as recounted in chapter two above) allowed legal actors to refer to, and deploy, national legal materials.[37]

According to the thinking behind this move, the European constitutional 'hermeneutical circle' that comprises the horizons of EU law and of national law as necessary for the work of interpretation is disposed of in that the normative positions of the relevant national legal actors are obliterated.[38] Legal actors are now placed under an obligation to comply with EU law that ends up with constraining and regimenting their modes of reasoning around economised balancing.

This must be called 'disciplining' not only in the hermeneutical sense of the EU order heteronomously imposing its (economised balancing) norms upon national legal systems – but also in the deeper sense of a subversion of the equally ordained hermeneutics entailed in the paradigm of constitutional autonomy that was. Moreover, as I explain in the following chapter, it is about 'disciplining' in the sense of imposing a totalising constitutional discipline through absolutising the private order: so that totality and not plurality becomes the key characterising trait of hermeneutics, giving rise to the oxymoron of hermeneutics as totality.[39] In chapter four I consider a number of major cases in which the Court expands its new jurisprudence of economisation relentlessly imposed on national private laws. Before proceeding with this step of the argument, I will recount the way in which scholarship has been participating, alongside the courts, in the shift from autonomy to heteronomy through devising the 'hermeneutics' of economised balancing: in other words, below I expand further on the aspect of heteronomy characterised as economised balancing.

[36] On these aspects, see L Niglia, 'Tra Europa e diritto privato. La questione del bilanciamento secondo il diritto civile comparato' (2018) 1 *EDP* 159.

[37] See ch 2 above.

[38] A hermeneutical circle, one may say, that is contingent on Europe's composite constitutional condition: see Niglia, 'Eclipse of the Constitution' (n 28).

[39] If taking hermeneutics as plural (see ch 1 above). The rest of the book refers to 'hermeneutics' in the limited (negative) sense of a juridical hermeneutics that subverts itself: see ch 1 above, at 'comparative hermeneutics', and ch 4 below (on 'trans-juridification').

III. A Scholarly Hermeneutical Transformation

This section considers the scholarly construction of a self-contained European private law discourse. 'Self-contained' designates the phenomenon of the insiders (the legal actors) to the private law field conjuring up a European private law made independent of, rather than reliant on, national private laws.[40] This is an intensive kind of new European private law discourse, characterised as it is by being centred on a balancing understood as economised rather than social. It is entirely about accommodating market imperatives.

This new transformation of the European private law discourse from national to European is in itself a reinforcement of the CJEU jurisprudence of constitutional heteronomy. Both have the effect of formally reordering the position of EU constitutional law (as encroaching upon privatistic materials) vis-à-vis national private laws' orders. This is because scholarship offers a hermeneutics that the courts can look at whenever conjuring up 'European' interpretations of the directives as,[41] contemporaneously, the courts are requested to detach themselves from the tradition of national private laws by resorting to a kind of balancing (economised) other than, and irreducible to, social balancing.[42]

The two moves are closely correlated: the Court engineers a decoupling of European Private Law norms from national private laws at the same time that it

[40] On 'self-contained' regimes, see ch 4 (on fragmentation of European law and of private law). For an illustration regarding the legal treatment of 'regimes', drawing on international law, see M Koskenniemi, *The Politics of International Law* (Oxford, Hart Publishing, 2011) ch 14; note and compare the judgment of *United States Diplomatic and Consular Staff in Tehran (United States of America v Iran)*, ICJ Reports 1980, p 40, para 86 (quoted in Judge Yusuf's dissenting opinion in *Immunities and Criminal Proceedings (Equatorial Guinea v France)*, Judgment, ICJ Reports 2020, www.icj-cij.org/en/case/163) with regard to the Vienna Convention on Diplomatic Relations, and as self-contained regime, as such having its own system of sanctions: 'The rules of diplomatic law, in short, constitute a self-contained régime which, on the one hand, lays down the receiving State's obligations regarding the facilities, privileges and immunities to be accorded to diplomatic missions and, on the other, foresees their possible abuse by members of the mission and specifies the means at the disposal of the receiving State to counter any such abuse'. This well-known international law phenomenon mirrors the case of private ordering as increasingly self-contained, and with its own procedures and system of sanctions (and, I argue, constitutionally so), which I consider in ch 4. On the methodology of comparative law (the analysis of the layers of the private law discourse, and of the relationships among the layers) through which one can capture private ordering as self-contained, see ch 1 above: through the looking glass of European law methodology, positivistic, one would be forced only to see the new positioning of private ordering limitedly, that is, as nevertheless belonging to, and as a function of, the EU order or the national order.

[41] On the argument from codification as part of this process, see Niglia, *The Struggle for European Private Law* (n 9). On knowledge and European private law, see L Niglia, 'On the "Rationalities" of European Private Law – Between the Internal Market and Law's Discourse' (2016) 22 *European Law Journal* 566; Niglia, *The Struggle for European Private Law* (n 9).

[42] The courts are 'requested' to do this in the mode of 'direct effect' (the interpretative obligation having become a proxy for direct effect, and through other constitutional-absorption technical means which I discuss in ch 4) and in the mode of the EU constructed related obligation to disapply any of the conflicting national norms.

constructs a new hermeneutics of balancing around economisation that blocks off any recourse to traditional private laws as a way to gain hermeneutical meaning from the latter. As a result of this decoupling from national private laws, and of the anchoring of law to economised balancing (efficiency), the praxis of constitutional heteronomy both comes into existence and gains in efficacy and effectiveness.[43]

As I shall explain in chapter four, it is a contingent kind of hermeneutical material (economised balancing) that then makes the jurisprudence of constitutional heteronomy intelligible as 'total law' – with the rising private order replacing the EU constitutional order and as a result totalising constitutional law.

One more aspect needs to be stressed:[44] the 'co-authorship' between the judiciary and scholarship as articulated in the age of the jurisprudence of constitutional autonomy[45] is also relevant here insofar as scholarship and the judiciary share the same vocabulary. In chapter four, I identify a further 'co-authorship' at the level of 'constitutional absorption' around the rising absolutising conception of the private order by the insiders (the legal actors) to the private law discourse.

In the rest of the chapter I argue that at a certain point in time the technique of (social) balancing, as previously developed in national private law and as positioned nationally under the paradigm of constitutional autonomy, was captured, appropriated and radically transformed by the actors in the European private law field – scholars and judges. This has been happening gradually over the course of the last 20 years or so, during which one has assisted to a transformation of balancing. Balancing has shifted from a hermeneutical technique, crafted and elaborated as part of a constitutional private law project informed to sociality and aligned along the constitutional orders of the EU and of the Member States, as discussed in chapter two above, to a self-standing technique accommodating market discipline (economisation) in four new balancing declinations – through recourse to *precontractual* (section B(i)), and to *principled* (section B(ii)) balancing, and to *rule-bound* (section B(iii)) and *teleological* (section B(v)) balancing. I will discuss each of the four declinations after having expanded on the background to new balancing (section A).

[43] Here the triad of efficacy, effectiveness and efficiency finds its full realisation. On efficacy and effectiveness of this praxis as 'total constitutional law', see ch 4. On the the deeper constitutional grounding of this interface between hermeneutical material and the jurisprudence of the CJEU, see ch 4 (explaining that economised balancing is a hermeneutical technique for the 'taking over' of the European constitutional order – as 'constitutional absorption').

[44] In this book, by 'jurisprudence' or 'jurisprudential forces' I mean both scholars and judges (for discussion, see Niglia, *The Struggle for European Private Law* (n 9) 2 et seq). On co-authorship, including the historical development of the law, see L Niglia, *The Transformation of Contract in Europe* (The Hague, Kluwer Law International, 2003); Niglia, *The Struggle for European Private Law* (n 9).

[45] See ch 2 above.

A. Background to New Balancing: A Context of Full Harmonisation and of Unification (Beyond Restrained Harmonisation)[46]

(i) Context (Harmonisation)

In 2004, the Commission called on the scholarly community to compile a Common Frame of Reference by way of merging the *acquis communautaire* with the received body of model rules such as those contained in the Lando Principles and similar common-rules-in-the-abstract writings.[47]

Read in parallel with the Directive on Consumer Rights,[48] the two Directives on Digital Contracting[49] and ancillary Commission documents,[50] this Commission's move amounts to requesting a redrafting of the private law script so as to accommodate the functionalist requirement of market integration in market libertarian terms. An example is the project of 'generalising'[51] a series of directive-generated rules, such as the test of fairness contained in the Unfair Terms Directive and the right of cancellation, so as to apply them not only to consumer contracts, but to all contracts.

[46] See ch 1 above.

[47] Commission, 'A More Coherent European Contract Law: An Action Plan', COM(2003) 68 final; Commission, 'European Contract Law and the Revision of the *Acquis*: The Way Forward', COM(2004) 651 final. For the broader spectrum of historic qua ideological reasons behind this shift, *cf* L Niglia, 'Constitutional Europe' (unpublished manuscript on file with author, 2022).

[48] Directive 2011/83/EU of the European Parliament and of the Council of 25 October 2011 on consumer rights, amending Council Directive 93/13/EEC and Directive 1999/44/EC of the European Parliament and of the Council and repealing Council Directive 85/577/EEC and Directive 97/7/EC of the European Parliament and of the Council Text with EEA relevance [2011] OJ L304/64.

[49] Directive (EU) 2019/770 of the European Parliament and of the Council of 20 May 2019 on certain aspects concerning contracts for the supply of digital content and digital services; Directive (EU) 2019/771 of the European Parliament and of the Council of 20 May 2019 on certain aspects concerning contracts for the sale of goods, amending Regulation (EU) 2017/2394 and Directive 2009/22/EC, and repealing Directive 1999/44/EC PE/27/2019/REV/1. See also Proposal for a Regulation of the European Parliament and of the Council on a Single Market for Digital Services (Digital Services Act) and amending Directive 2000/31/EC COM(2020) 825 final; Proposal for a Regulation of the European Parliament and of the Council on contestable and fair markets in the digital sector (Digital Markets Act) COM(2020) 842 final.

[50] COM(2002) 208, 17; COM(2005) 115, 10; COM(2006) 744, 4; COM(2007) 99, 4: *cf* also N Reich, 'Von der Minimal- zur Voll- zur "Halbharmonisierung"' [2010] *Zeitschrift fur Europaisches Privatrecht* 7, 15 (holding that the paradigm of protection of consumers is replaced by that of consumers as 'shoppers', this being generally speaking based on the template of the ECJ case law on the internal market); H-W Micklitz, 'The Visible Hand of European Regulatory Private Law. The Transformation of European Private Law from Autonomy to Functionalism in Competition and Regulation' (European University Institute, 2008) EUI Working Papers Law 2008/14; H Micklitz, 'The Visible Hand of European Regulatory Private Law' (2009) 28 *Yearbook of European Law* 3 (the average consumer is used as camouflage to dispense with mandatory standards of various sorts).

[51] On the role of the technique of 'generalisation' in European private law, see L Niglia, 'Beyond Enchantment: The Possibility of a New European Private Law (Instalment Two)' (2009) 28 *Yearbook of European Law* 60; N Jansen and R Zimmermann, 'Recasting the *Acquis Communautaire*? A Critical Evaluation of the Principles of the Existing EC Contract Law' [2008] *MLR* 505.

By 'libertarian' I mean the Commission's project of drafting private consumer law rules with a view to accommodating as much as possible business freedoms above consumer protectionist standards,[52] a project that the Draft Common Frame of Reference (DCFR)[53] had been intending to implement and to expand beyond just consumer law to apply to the whole of the private law sphere, from transactional interactions to non-contractual damages to unjust enrichment,[54] regardless of any of the 'subjective' denotations (merchant, consumer) of the parties involved in all such situations.

It should be stressed that the Commission's overall project of private law Europeanisation is not just ideological, but about the juridical hermeneutics itself,[55] as constantly reorganised by the community of private law scholars.[56]

Scholars have been explicitly asked to engage with the Commission's regulatory choices as embedded in its private law Europeanisation project as, specifically, the Commission would hope to convince scholarship to underwrite them all. In brief, the Commission has replaced the cryptic vocabulary of harmonisation with an open-ended vocabulary of full harmonisation and unification (codification)[57] of private law and related outright replacement of national private laws.

The DCFR, and even the related Common European Sales Law (CELS), albeit subsequently being dropped as a legislative proposal, remain the unquestioned benchmark against which to evaluate any moves from the Commission, such as the most recent move towards a European digital agenda.[58] Whilst the CELS legislative

[52] *cf* Niglia, *The Transformation of Contract in Europe* (n 44); Niglia, *The Struggle for European Private Law* (n 9).

[53] See critically below. On the DCFR, see C Von Bar and E Clive (eds), *Principles, Definitions and Model Rules of European Private Law. Draft Common Frame of Reference* (Oxford, Oxford University Press, 2009) (DCFR 2009) and the two previous editions without comments and notes: C Von Bar et al (eds), *Principles, Definitions and Model Rules of European Private Law: The Draft Common Frame of Reference* (Munich, Sellier, interim outline edition, 2008; outline edition, 2009).

[54] On contract and tort, see the rest of this chapter. On tort, see ch 5; and L Niglia,' A" European" Tort Law? Comparative Thoughts on an" Essentially Contested" Private Law Institution' in P Gilliker (ed), *Research Handbook on European Tort Law* (Cheltenham, Edward Elgar, 2017) 321.

[55] See ch 1 above (on methodology).

[56] Niglia, *The Struggle for European Private Law* (n 9).

[57] The naming of the project as Draft Common Frame of Reference as opposed to 'codification/code' has been widely considered to have been about camouflaging the move: see a synthesis of the relevant literature and discussion in Niglia, *The Struggle for European Private Law* (n 9). See also R Zimmermann, 'The Present State of European Private Law' (2009) 57 *American Journal of Comparative Law* 479, 491; for an author's argument that not to call the DCFR 'code' is a 'clever trick', see M Hesselink, 'The European Commission's Action Plan: Towards a More Coherent European Contract Law?' (2004) 12 *European Review of Private Law* 397, 402; see also C Von Bar, 'A CFR for European Private Law – Academic Efforts and Political Realities' (2008) 23 *Tulane European and Civil Law Forum* 37, 40 ('the nebulous term CFR serves as a camouflage'). De facto, one must consider the CFR to be about implementing a codification strategy. On the relatedness of this codification strategy to the broader governance plans of the European Commission, see L Niglia (ed), *Pluralism and European Private Law* (Oxford, Hart Publishing, 2013); Niglia, *The Struggle for European Private Law* (n 9).

[58] See H Micklitz, 'The COVID-19 Threat: An Opportunity to Rethink the European Economic Constitution and European Private Law' (2020) 11 *European Journal of Risk Regulation* 249. See also n 67 below and ch 4; for a discussion, see Micklitz (ibid).

project collapsed,[59] the law's trajectory towards a totalisation of European constitutional and European private law continues – as I argue in chapter four. The legal culture, in terms of the juridical hermeneutics, of European constitutional and private law is firmly on its economisation path.[60]

(ii) Context (Federative)

This chapter discusses substantive and structural aspects that are part and parcel of a broader set of changes towards what one can call a 'federative consciousness', that is, changing federalising dynamics as a result of the new ways of engagement of private law actors vis-à-vis, and in interaction with, not only the work of the EU Commission, but also the jurisprudence of the CJEU. In fact, in a series of writings that have developed over the last 20 years or so, it has been submitted, both in general EU law scholarship and in scholarship that discusses the implications of general EU law for private law, as well as in European private law scholarship, that private law must 'think federally'.[61]

Any such federalising positions have since been challenged by nationalist and populist voices articulating their criticism of the EU, which they see as over-powerful insofar as it is expanding and exceeding its competences. Yet, it is exactly in the context of the ritual crises of the EU that 'thinking federally' has acquired a new importance – as emerges in the rest of this book. This is in relation to the heavy intervention of the EU in the crisis management of the coronavirus pandemic, including the structural reforms that affect the once autonomous (in the sense of the 'constitutional autonomy' paradigm) private law, as well as the digital agenda and the greening and recovery policies promoted at the EU level in the context of the new economic governance structures.[62]

[59] Codification is to be critically considered (see Niglia, *The Struggle for European Private Law* (n 9)) in the broader context of crisis in Europe: on European integration and 'crises', see C Joerges, 'Integration through Law and the Crisis of Law in Europe's Emergency' in D Chalmers, M Jachtenfuchs and C Joerges (eds), *The End of the Eurocrats' Dream: Adjusting to European Diversity* (Cambridge, Cambridge University Press, 2016); D Chalmers, 'Crisis Reconfiguration of the European Constitutional State' in Chalmers et al (ibid); A Menéndez, 'The Crisis of Law and the European Crises: From the Social and Democratic Rechtsstaat to the Consolidating State of (Pseudo-)Technocratic Governance' (2017) 44 *Journal of Law & Society* 56, 73; Niglia, 'Europe and "Crisis" (First Part)' (n 16) (special section edited by Leone Niglia).

[60] See also L Niglia, 'The New Transformation of Europe. Arcana Imperii' (2020) 68 *American Journal of Comparative Law* 151. By legal culture I mean (see ch 1 above, at methodology) legal culture as juridical hermeneutics, as comparative juridical hermeneutics; the hermeneutical approach chosen here equally contributes to portraying legal culture in its own ways: compare and contrast the works on legal culture of P Legrand (eg P Legrand, 'Jameses at Play: A Tractation on the Comparison of Laws' (2017) 65 (suppl 1) *American Journal of Comparative Law* 1).

[61] *cf* R Brownsword, H Micklitz, L Niglia and S Weatherill (eds), *The Foundations of European Private Law* (Oxford, Hart Publishing, 2011); W Van Gerven, 'European Private Law: Unification, Harmonisation or Coordination?' in Brownsword et al (ibid) 338. In critical perspective on European private law and federalism, for the beginnings of the reflection on European private law as related to federalism as constitutional project, see Niglia, 'Beyond Enchantment' (n 51).

[62] On crisis, see Niglia, 'Europe and "Crisis" (First Part)' (n 16); Niglia, 'The New Transformation' (n 60); see also ch 4 below (on the ECB asset buying programme); I refer to the Next Generation EU, *https://ec.europa.eu/info/strategy/recovery-plan-europe_en#nextgenerationeu*.

The traits of this persistent federalising legal consciousness can be summarised as follows: it has become increasingly felt that private law must justify itself functionally in relation to the complex demands of the European multi-level system of governance.[63] Over the last two decades, key steps in this turn towards reframing private law through governance[64] have been, in no order of importance: the introduction of maximum harmonisation through the Directive on Consumer Rights;[65] the CJEU jurisprudence that purports to establish the horizontal direct effect of general principles of law;[66] the codification project through the DCFR and then the CELS proposal; the Directives on Digital Contracting of 2019 and subsequent directives' proposals;[67] the judicial activism of domestic courts over-reading directives and extending them to disputes that were not originally in the mind of the legislature;[68] an increasing awareness of private law scholarship regarding the interconnectedness between EU private law and the rest of EU law;[69] and the critical concerns in legal comparative terms regarding the claims to sameness of private law rules throughout legal traditions as allegedly justifying a trans-state (EU) common governance regime.[70]

What is striking is that all the actors (judges, scholars, legislators), whatever their positions (whether more or less inclined towards the integration project), share this new hermeneutical consciousness.[71] This is a 'new federal consciousness for private law', given that it repositions private law in the newly re-constituted federal, multi-level system, away from the constitutionally autonomous position

[63] Niglia, 'Beyond Enchantment' (n 51); Micklitz, 'The Visible Hand of European Regulatory Private Law' (2008) (n 50) (discussing private law's increasing economisation and politicisation processes); W Van Gerven, 'European Private Law: Unification, Harmonisation or Coordination?' in R Brownsword, H Micklitz, L Niglia and S Weatherill (eds), *The Foundations of European Private Law* (Oxford, Hart Publishing, 2011) 338 (agreeing with Micklitz that 'in order for the study of private law to have a truly European dimension, it must also focus on what he calls 'the Visible Hand of European Private Law', that is, private law in its transformation, in a European context, from autonomy to functionalism in economic and governance matters).

[64] On governance, see Eriksen, EO, and Fossum, JE 'Europe at a Crossroads: Government or Transnational Governance?' in C Joerges, I Sand & G Teubner (eds) *Transnational Governance and Constitutionalism* (Oxford, Hart Publishing, 2004) 115–146.

[65] See Niglia, 'Eclipse of the Constitution' (n 28) and see n 48 above.

[66] See ch 4; see also below on Case C-684/16 *Max-Planck* of 6 November 2018 ECLI:EU:C:2018:874; Case C-414/16 *Egenberger* of 17 April 2018 ECLI:EU:C:2018:257.

[67] See the two proposals ('new deal for consumers'), that is, Proposal for a Directive amending Council Directive 93/13/EEC, Directive 98/6/EC, Directive 2005/29/EC and Directive 2011/83 as regards better enforcement and modernisation of EU consumer protection rules, https://eur-lex.europa.eu/legal-content/EN/TXT/?qid=1573719288581&uri=CELEX:52018PC0185 (on 'fundamental rights', freedom of contract and on national laws and practices), and Proposal for a Directive on representative actions for the protection of the collective interests of consumers and repealing Directive 2009/22/EC. See M Durovic and T Tridimas (eds), *New Directions in European Private Law* (Oxford, Hart Publishing, 2021); S Weatherill (ed), *Better Regulation* (Oxford, Hart Publishing, 2020).

[68] See the rest of this chapter.

[69] Niglia, 'Of Harmonisation and Fragmentation' (n 16).

[70] See Niglia, 'Taking Comparative Law Seriously' (n 33); Niglia, 'Beyond Enchantment' (n 51); Niglia, 'Of Harmonisation and Fragmentation' (n 16); ch 1 above; in parallel, see Legrand (n 60).

[71] See, critically, Niglia, *Pluralism* (n 57) (on complex pluralism); see also Niglia, 'Beyond Enchantment' (n 51).

relative to the federal dynamics in which it found itself for a long time until the changes recounted here. Such constitutional autonomy used to manifest itself in various ways – whether by gravitating around nation states as the true and only source for the common rules,[72] engaging in building a new common legal culture independently of EU legislative developments[73] or, regarding EU legislation, by emphasising the relative intensity of the EU interventions by pointing to the minimal character of the harmonisation project (the so-called 'minimum harmonisation clauses').[74]

Broadly speaking, I am referring to, and recounting, regulatory changes as manifested in a new turn in the case law of the CJEU (including, among the many, *Laval* and *Mangold*),[75] at times supported by the national courts, and a new strategy adopted by the Commission in the area (see section (iii)). It is a sequence of revolutionary European-led regulatory interventions that have been remapping European economic law, effectively placing private law at the core of economic constitutional reforms and making key organising tools of the private law script less autonomous and more federative and regulatory in outlook.[76]

The importance of this shift cannot be underestimated. In much the same way as in other policy arenas, as they have become part of the EU multi-level regulatory suite, private law has been shifting away from what I have elsewhere labelled as an age of enchantment,[77] characterised by positivistic preoccupations with legal details. It now increasingly shows signs of maturity, whereby dilemmas regarding the 'social embeddedness' of markets and law (in the vocabulary of Karl Polanyi[78]) have become evident and can no longer be denied. Quantitative issues of how much room there is for intervention and for market processes, as well as qualitative issues of 'how and for what ends should markets and states be combined',[79] inevitably become pressing and require explicit answers, much as in other fields of market integration. The internal market project is now taken to be in need of a sophisticated apparatus of private law rules and principles to work properly,[80] no longer

[72] In legal cultural terms, see Legrand (n 60).

[73] See, eg R Zimmermann, 'The Present State of European Private Law' (2009) 57 *American Journal of Comparative Law* 479.

[74] See, eg Directive on Unfair Terms.

[75] Case C-341/05 *Laval* [2007] ECR-I 11767 and Case C-144/04 *Mangold* [2005] ECR I-9981.

[76] For a synthesis *cf* H Micklitz, 'The Visible Hand of European Regulatory Private Law' (2009) (n 50), with a focus on regulatory aspects; Niglia, 'Beyond Enchantment' (n 51), with a focus on constitutional federative aspects.

[77] On formalism qua enchantment, *cf* Niglia, 'Beyond Enchantment' (n 51).

[78] *cf* K Polanyi, *The Great Transformation* (New York, Farrar & Rinehart, 1944). See C Joerges and J Falke (eds), *Karl Polanyi, Globalisation and the Potential of Law in Transnational Markets* (Oxford, Hart Publishing, 2011).

[79] See F Block, 'Towards a New Understanding of Economic Modernity' in C Joerges, B Strath and P Wagner (eds), *The Economic as a Polity: The Political Construction of Modern Capitalism – An Interdisciplinary Perspective* (London, UCL Press, 2005), also interpreting Karl Polanyi as arguing that the disembedding of socially embedded markets cannot be successful. The contribution by T Wilhelmsson, 'Varieties of Welfarism in European Contract Law' (2004) 10 *European Law Journal* 712 is path-breaking in pointing to the manifold implications of the private law harmonisation project. See also Niglia, 'Beyond Enchantment' (n 51).

[80] Explicit in this sense has always been Micklitz, 'The Visible Hand of European Regulatory Private Law' (2009) (n 50); see the previous work (on 'contest of disciplines') of C Joerges, 'The Europeanization

satisfied with promoting market integration through free movement and competition only. It should be noted that the broader context to this rising consciousness consists of a shift from 'nation state' to 'market state', which is, in my view, more a project (an ideological project) and less a taken-for-granted process – for it is a project that the Commission is carrying on (most recently in the area of digital private law) through private law, but that, as I argue in the rest of this book, meets with resistance of various kinds.[81]

(iii) Three Kinds of EU Interventions

There is a range of three-layered EU interventions that I would now like to consider and that encroach upon, and alter, the structures of what conventionalism labels 'negative' (cases) and 'positive' (legislative) market integration as relevant to private law.

First, a pervasive line of jurisprudence from the CJEU (*Viking*, *Laval*, *Mangold*, *Kücükdeveci*)[82] entails a reassessment of the substantive rationality of private law rules in relation to market building, with a view to instrumentalising it for the establishment of a competitive, pan-European market based on access to the 'least regulative state'.[83] Private law is no longer kept away from the 'regulatory synergies' of the integration project,[84] but becomes part and parcel of it. The expansion of the European project, both in scope and depth, encompasses a private law which, for the first time, needs to rethink its very rationality in relation to those synergies. Consequently, the private law script needs to be explicitly justified against the new requirements of market integration – otherwise other actors will write it on their own, from constitutionalists to policymakers.

The expansion is twofold. As to depth, groundbreaking substantive changes are being superimposed upon private law towards favouring a competitive and deregulatory framework. As to scope, the core areas of domestic private laws are no longer sheltered from the encroachment of European integration.[85] *Mangold* is one

of Private Law as a Rationalization Process and as a Contest of Disciplines: An Analysis of the Directive on Unfair Terms in Consumer Contracts' (1995) 3 *European Review of Private Law* 175.

[81] See, eg H Micklitz and D Paterson, 'From the Nation State to the Market: The Evolution of EU Private Law' (2012) EUI Working Paper 2012/15. On digital private law and on patterns of 'resistance', see the rest of this chapter and chapters 4 and 5.

[82] *Laval* (n 75); *Mangold* (n 75); C-438/05 *The International Transport Workers' Federation (ITF) & The Finnish Seamen's Union (FSU) v Viking Line ABP and Oü Viking Line Eesti* [2007] ECR I-10779 (*Viking*); Case C-555/07 *Kücükdeveci*. See Niglia, 'Eclipse of the Constitution' (n 28). For a discussion, see ch 4 below.

[83] *cf*, eg S. Deaki, 'Regulatory Competition after Laval' (2007) 10 *Cambridge Yearbook of European Legal Studies* 581; M Everson, 'Vom *effet utile* zum effet néolibéral: Warum setzt der EuGH die Integritaet des Europrechts aufs Spiel?' in C Joerges and T Pinkel, *Europaeisches Verfassungsdenken ohen Provatrecht – Europaeisches Privatrecht Ohne Demokratie?* (ZERP, 2011) Disckussionpapier 1/2011.

[84] 'Regulatory synergies' is how I would call the European private law sectorial regimes: see ch 4 below.

[85] It is notoriously difficult to justify such an expansive agenda in terms of the actual competences conferred upon the EU (*cf* S Weatherill, 'Competence and European Private Law' in C Twigg-Flesner (ed), *The Cambridge Companion to European Union Private Law* (Cambridge, Cambridge University Press,

key case in this sense, displacing as it does (or at least attempting to)[86] the established competence boundaries between the national and the European levels in relation to social policy and private law whilst superimposing on domestic regimes the EU law-fabricated principle of (age) equality – here, an 'erosion' of competence boundaries is taking place through the application, horizontally, of fundamental rights.[87] For, as a result of *Mangold*, social policy and private law (including consumer protection) are no longer left in the national realm but are fully caught up in the dynamics of Europeanisation through an argument presented as if it apodictically descended from EU law worked out as a law of (general) principles.

Whilst there remains deep uncertainty as to the status of *Mangold* and similar cases,[88] given their controversial character, it is clear to all that through such cases in which fundamental rights are applied horizontally the CJEU has been displacing previously established constitutional conventions.

I refer to those conventions grounded on competence boundaries and under the broad paradigm of constitutional autonomy considered in the previous chapter, whereby it is concurrently and ultimately a decision of the nation state whether or not to adapt domestic private law to EU law. The dynamics of 'constitutional absorption' explain these trends, as I argue in chapter four.[89]

Second, and in parallel to the noted judicial developments, legislative developments are no less important. The directives pertaining to contract law have been expanding in both scope and intensity – in scope, through the broadening of their reach by merging a few of them, as in the case of the Directive on Consumer Rights; and in intensity, through the introduction of maximum harmonisation, as in the case of the Unfair Commercial Practices Directive and the Directive on Consumer Rights.[90] Also, the European Commission has been supporting networks of scholars advising on how to instrumentalise contract and tort law

2010), but it is equally notorious how firmly the CJEU and the EU Commission proceed in their work of reconfiguration of market integration by incorporating private law in their range of activities – the shift of scholars towards insisting on the need for private law to 'think federally', whilst understandable on the grounds explained in the text, plays an ambiguous role in relation to this problematic aspect. I note later in the book (see ch 4) that there is another aspect (proportionality) that must be placed alongside that of 'competence' as another unresolved issue in the Europeanisation of private law.

[86] See Niglia, 'Eclipse of the Constitution' (n 28).

[87] On 'erosion', see ch 4.

[88] See Niglia, 'Eclipse of the Constitution' (n 28); see also *Max-Planck* and *Egenberger* (n 66) (holding for the horizontal effects of the EU Charter of Fundamental Rights' provisions). The proposed reading, in the light of the framework for analysis of the jurisprudence of constitutional autonomy, suggests (in relation to *Mangold*, *Max-Planck* and *Egenberger*; see also Case C-555/10 *Kucukdeveci* of 19 January 2010) a process of 'erosion' of jurisdictional demarcation. On erosion, see ch 4 below.

[89] For more discussion, see also Niglia, 'Eclipse of the Constitution' (n 28). For an account of this situatedness of the private law discourse, *cf* Niglia, *The Transformation of Contract in Europe* (n 44).

[90] See, respectively, Directive 2005/29/EC of the European Parliament and of the Council of 11 May 2005 concerning unfair business-to-consumer commercial practices in the internal market and amending Council Directive 84/450/EEC, Directives 97/7/EC, 98/27/EC and 2002/65/EC of the European Parliament and of the Council and Regulation (EC) No 2006/2004 of the European Parliament and of the Council ('Unfair Commercial Practices Directive') [2005] OJ L149/22; Directive 2011/83/EU (n 48).

towards the market-orientated competitive project, with the result that consolidation (Directive on Consumer Rights – notably merging four directives) and codification (the DCFR project) techniques have gained centre stage for a long time, until the digital agenda was embraced whilst keeping the market-orientated competitive project central to its policy work.[91]

One must also note an increasing awareness over time that the private law script is no longer national but European *in the first instance*, whilst the problematic 'modernisation' of the private law script through adaptation to economic developments increasingly takes place less nationally and more supranationally, as if the EU were an agency enjoying exclusive powers in matters of 'innovation' and 'modernisation'[92] – as demonstrated by debates about the two Directives on Digital Contracting.

Third, as I discuss in the remainder of the book, reversing previous trends,[93] domestic courts, in their interpretation of the many directives in the field, have been overcoming methodologies based on literal readings, with a view to applying them to disputes that were unthinkable when the relevant directives were enacted – the application of the right of cancellation to the issue of guarantees (*Dietzinger*) and to that of loan agreements (*Schulte*) in Germany respectively being the case in point.[94]

Let me give an example that draws on only one of the three processes under consideration (the legislative) as a way of showing how the three processes take us to the same destination, that is, towards a private law that needs to be explicitly justified in terms of the value tensions caused by the expanding market integration project and its increasing degree of encroachment on private law. It is the case of maximum harmonisation, as included in the Directive on Consumer Rights, implying a true reversal of the burden of proof and of the related power relationships between the EU and the Member States. For, for national legal systems to keep their laws, in relation to the ongoing impact upon them by the proposed directive, they will have to justify it through the vocabulary of market integration – a reversal of the burden of argumentation would take place, if contrasted to the age

[91] See (i) and (ii) above. Note pathways of convergence between general contract law and sectorial law in N Jansen and R Zimmermann (eds), *Commentaries on European Contract Laws* (Oxford, Oxford University Press, 2018).

[92] 'Modernisation' is a word that is key to the Commission strategy in the area: *cf*, eg www.ec.europa.eu/consumers/rights/cons_acquis_en.htm. For a reconstruction of the making, implementation and enforcement of the Unfair Terms Directive in national systems, as modernisation and with a critical approach, see Niglia, *The Transformation of Contract in Europe* (n 44). See also N Reich, 'Balancing in Private Law and the Imperatives of the Public Interest' in Brownsword et al (n 63) 221.

[93] L Niglia, 'The Non-Europeanization of Private Law' (2001) 4 *European Review of Private Law* 575. and see above at ch 2.

[94] See, respectively, CJEU Judgment of the Court (Fifth Chamber) of 17 March 1998, Case C-45/96 *Bayerische Hypotheken- und Wechselbank AG v Edgard Dietzinger* ECR I-01199; CJEU Judgment of the Court (Grand Chamber) of 25 October 2005, Case C-350/03 *Elisabeth Schulte and Wolfgang Schulte v Deutsche Bausparkasse Badenia AG*. Reference for a preliminary ruling: *Landgericht Bochum – Germany* ELI:ECLI:EU:C:2005:637. On Dietzinger, see Niglia, *The Struggle for European Private Law* (n 9) (right of cancellation applied to cases of guarantees). On Schulte, see ch 2 above.

of constitutional autonomy (eg the interpretative obligation); in fact, 'full harmonisation' means that the Member States will have to justify their deviation from the maximum standards whilst, under minimum harmonisation, 'the Commission has to prove that Member States' legislation reaching beyond the minimum is incompatible with EC law principles'.[95] This affects the deep nature of the federative interchange between the national and the supranational in matters of private law. The point of that interchange is no longer about designing minimum harmonised rules whilst leaving it to the national level to provide for, or maintain, an increased level of protection, if there is willingness to do that; rather, the point is to compel legal actors to deal with 'maximum rules' that, whenever they provide for a level of protection for consumers that is lower than the national one, may bring about a true 'race to the bottom' in private law regulation in Europe.[96]

In brief, private law actors are inevitably involved, and required to participate, in a process that is less about form and more about substance – they have to make choices about 'how much' intervention to make in markets and 'what sort' of intervention is desirable, which, in turn, takes them to justifying private law rules in the broader vocabulary of market integration borrowed from scholarship on free movement and competition law (including proportionality, efficiency, competitiveness and efficacy).

(iv) A New Kind of Scholarship

As a result of this turn of events, what I called at the start of the first decade of this century *market-orientated contract law* – and another author called *competitive contract law*[97] – in an attempt at synthesising the meaning of the whole of the Commission agenda in the area, has now become the bread and butter of scholarly deliberation, replacing the contemplative kind of scholarship to which we had become used to up until the end of the last century.[98]

One notes the new movement of thought at work not only among the insiders (the legal actors) to the DCFR but also outside it – looking at the last 20 years,

[95] H Micklitz, 'The Concept of Competitive Contract Law' (2005) 23 *Penn State International Law Review* 549, 584. Note Art 4 of Directive 2011/83/EU (n 48): 'Member States shall not maintain or introduce, in their national law, provisions diverging from those laid down in this Directive, including more or less stringent provisions to ensure a different level of consumer protection, unless otherwise provided for in this Directive.'

[96] L Niglia, 'Review of *The Cambridge Companion of European Union Law*' (2011) 36 *European Law Review* 760. On *Optional Instrument* and 'social dumping', *cf* M Hesselink, 'An Optional Instrument on EU Contract Law: Could it Increase Legal Certainty and Foster Cross-Border Trade?' (European Parliament Policy Department, 2010) PE 425.642; J Rutgers, 'An Optional Instrument and Social Dumping' [2006] *European Review of Contract Law* 199.

[97] Niglia, *The Transformation of Contract in Europe* (n 44); Micklitz, H, 'The Concept of Competitive Contract Law' (2005) 23 *Penn State International Law Review* 549.

[98] *cf*, eg the critical contributions of Reich, 'Von der Minimal-' (n 50) and Reich, 'Balancing in Private Law' (n 92); Niglia, 'Taking Comparative Law Seriously' (n 33). See now Hesselink, M, *Justifying Contract* (Oxford, Oxford University Press, 2021) (discussing private law in terms of justice).

one such movement of thought was the dispute between scholars belonging to the 'social' school of thought and those belonging to another group of scholars, operating within the DCFR.[99] Another new movement of thought consisted of the criticism coming from 'the outside', that is, from scholars who have not participated in the workings of the DCFR, and specifically a number of German scholars who are highly representative of their country's legal culture.[100] It suffices here to note how both movements of thought are paralleled in scope and importance only by previous sporadic scholarly writings coming from national jurisdictions, and critically written in relation to specific directives.[101]

What is striking is that scholars and judges have openly started addressing the normative considerations that underlie the Europeanisation process as a way to face the normative tensions caused by the new federative circumstances of increasing contestation taking place in the context of an EU seen as more and more powerful – and with the succession of crisis situations, from financial to pandemic, having made it ever more powerful through the European Central Bank buying bonds, and the Next Generation EU crisis resolution interventionist, programmes.[102] As domestic private law rules and principles come under pressure given the new strategies of the EU institutions as they intersect private law, scholars and judges increasingly employ balancing techniques, as defined in the rest of this chapter, aimed at re-rationalising private law around these concerns. It seems to me that increasingly more scholars and judges are participating in the new developments, with varied degrees of awareness, as the rest of the chapter will show, and yet as part of a shared path towards a self-referential kind of balancing, centred on concerns for accommodating market imperatives, and no longer 'social balancing'.

B. New Balancing in Contemporary Juridical Hermeneutics: Four Types

In this section, I consider strands of scholarship, including any representative case law that matches scholarly thinking, that have been adopting a distinctive kind of

[99] Hesselink, M, 'If You Don't Like Our Principles We Have Others' in R Brownsword, H Micklitz, L Niglia and S Weatherill (eds), *The Foundations of European Private Law* (Oxford, Hart Publishing, 2011) 59.

[100] H Eidenmüller, F Faust, H Grigoleit, N Jansen, G Wagner and R Zimmermann, 'The Common Frame of Reference for European Private Law – Policy Choices and Codification Problems' (2008) 28 *OJLS* 659.

[101] See, eg HE Brandner and P Ulmer, 'EG-Richtlinie über missbräuchliche Klauseln in Verbraucherverträgen. Kritische Bemerkungen zum Vorschlag der EG-Kommission' [1991] *Betriebs Berater* 701 (on which, see the reconstruction in Niglia, *The Transformation of Contract in Europe* (n 44); Micklitz, 'The COVID-19 Threat' (n 58); Niglia, *The Struggle for European Private Law* (n 9)).

[102] Niglia, 'Europe and "Crisis" (First Part)' (n 16).

European private law hermeneutics of balancing other than 'social balancing', as discussed in chapter two.

As the rest of the chapter will show, in giving rise to the considered types of balancing, the relevant legal actors have been acting not out of creativity, or of simply borrowing from other fields (that is, constitutionalism), but out of rediscovery, or invention (from the Latin: *invenire*). Here, 'invention' is used in the sense of finding out what is out there in terms of past narratives and techniques, as they have accumulated over the last two centuries or so in the private law area, then altering and transforming them primarily with the objective of designing a law that accommodates market imperatives, as I will further explain below.

I will call the proposed kind of reasoning of these strands of scholarship 'balancing', by which I mean less a monolithic mode of reasoning and more the designation of a variety of hermeneutical balancing models or ideal types becoming the new normal of European private law discourse. I will now discuss the variety of balancing types in turn.[103]

(i) Preliminary – Two Instances of Arguments for Balancing Applied to the Precontractual Stage

Adopting a micro-perspective that focuses on two specific problematic situations that arise in precontractual settings, some authors have noted that encapsulating fixed solutions in common rules may be counterintuitive. This argument has been put forward with regard to two key sets of contractual rules, that is, those on information duties and those on cancellation of contracts.

As far as information duties are concerned, it has been argued that it does not always make sense to impose rules that oblige one contractual party to give all sorts of information to the consumer. Relying on the rich Germanic literature on law and economics,[104] it has been submitted that there are a number of criteria that represent 'adequate tools for specifying information duties', including 'the relevance of the information at issue, the relative costs and accessibility of information as between the parties, and an assessment of the information gathering incentives'.[105] It is on the basis of these very tools, ranging from costs entailed in obtaining information to incentives to the actual relevance of the information depending on the

[103] On 'balancing', see, in comparative constitutional literature, J Bomhoff, *Balancing Constitutional Rights: The Origins and Meanings of Postwar Legal Discourse*, Cambridge Studies in Constitutional Law (Cambridge, Cambridge University Press, 2013) (mapping convergence and divergence of balancing in comparative constitutional perspective in Europe and in the US); Bomhoff, J, 'Review of Alec Stone Sweet & Jud Mathews, *Proportionality Balancing and Global Governance: A Comparative and Global Approach* (Oxford University Press, 2019)' (2021) 69 *American Journal of Comparative Law* 168.

[104] See, eg H Eidenmüller, 'Recht als Produkt' (2009) 64 *Juristenzeitung* 641; see now, critically, R Michaels, 'Vorwort zum Symposium: Der Code des Kapitals' (2021) 85 *Rabels Zeitschrift* 852.

[105] Eidenmüller et al (n 100) 696 (also arguing that such criteria have been neglected in the DCFR, which is at odds with what the DCFR really provides for: *cf* below under 'rule bound' balancing).

contractual circumstances, that one should decide whether or not to implement the information duty requirement on contractual parties in each specific instance. It appears that these scholars are calling for a flexible assessment that balances all such considerations in any decision regarding the extent of information duties being imposed on businesses, as opposed to an integral implementation of an abstract command to superimpose duties whatever the contractual circumstances and whatever the type of parties involved (consumers or businesses).

Equally, it has been submitted, it does not always make sense to provide for a right of withdrawal from contracts in any case – rather, it should depend on the circumstances.[106] Arguably, here, one should also take seriously, if not cost- and incentive-related factors such as those that these scholars consider in relation to information duties (as discussed above), at least contingent problematic situations, such as being 'caught off-guard' or contracting taking place entirely by means of 'distant communication' as opposed to 'away from the business premises' only.[107] In this view, one should keep the current fragmentary state of the directive-based harmonisation project, albeit now moderated by the Consumer Rights Directive, rather than generalising all of the contractual situations under the single common-rule requirement of the right of cancellation for the case of the consumer's acceptance taking place 'away from the business premises'.[108]

The underlying point being made here is that there should be some kind of balancing, rather than outright implementation of fixed texts (with the qualification that the role of texts is defended by the upholders of both the 'rule-bound' and 'principled' types of balancing that I discuss below). In the sense that this strand of scholarship seems to stand for the employment of a kind of *factors-based balancing*, considering that they mention circumstances that may be relevant to an ad hoc assessment, and that turn against the imposition of the common rules on information duties or on cancellation of contracts.[109] Note that scholars make the case for balancing only in relation to information duties and the right of cancellation – for other matters they express suspicion of any opening up towards discretionary standards.[110] Generally speaking, they argue that, as standard practice, one should construct 'rules' that define as much as possible the tasks of the judges in applying them. They also show concerns about the ways in which the general doctrines of law could be re-engineered to accommodate such

[106] ibid; Jansen and Zimmermann, 'Recasting the *Acquis Communautaire*?' (n 51).

[107] Eidenmüller et al (n 100) 697 et seq. Arguably the law and economic literature in Germany focuses on information duties rather than on cancellation rights, but their arguments lend themselves, at least in principle, to be applied across the board of both sets of rules. This is not, however, the case of the scholarship under consideration, which proposes to balance the 'sanctity of contract' rules whereby concluded agreements cannot be altered against off-guard and distant communication contractual situations for the sake of providing for cancellation rights.

[108] Consumer Rights Directive and DCFR 2009, Art II.5:201(1).

[109] I say 'seem' since there are scholars who articulate a strong belief in system and formal interpretivism, much as the DCFR that they criticise.

[110] *cf* Eidenmüller (n 104) 678 et seq.

particularised types of judgments – for example, arguing that the traditional will theory of contractual conclusion should be redrawn so as to be applied at the point of conclusion of the contract, that is, at the completion of the 14th day by which the right of cancellation can be exercised (Directive on Consumer Rights).[111]

Alongside the above scholarly endorsement of some kinds of balancing approaches only in relation to the two sets of rights (right of cancellation and right to information), arguments for balancing have appeared in one more place – the Draft Common Frame of Reference.[112] Here, balancing is not episodic, that is, limited to two cases only, but comprehensive, that is, applied throughout the whole body of model rules contained in the DCFR.

Specifically, the DCFR is in itself a major intellectual effort preluding to a desired (albeit then ultimately failed) codification of private law in Europe. Woven into it is a form of balancing that is both 'high level', that, is operationalised through principles (*principled balancing*), and 'low level', that is, balancing explicitly made within the body of individual rules (*rule-bound or local balancing*). I will discuss each of these two types of balancing in turn, for they are different sides of the same coin (they deploy the balancing technique) but may be analytically distinguished for the purpose of my analysis.

(ii) Principled Balancing

Almost 20 years ago, in its Communications in 2003 and 2004,[113] the EU Commission called for a Common Frame of Reference that would provide for 'fundamental principles, definitions and model rules'.[114] By 'principles', as indicated in the Commission's documents, the authors of the DCFR understood neither 'rules which do not have the force of law' (such as the Lando Principles) nor 'rules of a general nature' (such as good faith or freedom of contract), but 'fundamental principles', given that the word 'principles' surfaces occasionally in the Commission's communications with the prefix 'fundamental' attached.[115] The authors of the DCFR argued that 'That suggests that it may have meant to denote essentially abstract basic values'.

The 2008 DCFR edition mentioned 'some possible fundamental principles' identifying

> no fewer than fifteen items – justice; freedom; protection of human rights; economic welfare; solidarity and social responsibility; establishing an area of freedom, security

[111] *cf* Jansen and Zimmermann, 'Recasting the *Acquis Communautaire*?' (n 51).

[112] It is remarkable how substantive balancing has been put forward as an alternative path for private law, in the context of a critique of the DCFR, and yet there are common threads between the two positions in the sense of adopting forms of balancing as discussed in the text.

[113] EU Commission, 'A More Coherent European Contract Law – An Action Plan' COM(2003) 0068 final [2003]OJ C63/1; EU Commission, 'European Contract Law and the Revision of the Acquis: The Way Forward' COM(2004) 0651 final.

[114] DCFR 2009 (n 53) 4 et seq.

[115] ibid 5.

> and justice; promotion of the internal market; protection of consumers and others in need of protection; preservation of cultural and linguistic plurality; rationality; legal certainty; predictability; efficiency; protection of reasonable reliance; and the proper allocation of responsibility for the creation of risks.[116]

Such principles 'were not ranked in order of priority' and 'It was stressed that the principles would inevitably conflict each other and that *it was the function of the model rules to find an appropriate balance*' (emphasis added).[117] What is self-evident is that the 2008 text empowered the judges to make balancing choices among the principles, but within the interpretative boundaries of the individual model rules.

The 2009 edition of the DCFR dropped some of the 'principles' mentioned in the earlier version, leaving the balancing mechanism in place in relation to only the four remaining principles – freedom, security, justice and efficiency.[118] The rationale for this choice of reorganising and 'presenting better' by reframing the introduction of the 2008 interim outline edition is the following:

> [A] small group of them … are all-pervasive within the DCFR. They can be detected by looking into the model rules. They are underlying principles. They furnished grounds for arguments about the merits of particular rules. The remaining principles mentioned in the introduction to the interim outline edition are generally of a high political nature. They could be said to be overriding rather than underlying.[119]

Note how the authors here have chosen to shift away from a type of balancing exercised in relation to a wide range of principles, and conveying a variety of conflicting normative considerations, to a balancing limited to a range of rather homogeneous principles.[120] This is implicit in the statement whereby 'it was the function of the model rules to find an appropriate balance'.[121]

This statement reformulates the balancing command to operate only within the limited range of (the then admitted) principles. What remains in place is a mode of balancing principles that applies to only four of them, and that incorporates that balancing act in the individual model rules, rather than leaving it up to the decision-maker to decide how to do the balancing.[122]

Among the four principles, that of efficiency is crucial for understanding the policy rationale behind the DCFR.[123]

[116] ibid 5 (summarising the 2008 interim outline edition).
[117] ibid 5–6.
[118] ibid 37 et seq.
[119] ibid 7.
[120] Critically, *cf* M Hesselink, 'If You Don't Like Our Principles We Have Others' in Brownsword et al (n 63) 59; D Kennedy, 'A Transnational Genealogy of Proportionality in Private Law' in Brownsword et al (n 63) 185.
[121] DCFR 2009 (n 53) 5–6.
[122] Contrast Eidenmüller et al (n 100). But note that what the DCFR has done is to introduce *not* a full balancing model, but one that, in the understanding of its proponents, somehow leaves it to the text, that is, the incorporated directives, to speak for the judge, in the mode of interpretive formalism – something which in the text I call 'rule-bound balancing'.
[123] See L Niglia, 'Of Constitutionality and Private Consumer Law in Europe' (2012) 4 *Journal of European Consumer and Market Law* 223 (on efficiency and market libertarianism).

I now turn to the next type of balancing – how such individual model rules implement the balancing act, given that the 2009 edition of the DCFR conflates principled and rule-bound balancing.

(iii) Rule-Bound Balancing

The DCFR implements the choice, stated in its introduction, of designing rules that encapsulate a certain balancing act at the very level of the text itself, commanding the interpreter to automatically implement it. I could find at least four such examples of what is called 'local balancing' – or balancing made at the 'local' level of the individual model rules.[124] Here, I consider each of the four in turn.

(i) First is Article II.7:205, on disclosure of information in contractual situations involving fraud. The article holds that:

> [A] party may avoid a contract when the other party has induced the conclusion of the contract by fraudulent misrepresentation … or fraudulent non-disclosure of any information which good faith and fair dealing, or any pre-contractual information duty, required that party to disclose.

However, it also holds at Article II.7:205(3)(b) that 'In determining whether good faith and fair dealing required a party to disclose particular information, regard should be had to all the circumstances, including … the cost to the party of acquiring the relevant information.'[125]

This means that the decision-maker/interpreter is required to balance such costs against the case for fraud. It may well be the case that disclosure of information, however required under good faith and fair dealing, may be disregarded as a ground for 'avoiding the contract' on the basis of a straightforward cost–benefit analysis that looks at the actual costs saved by the contractual party in not providing the relevant information. The 'general policy' that 'in a case of fraud there is no reason to protect any interest the fraudulent party may have in upholding the contract; nor is the risk of being deliberately misled one that a party should be expected to bear'[126] may *ex hypothesi* be sacrificed on the altar of a straightforward cost–benefit analysis by balancing it against the actual costs saved.

However, one should note that the commentary clarifies the meaning of the provision, saying that 'there may not be any obligation to disclose the information which concerns the other party's performance and which the informed party had to make a great investment in order to acquire',[127] which limits the potential sphere of operation of the provision to the case of information regarding 'the other party's performance' and the involvement of a 'great investment to acquire the relevant

[124] I disagree with the statement that the DCFR fails to implement the stated choice of indicating what compromise should be made within the body of the individual rules.
[125] *cf* Eidenmüller et al (n 100) 673.
[126] DCFR 2009 (n 53) 492 (under comments).
[127] ibid 494 (adding that 'the list in para 3 is not intended to be exhaustive').

information', rather than any hypothetical situation in which to balance costs. Whilst the list of circumstances is 'not intended to be exhaustive', as far as costs are involved it looks as if it were.[128]

(ii) Second is Article IV.C.2:105, on services contracts.[129] The article provides for the obligation on the service provider to 'perform the service with the case and skill which a reasonable service provider would exercise under the circumstances' and also provides, at Article IV.C.2:105(4)(b), that 'in determining the care and skill the client is entitled to expect, regard is to be had, among other things, to … if damage has occurred, the costs of any precautions which would have prevented that damage or similar damage from occurring'. Precaution costs are therefore required to be balanced against the assessment of liability of the provider, but only for the case of damages. Again, the list is not exhaustive,[130] but, as far as the requirement of costs is involved, it appears as if it were.[131]

(iii) Third is Article VI.6:202, on reduction of liability, a 'reduction clause' in tort liability cases. It provides for the discretionary power of the judge to reduce, or even nullify, a tort liability claim that is otherwise valid on the ground of any of three factors, assuming that 'the damage is not caused intentionally':

> Where it is fair and reasonable to do so, a person may be relieved of liability to compensate, whether wholly or in part, if, where the damage is not caused intentionally, liability in full would be disproportionate to the accountability of the person causing the damage or the extent of the damage or the means to prevent it.

There follows, as usual, a comment limiting the potential scope of application of the article, that is:

> Grounds for and prerequisite of a reduction of liability … The decisive ground for the solution chosen here is mentioned in the Article itself. Such abnormal discrepancies between the basis of liability and the extent of the damage may arise as to make it seem intolerable to let the liable person bear liability for the entire damage. There should therefore be an instrument available to allow a final check of the decision against

[128] ibid.

[129] *cf* Eidenmüller et al (n 100) 674.

[130] DCFR 2009 (n 53) 1648 ('The criteria provided for in para 4 are to be taken into account in determining the standard of care and skill to be demonstrated by the service provider. They are not to be regarded as the only criteria that have to be looked at, but they are thought to be the most relevant ones').

[131] Note that the DCFR 2009 (n 53) 1656, in commenting on Art. IV.C.2:106 on 'obligation to achieve result', opts for a flexible solution other than the dogmatic one (that is, reasoning along the lines of either obligations of means *or* obligations of result), considering the fact that to impose a plain obligation of result on some service providers (unable to fully control the outcome of the service process) would 'make their services much more expensive for the client, given that the service provider would have to buy insurance for the coverage of uncontrollable risks. Where insurance cover cannot be obtained or can be obtained only at very high costs, this might cause service providers to withdraw from the market, leading to the disappearance of such services altogether.' This, it should be noted, is in line with the welfare-efficiency principled policy that is at the core of the DCFR – one more illustration among the many of how rule-bound balancing operates.

> general considerations of justice and fairness. This is mainly significant where a slight oversight or a technically negligent but morally unobjectionable act leads to damage, the reparation of which would disproportionately burden the injured person, there being other possibilities for reparation open to the injured person. The rule can play a role in certain emergency situations requiring self-defence and it may also be the only way of achieving a reasonable result in cases coming under Chapter 3, section 2 (Accountability without intention or negligence).[132]

Illustrations follow clarifying that children aged eight and nine playing in a farm and burning down the entire premises as a result of a campfire that they had lighted would see their liability reduced considering that they would have to work until they are middle aged to pay it off; and liability would be reduced so as to consider the 'extraordinary risk of damage' in the case of a water pipe that bursts in a flat and causing damage in another apartment directly below it.[133]

This article flies in the face of the ways in which traditional domestic laws arrange tort claims. Taken literally, it could mean that tortuous claims would be decided on equitable grounds rather than under the law.[134] It is also an indication of how the DCFR tends to circumscribe the balancing act, in this case limiting the operation of a reduction clause to cases of discrepancy between the grounds of liability and the extraordinary risk of damage that require balancing out, rather than any case in which the judge may feel that he should reduce liability on straightforward equity grounds.[135]

(iv) Fourth is Article II.7:201(2)(b), on avoidance of contract for mistake.[136] This article stipulates that a party 'may avoid a contract for mistake of fact or law existing when the contract was concluded' unless 'the risk of the mistake was assumed, or in the circumstances should be borne, by that party'. The commentary clarifies that such provision applies in situations in which

> [t]here are some contracts under which the parties are deliberately taking the risk of the unknown, or should be treated as so doing. One example of this is where one party is well aware that the contract is being concluded without knowledge of an important matter but proceeds to conclude the contract anyway.

An example, in the illustration that follows in the DCFR, is the case of someone who sold inherited goods, having deliberately decided not to value them, being

[132] DCFR 2009 (n 53) vol IV, 3785.
[133] ibid 3785.
[134] For this criticism, *cf* Eidenmüller et al (n 100) (also in relation to contract versus tort law claims). Recall T Weir, *An Introduction to Tort Law* (Oxford, Oxford University Press, 2006) (for whom the only thing that holds the subject of tort law together is the binding of the textbook), referred to in G Samuel, 'Is Legal Neo-Formalism Nothing but Pastiche?" [2020] *Journal of Contract Law* 347, 368 (for whom it 'is not an unreasonable assertion given how the subject was formed historically') and in Niglia,' A" European" Tort Law?' (n 54).
[135] DCFR 2009 (n 53) 3785; Eidenmüller et al (n 100) (arguing that there is no such a limitation).
[136] *cf* Eidenmüller et al (n 100) fn 73.

barred from avoiding the contract in relation to a picture by Constable sold at a lower than market value.[137] Again, the DCFR is setting interpretative boundaries to the balancing exercise.[138]

[137] DCFR 2009 (n 53) 463 (under comments).

[138] Further examples include the *test of unfairness*. *cf* DCFR 2009 (n 53) II.9:401 et seq – at p 650 on individual versus overall assessment and on price (setting boundaries as to the overall balancing); at p 650 (under Art II.9:407): 'The list of factors to be taken into account when assessing the unfairness of a contract term is based on Directive 93/13EEC art 4(1)' (note the comment at Art I.9:407: Factors to be taken into account in assessing unfairness. It has to be borne in mind that the starting point and the subject of the unfairness test is an abstract assessment of the relevant single term in question and not the 'overall acceptability' of the contract as a whole. Nevertheless, other terms of the contract and terms of any other contracts on which the contract depends are also included in the assessment. This approach, however, may not compromise the principle that the subject of control is each individual term. Thus, in principle, each term has to be considered separately. An 'overall acceptability' of the contract as a whole is irrelevant. Consequently, the supplier of terms is not allowed to justify an unfair term by including other terms which are favourable to the other party unless there is a close connection between the subject matter of both terms so that the favourable term constitutes an effective compensation. In particular, a lower price cannot justify an unfair term unless this arrangement is the result of individual negotiations. In summary, the reference to other terms in paragraph (1) only means that the effect of one term may be influenced by other terms'). For the DCFR, the 'subject matter' of the contract is, 'in most cases', the goods or services to be delivered (p 647). Clearly the above allows the balancing for the most important event of a lower price accompanied by the delivery of goods or services (the two being clearly connected): note similarly *Freiburger* (n 14). And note the DCFR 2009 (n 53) II.9:401 et seq, at p 650: 'As the unfairness test starts from an abstract assessment of an individual term, the "circumstances prevailing during the conclusion of the contract" might only influence the result of the test in exceptional cases. For instance, if the abstract fairness test has the result that the term in question lies on the borderline between fair and unfair, the term may be considered as "only just fair", if the party supplying the term has made a particular effort to explain the consequences of the term to the other party.' This appears to me to be about incorporating the circumstantial test in pro-market fashion as per the UK Supreme Court judgment of *National Bank* (see the rest of the chapter) Note also the DCFR 2009 (n 53) II.9:401 et seq, at p 651: 'According to para 1' in 'assessing the unfairness of a contract term regard is to be had to the duty of transparency … Thus, one of the factors to be taken into account is whether the term has been drafted in plain, intelligible language. This question has to be distinguished from the question regulated in para (2), according to which (in consumer cases), another relevant factor is the extent to which the consumer was given a real opportunity to become acquainted with the term before the conclusion of the contract. This rule is based on several provisions of the acquis communautaire which confirm that this aspect is a key fairness requirement (at least) in business to consumer contracts. Para 2 stipulate an intensification of the general rule in II.9:103 (Terms not individually negotiated), according to which the supplier of non-negotiated term has to draw the other party's attention to the terms before the conclusion of the contract.'. Specifically: 'Para. 2 requires the business to do more, namely to give the consumer a real opportunity to become acquainted with the term … It should be noted that the consequences of II.9:103 … and of the para 2 of the present Article [II.9:407] are different. If the supplier of the terms does not take reasonable steps to draw these terms to the attention of the other party, the supplier may not invoke the terms against the other party. Thus, the terms are not part of the contract unless the other party so desires. However, if the business takes reasonable steps to draw the attention of the consumer to the terms, but the consumer is not given a real opportunity to become acquainted with the terms, the terms become part of the contract. Nevertheless, the lack of this opportunity is a factor which has to be taken into account when assessing whether a term is to be considered unfair.' Under para 2, the supplier has to ensure that the consumer actually takes notice of the terms and has a real opportunity to read them. A real opportunity to read is both necessary and sufficient. Whether the consumer takes this opportunity or not is irrelevant (at p 651). It is then added (at p 652) that 'In most cases, it will be necessary to provide a readable print version of the terms prior to the conclusion of the contract and to give the consumer enough time to carefully read the terms'. This means that an incorporation of the terms into the contract may happen if standard terms are drawn to the consumer's attention (a notice at a cashier indicating the terms, even

(iv) An Intermediate Point: On the Precontractual, Principled and Rule-Bound Balancing as 'Minimal' ('Maximal' v 'Minimal' Balancing)

To continue the analysis of the state of the art of the technique of balancing as identified in contemporary legal discourse in Europe: all of the above types of balancing that one can find in current writings – whether precontractual,

though there is no time to read them because of the queue), but more needs to be done. This appears to be favourable to the consumer, but it is in fact favourable to the business, who can escape being accused of unfairness on the basis of the 'real opportunity' rationale (note the argument for printed copy as necessary, and therefore sufficient, at p 652). The DCFR is explicit on this, but does not address the issues relevant to bank charges (see *Director General of Fair Trading v First National Bank plc* [2000] 1 WLR 98, 32: see section B.v.b below), and from Art II.9:407, para 1 one understands that its position is rather pro-market. Therefore, the above means that a transparent term (ex para 1) *or* a real opportunity (ex para 2) saves the term from unfairness. This seems to me an endorsement of market libertarian solutions: as individual terms are exempted from control just because they are transparent or because of the situation of a 'a real opportunity to read' rather than subject to control under the test of unfairness understood as overall evaluation (*cf* for this opinion Reich, 'Balancing in Private Law' (n 92)). The comprehensive grey listing and the exclusion of blacklisting in Art II.9:401 (with the exception of exclusive jurisdictional clauses, which are blacklisted in Art II.9:409) does the final job of confirming the market rationale approach behind the unfairness test; and the DCFR omits to mention from the illustrative directive-originated (UCTD) list para 1, lit I of the Annex (terms which the consumer had no real opportunity to become acquainted with) 'since this provision is sufficiently reflected in the above noted II.9:407' (see DCFR 2009 (n 53) 663). As to the test of *liability in obligations*, in relation to the classical divide between obligations of means and of results, see above. As to the meaning of *legally relevant damage*, the authors of the DCFR understand it not to be a general clause: on the one hand, they reject interpreting it as a 'general clause', whilst, on the other, they seem to be open to compensation for any 'interest worthy of'. However, they indicate a number of guidelines for the implementation of the test of liability in tort that limit the interpreter in implementing the meaning of 'legally relevant damage'. Note the DCFR 2009 (n 53) at p 3087: 'what we have here is not a general clause in the strict sense, but rather a provision whose component elements are later filled out with more precise content'. That does not exclude the prospect that, alongside others with sharply drawn contours, the following Articles may contain rules which have deliberately been left open and flexible: VI.2:101 (Meaning of legally relevant damage) and at VI.4:101 (General rule on causation) provide examples of this. One should note how, however, the DCFR is at pains in trying to delimit the potentially arbitrary use of the notion that "the loss or injury results from a violation of an interest worthy of legal protection". It attempts to do that in two ways at least. First, by arguing that "the practical significance of the distinction between 'rights' and 'interests which are worthy of legal protection' is not especially great. It has little significance because … the legal penumbra of non-contractual liability is not yet harmonised and therefore the European legal systems may have completely diverse perceptions of what qualifies as 'right' and what is merely an interest … the concern here is with rights and interests which enjoy protection against all and which therefore are generally capable of being infringed by anyone. A mere contractual interest in some performance, for example, is excluded from the scope of application of Article VI.2:101 for this reason alone" (at p 3143). The DCFR then goes on to enumerate guidelines for decoding 'interests', that is, grounds of accountability (such as intentional or negligent), nature of damage (that is, loss of quality of life for pollution not being an interest worthy of protection), damage suffered in business competition, proximity of damage and reasonable expectations on the part of the injured person, all qualified with examples of what is, and what is not, an interest (DCFR, pp 3146–48). Note that almost 200 pages (DCFR, pp 3194–389) follow detailing the 'particular instances of legally relevant damage'. Key choices are being made on controversial issues such as: 'the loss of quality of life which is inflicted on residents in a given region because, as a result of an industrial accident, they are no longer able to enjoy the spectacle of particular wildlife, be it animals or plants, affected by the pollution [would not be recoverable]'; 'There are interests … which are in essence only assigned to the commonality as a whole and therefore are not capable of constituting a legally relevant damage in relation to any particular individual' (DCFR, p 3146); 'If somebody is so bodily disfigured as a result of an principled or rule-bound – are inherently 'limited' when compared to a distinct model of balancing that has emerged in the EPL literature, in particular in a co-edited collection of works from a conference gathering leading scholars in the field – the *Foundations of European Private Law*.[139]

Each of the above types of balancing (precontractual, principled and rule-based) is an ideal type that is premised on setting well-defined boundaries to an otherwise integral implementation of the balancing exercise centred entirely on the compromising among, or the combination of, the conflicting normative considerations at stake. I am referring here to a further, distinctive ideal-type balancing technique that knows no such boundaries, and that has been elaborated in a line of writings of leading French and German private law scholars – as well as being employed in subaltern yet remarkable lines of decisions in some domestic legal systems (independently of Europeanisation),[140] and now re-emerging here in all its strength out of the depths of the intellectual history of ideas.[141] It goes without saying that, in contemporary law, this is a kind of technique typically employed in the cases of constitutional courts,[142] as well as in cases of transnational, regionally

accident that his spouse cannot endure life with him and they divorce', the stresses and strains on the marriage may mean liability for he who caused the damage to cover such event, and the same 'if the marriage breaks down because as a result of the accident the injured person has lost the capacity for sexual intercourse' (DCFR, p 3146) – 'if the marriage remain intact on the other hand, then the uninjured spouse suffers a legally relevant damage since he or she is adversely affected in respect of an interest worthy of legal protection. Somebody who only stands in a loose relationship to the injured person, however, does not suffer a legally relevant damage. In that latter situation there is merely an insubstantial reflected damage' (DCFR, p 3146); damage to mental or psychiatric health can only be recoverable (that is, it is legally relevant) if 'it calls for treatment … according to medical science' (DCFR, p 3197); loss of chance may be recoverable and should not be excluded altogether (DCFR, p 3195). There may be either radical environmentalists or libertarians who may not be entirely happy with all such choices, but it is striking how they are set in stone as if they were unquestionable truths in a neutralising mode of depoliticisation.

[139] See the contributions in the section introduced by L Niglia in Brownsword et al (n 63)).

[140] I am thinking of certain judicial decisions on unfair terms, and related literature, in France and Germany: see Niglia, *The Transformation of Contract in Europe* (n 44).

[141] For full discussion, see Brownsword et al (n 63); see also nn 142–45 below.

[142] Balancing is a well-known technique used in constitutional and international law courts: see Bomhoff, *Balancing Constitutional Rights* (n 103); for balancing in the English common law, with regard to both judges and jurists, see, eg S Greer, '"Balancing" and the European Court of Human Rights: A Contribution to the Habermas–Alexy Debate' (2004) 63 *CLJ* 412, 412 et seq: 'It is common-place for judges to seek to resolve conflicts between "constitutional", "fundamental", or "human" rights – and between these rights and competing public interests – by "balancing" one against the other. In their turn, jurists have uncritically endorsed the practice in spite of the fact that courts have generally been very reluctant to reveal how it occurs.' Then, quoting the then Lord Chancellor Lord Irvine of Lairg 'The Impact of the Human Rights Act: Parliament, the Courts and the Executive [2003] *Public Law* 308, 310, 313–14, 316, 319, 323, holding that: 'The present arrangements … represent our reconciliation of effective rights protection with parliamentary sovereignty. The balancing of these is central to the Act … In examining what impact the Act has had on the courts, and on our system of law, the overriding theme that has emerged is balance: balance between scrutiny and deference; between the individual and the community; and between interpretation and declarations of incompatibility … The balance between intense judicial scrutiny and reasonable deference to elected decision-makers is a delicate one to strike. But the judiciary has struck it well … In drafting … (sections 3 and 4 of the Human Rights Act 1998) … as we did, we were again asking courts a careful course between two extremes. Once again they are doing that well; they are striking a sound balance … (The Human Rights Act) … was drafted sensitively to the balance of forces within our substantially unwritten constitution.'

based courts.[143] Yet, it should be noted that private law has its own idiosyncratic variation on this theme.

Such an ideal-typical balancing exercise, which we can label 'maximal', rests on the compromising among conflicting considerations, and specifically, in the words of Duncan Kennedy:[144]

'In balancing, we understand ourselves to be choosing a norm (not choosing a winning party) among a number of permissible alternatives on the ground that it best balances or combines conflicting normative considerations.'[145]

I will now highlight two aspects ((a) and (b)) that should convince us to classify the precontractual, principled and rule-based forms of balancing as 'minimal', as opposed to the 'maximal' ideal-type, emerging in the context of the new hermeneutics of private law that is being considered – signifying the presence of key tensions from within the EPL discourse.

(a) Minimal v Maximal Hermeneutics of Balancing I

Despite embracing balancing, the three approaches (precontractual, principled and rule-based) are a long way from allowing a compromise among the considerations at stake, such as those contemplated in the above-noted maximal ideal-typical balancing.

Precontractual balancing is, on close inspection, proposed in a way that excludes compromising, for it only admits of an either/or situation – either one concludes that, in the circumstances, one should give relevance to certain costs or incentives, and thus relax precontractual information duties and cancellation rights, or one should uphold the latter. One does not read in these writings any opening towards compromising among costs, incentives, rights and duties. Indeed, these scholars believe that balancing should be made once and for all (at the legislative level) – by

[143] *cf* respectively, in Germany, Reich, 'Balancing in Private Law' (n 92) and the debate on balancing in relation to the decisions of the European courts such as the remarkable judgment of 21 September 2005 in Case T-315/01 *Yassin Abdullah Kadi v Council of the European Union & Commission of the European Communities* [2005] ECR II-3649 (*cf*, eg G de Búrca, 'The European Courts and the Security Council: Between Dédoublement Fonctionnel and Balancing of Values: Three Replies to Pasquale De Sena and Maria Chiara Vitucci' (2009) 20 *European Journal of International Law* 853).

[144] I am drawing here on previous writings: Kennedy, 'A Transnational Genealogy of Proportionality in Private Law' (n 120); L Niglia, 'Of Jurisdictional Balancing' in Brownsword et al (n 63) 309; Reich, 'Balancing in Private Law' (n 92). This literature refers to the private-law understanding of 'balancing'. For 'public-law' understandings, see n 142 above.

[145] According to Reich, 'Balancing in Private Law' (n 92), balancing is more about choosing principles and less about compromising among conflicting considerations (as well as being more descriptive/analytical and less normative) than in Duncan Kennedy's synthesis in Kennedy, 'A Transnational Genealogy of Proportionality in Private Law' (n 120) – despite the fact that both highly value the role of ideologies/values in legal determinations in post-formalist mode. Indeed, Reich adopts Joseph Esser's *Vorverstandniss* approach (see J Esser, *Vorverständniss und Methodenwhal in der Rechtsfindung* (1970, 1972)) rather than relying on the work of Demogue (R Demogue, *Les notions fondamentales du droit privé: essai critique pour servir d'introduction à l'étude des obligations* (Paris, Rosseau, 1911)); for discussion, see also L Niglia, 'The Political Foundations of European Private Law: Editorial Introduction' in Brownsword et al (n 63) 177), which sets the stage for this difference in outlook.

choosing whether (information) duties *or* (cancellation) rights should prevail over costs or incentives calculations – as set in stone in the legislative texts. Nothing could be thought of that is farther from maximal discretionary balancing.

In relation to duties of information, it has been argued that such (information) duties represent 'intrusions' in the parties' autonomy and that, as such, they should be exceptionally implemented, carefully identified and delimited at the 'level of the rules' in much the same way as Art III.1:110 DCFR provides for change of circumstances – a rule that the proponents consider to be a standard model setting a high threshold for judicial intervention altering party autonomy as concretised in contractual arrangements. Art III.1:110 DCFR, it should be noted, allows for judicial intervention, aimed at altering standard performance obligations rules, only in cases of 'exceptional change' or of 'manifestly unjust' circumstances.[146] In regretting that a mass of generalised information duties are being placed on contractual parties through the DCFR, whatever the circumstances and the type of contracts, scholars proposing precontractual balancing also convey the idea that the criteria for balancing should be implemented at the 'level of the rules'. In relation to the right to withdrawal, the same kind of 'over-expansive' approach as adopted in the DCFR is equally criticised for similar reasons.[147]

The further positions of principled balancing and its rule-bound application equally exclude compromising in that, first, they admit of the possibility of a conflict among the principles, but they resolve them all by limiting the principles to a few ones that are homogeneous. This is the outcome of the 'exchange' between the DCFR authors and their critics which has led to the *reductio ad unum* of the wide range of principles initially put forward in the 2008 edition of the DCFR and then abandoned in the 2009 edition. Second, compromising is excluded also in that scholars encapsulate the balancing among the principles in the text of the model rules, in much the same way as scholars do when they support forms of balancing limited to the precontractual stage (so-called 'local balancing').

Needless to say, it is part of the scholars' resistance to compromising that they also resist the 'combining' of normative considerations as proposed in the maximal ideal type. Therefore, the same set of arguments mentioned above must apply.

(b) Minimal v Maximal Hermeneutics of Balancing II

Despite their embracing the above-noted declinations of the balancing technique, whether precontractual, rule-based or principled, scholars nevertheless resist acknowledging the highly discretionary judicial powers involved in the maximal balancing position.[148]

[146] Eidenmüller et al (n 100) 696, fn 141.

[147] ibid 697 et seq.

[148] On 'discretion' in balancing as understood to be an entirely 'rational operation', that is, one that takes place through rational steps and within rational constraints, *cf* notably the work of R Alexy: see L Niglia, 'Between "Institutionalizing Reason" and Private Law. A Comparative Map of Influences' in M La Torre, L Niglia and M Susi (eds), *The Quest for Rights* (Cheltenham, Edward Elgar, 2019).

For, according to the maximal balancing reading, one can *ex hypothesi* consider delegating to the judge fully interpretive powers to balance – including whether or not to compromise among, and combine, the underlying normative considerations – rules against contractual circumstances, applying or disapplying them intermittently, thus leaving it to the judge to apply different sets of rules to different situations. Examples include the case of information duties applied to consumers as opposed to commercial contracts; or of cancellation rights applied to consumers caught off-guard as opposed to all 'away from business premises' consumer contracts. Yet, this is what scholarship adopting the precontractual, rule-based or principled position does *not* allow. Instead, they opt for the intermittent application of certain rules by clinging on to their belief in a 'text' that would do the job of identifying where and when to apply (or not) certain rules once and for all. From this viewpoint, theirs is a *legislative* as opposed to *judicial* balancing.

Specifically, supporters of precontractual balancing are sceptical of full judicial discretion. Their understanding of balancing is presented in a way that only admits of it insofar as such balancing is encapsulated in a text, for in that way it will be entrenched 'at the level of the rules' and not surrendered into the hands of the interpreter-judge – a prospect that the proponents of this view outrightly reject.

Principled balancing proponents are equally sceptical of full discretion insofar as they reduce the number of principles to a few homogeneous ones around the objective of welfare maximisation. Thus, scholars have rightly noted how the shift away from a plurality of principles as enumerated in the 2008 outline edition entails not only a 'betrayal' of social justice principles, but also a sacrifice of a broader ('maximal') kind of balancing.[149]

Proponents of rule-bound balancing are no less sceptical of full discretion in that they place in the text any of the balancing act they can conceive of, in much the same way as do scholars who support precontractual balancing. Moreover, in this view, were the model rules to fail to indicate how that balancing should be made, the judge is supposed to follow the overarching range of homogeneous principles rather than his own discretion – for we are told that only four principles are 'legal' ('underlying'), the rest of them being instead placed outside the legal realm for being 'political' ('overarching'). Here, all comes full circle. Balancing is thus intended to be about applying the choices made in the model rules *or*, where not explicitly made, by leaving to the judge the power to implement only the four homogeneous principles that revolve around the objective of welfare maximisation – which ultimately is about commanding less judicial discretion and more a defined obligation for the judge to act within the principled constraints.

As to rule-bound balancing, the balancing is implemented via fixed rules rather than leaving it to the judge to do the job at his discretion. Interpretive formalism[150] (the belief that decisions derive from rules) operates here much as it does in the

[149] *cf* Kennedy, 'A Transnational Genealogy of Proportionality in Private Law' (n 120).

[150] See, eg D Kennedy, 'Legal Formalism' in NJ Smelser (ed), *Encyclopedia of the Social & Behavioral Sciences* (Amsterdam, Center for Advanced Study in the Behavioral Sciences, 2001) 13, 8634–38.

other strands of scholarship, for there is room for interpretation – as, for example, in relation to fraud, with regard to which the list of circumstances by which to avoid it is not exhaustive, which points in the direction of a broader kind of balancing (although, it should be noted, the provision on costs is qualified rather than left indeterminate). Here, clearly the interpreter will step in on the basis of the usual interpretative techniques. Yet, interpretive formalism lurks behind, in that it is held that decisions are nevertheless to be based on the fixed rules. This transpires from the way in which the authors of the DCFR understand the operation of the balancing of principles. That is:

> It is characteristic of principles such as those discussed here that they conflict with each other. For example, on occasion, justice in a particular case may have to make way for legal security or efficiency, *as happens under the rules of prescription*. Sometimes, on the other hand, rules designed to promote security have to be balanced by considerations of justice, *as happens under the rules in Books V and VI which allow for a reduction of liability on equitable grounds*. (emphasis added)[151]

Here, the balancing of principles is held to have been done in the text itself (that is, within the structures of the individual model rules), rather than being delegated to the decision-maker – this being a model that appears to me to be followed in relation to local balancing as well, considering the illustrations given above.

(v) The Hermeneutics of Market-Orientated Balancing (Teleological)

A variation on the theme of the hermeneutics of balancing is balancing *teleologically* orientated to market efficiency. In embracing this type of balancing, both scholars and judges acknowledge that there are policy choices at stake, choices that need to be made among 'alternatives on the ground'. Balancing orientated to market efficiency differs from the three previous forms of balancing (precontractual, principled and rule-based) in that it is the judge that is given full discretion to resolve conflicts between normative considerations by implementing, teleologically, the singular end-goal of economisation – rather than the legislature ex ante making that choice once and for all. This type of balancing, implying a single normativity made out of efficiency objectives, both predates and crosses through the currents of thought and related practices of the last decades considered above.

In the 1990s, the European Commission had already developed a mode of regulating contracts centred on the employment of balancing techniques orientated to market efficiency. This is a critical reading that I had proposed in 2003 in *The Transformation of Contract in Europe*. It was initially met with criticism by certain strands of scholarship, but now has become widely accepted – which confirms, with regard to scholarly consciousness, the thesis of a structural transformation of EPL from autonomy to heteronomy.

[151] DCFR 2009 (n 53) 37.

Specifically, the European Commission formulated a proposal for a directive on unfair terms in consumer contracts revolving around a 'test of fairness'. Circumstances such as a lower price, compared to a higher price in the context of a contract with less burdensome terms for the consumer or guarantees in place of protectionist terms – *à la Freiburger* – were, in the body of the Commission's proposal, meant to empower the judge to dismiss claims of unfairness of one or more contractual terms. This is largely at odds with traditional protectionist legislation and case law (for example, in Germany) centred on strict and inflexible protection of consumers from burdensome contractual terms.[152] The judge is supposed to balance any circumstance against the argument for unfairness of one or more of the contractual terms, with a view, on this basis, to avoid declaring the unfairness of one or more burdensome terms. It is a balancing of a teleological kind considering, first, that the judge is given the power to balance on the basis of the general clause composing the fairness test; and, second, that that power is given for the purpose of lifting the contractual liability of the drafter of the contractual terms in relation to major contractual risks, rather than for other potential purposes of a different colour, such as the purpose of increasing the protection of the consumer. Note that here discretion is meant to be actualised for the purpose of implementing business-orientated objectives, with the aim of freeing transactions from the protectionist constraints involved in national contractual regimes. This is what one must call a market-orientated or, as one wishes, a 'competitive' model of contract law regulation.

After an initial dismissal of the importance of this kind of balancing as related to the directive through clinging on to formalistic positions, various scholars have been endorsing this kind of balancing – ranging from full to moderate 'acceptance'.[153] Writings on the Unfair Terms Directive have been arguing in favour of such balancing *or* criticising it for being at odds with the heritage of domestic laws,[154] restating the respective strands of the hermeneutics of balancing as considered in the above and never proposing to break out of the teleological mode of economised balancing based on market end-goals, as opposed to a more open, maximal kind of balancing that would also incorporate non-efficiency normative considerations. Some courts have been particularly active in endorsing this mode of balancing – acting as true *balancing (economised balancing) courts*. Two key decisions, respectively of the Court of Justice of the European Union and of the (then called) House of Lords (now the UK Supreme Court), illustrate this endorsement and summarise well a series of recurring narratives with which some scholars have encapsulated the directive-mandated balancing exercise in their works. Here the intersection between the line of cases noted at the start of this chapter and the broader scholarly balancing hermeneutical material that one can

[152] See Niglia, *The Transformation of Contract in Europe* (n 44).

[153] For relevant literature, see ibid.

[154] In the context of a move of legal thought towards substantive reasoning and balancing.

identify across Europe is particularly evident. I will start with the CJEU judgment before considering a major (pre-Brexit) judgment of the UK Supreme Court.

(a) In *Freiburger*, the CJEU dealt with a dispute between the buyers of a parking space located in a multi-story car park and the construction company acting as seller. According to the terms of the contract, the payment was due not, as normal practice, at the moment of acceptance of the work – as stated in paragraph 641 of the Bürgerliches Gesetzbuch (BGB) – but upon delivery of a security in the form of a bank guarantee. The guarantee was given to Mr and Mrs Hofstetter 15 days after the conclusion of the contract. Under the terms of the contract, the guarantor undertook to compensate the buyers for any claims that they might assert against the construction company in respect of a defective performance or non-performance of the contract. The buyers refused to make the payment at the time indicated in the contract (the moment of delivery). Instead, they paid after 'accepting' the parking space 'free of defects'. This infringed Article 5 of the contract, which provided for the sanction of default interest in case of non-performance of the obligation to pay at the moment of delivery.

The construction company sued the buyers, claiming contractual damages for default interest on the late payment and invoking the liability expressly provided for under Article 5 of the contract. The company's claim was successful before the Regional Court of Freiburg but not on appeal, before the Oberlandesgericht – the Regional Court of Karlsruhe. The company's appeal to the Bundesgerichtshof was favourable to them, for the Supreme Court was inclined to view Article 5 as not unfair under German law – as reformed as a result of the implementation of the Unfair Terms Directive. In relating its decision to the 'wide variety of rules applying in the Member States', it decided to stay the proceedings and refer the following question to the European Court of Justice (ECJ) for a preliminary ruling:

> Is a term, contained in a seller's standard business conditions, which provides that the purchaser of a building which is to be constructed is to pay the total price for that building, irrespective of whether there has been any progress in the construction, provided that the seller has previously provided him with a guarantee from a credit institution securing any monetary claim the purchaser may have in respect of a defective performance or non-performance of the contract, to be regarded as unfair within the meaning of Article 3(1) of Council Directive 93/13/EEC of 5 April 1993 on unfair terms in consumer contracts?

The ECJ both acknowledged and endorsed the value of the circumstances-based style of regulation that emerged out of the Community decision-making process.

Firstly, at paragraphs 16 and 23 of the judgment, read in combination, the ECJ adopted an interpretation of the fairness test that rested on a straightforward consideration of the circumstances surrounding the transaction. In particular, the two passages focus upon the crucial factor of the balancing impact of the builder's bank guarantee on the overall deal, and highlight the fact that the guarantee was given for the benefit of the buyers. Specifically, this contractual arrangement, as opposed to one that contemplates payment at the moment of execution of the parking space, *both* reduces the price for the work, in that it reduces the need for the builder to finance the building work through use of borrowings, *and* limits the disadvantages faced by the buyers, in that it ensures the return of the sum paid in the case of non-performance, defective performance or insolvency of the builder. Therefore, the disadvantage of the payment being due before the conclusion of the contract – which stems, in the words of the defendants in the main proceedings, from the derogation of the fundamental rule-principle 'recognized in all systems of civil law, that mutual obligations must be performed contemporaneously' – is unfair only in the abstract, and not in the circumstances at stake. The distance between this type of decision and a decision that would instead rely on the rule-based approach is self-evident. This is particularly true if one takes into account one aspect of the decision: the German Supreme Court, in referring the case to the ECJ, was motivated by the need to assess whether a hypothetical declaration of fairness of the term at stake would be compatible with 'the wide variety of rules that apply in the Member States'; yet the ECJ ignored such an approach in that it played down the 'rule language' and, indeed, strongly directed its attention to the concrete substantive factors.

Secondly, at paragraph 19 of the judgment, the ECJ held that:

> In referring to concepts of good faith and significant imbalance between the rights and obligations of the parties, Article 3 of the Directive *merely defines* in a general way *the factors that render unfair a contractual term* that has not been individually negotiated (emphasis added).

This approach disentangles good faith from the protectionist ideology from which it derives, in legal comparative terms, in that it reinterprets good faith in the vocabulary of the circumstantial test. In fact, the ECJ does not reconstruct good faith as a proxy for protectionist rules but rather as being instrumental to the factorial judgment based on the substantive reasons involved in the decisions.

Thirdly, at paragraph 20 of the judgment, the ECJ held that the list of unfair terms that the directive provides is only 'indicative and non-exhaustive'. This restates what Article 3(3) of the Unfair Terms Directive provides for, and can be held to be another indication of the weight that the ECJ gives to its option for a circumstantial decision-making style, for to hold that the listed terms are mandatory, rather than indicative, would have gravely limited the operation of the fairness test by taking away from the decision-maker, in disputes where the listed terms were at stake, the power to make judgements in light of the circumstances.

Fourthly, at paragraph 21 of the judgment it is stated that in assessing fairness reference must be made 'to all the circumstances attending to the conclusion of the contract'. As a detailed analysis of the decision-making process that led to the directive shows, a point that I have made elsewhere,[155] 'circumstances' is a proxy for the factors surrounding the transactions – for example, the guarantee given

[155] Niglia, *The Transformation of Contract in Europe* (n 44).

in support of the transaction in *Freiburger*. Reference is also made to 'the nature of the goods or services for which the contract was concluded', which entails that judges are to adjust their decisions depending on the type of goods and services at stake. This passage restates the choice for disentangling the assessment of fairness from the rules in that (un)fairness is made contingent on the characteristics of the goods and services: which, in turn, means that decision-makers will be able to diversify decisions of fairness for similar terms inserted in contracts that have distinct goods or services as their object. For example, an exclusion of liability may be unfair in a highly risky investment contract in securities, but not in a contract for the sale of books.[156]

In summary, the ECJ reads the relevant text of the directive in relation to the substantive stakes relevant to the dispute, ending up by supporting a reading entirely in line with the Commission's project as approved by the then Council of Ministers, the Unfair Terms Directive being based on a circumstantial model aimed at promoting the interests of entrepreneurs in enabling them to draft contracts that minimise their risks as much as possible.

Océano Grupo Editorial is another illustration of this approach, albeit one read through the lens of the *Freiburger* judgment, for in the latter the CJEU holds that *Océano* was decided in favour of the consumer because there was no competing interest ('solely to the benefit of the seller') at stake, implying that the Court is ready to balance the consumer's interests with those of the counterparty.[157] In the words of the Court (at paragraph 23):[158]

> It is true that in Joined Cases C-240/98 to C-244/98 *Océano Grupo Editorial and Salvat Editores* [2000] ECR I-4941, paragraphs 21 to 24, the Court held that a term, drafted in advance by the seller, the purpose of which is to confer jurisdiction in respect of all disputes arising under the contract on the court in the territorial jurisdiction of which the seller has his principal place of business, satisfies all the criteria necessary for it to be judged unfair for the purposes of the Directive. Nevertheless, that assessment was reached in relation to a term which was solely to the benefit of the seller and contained no benefit in return for the consumer. Whatever the nature of the contract, it thereby undermined the effectiveness of the legal protection of the rights which the Directive affords to the consumer. It was thus possible to hold that the term was unfair without having to consider all the circumstances in which the contract was concluded and without having to assess the advantages and disadvantages that that term would have under the national law applicable to the contract.

(b) I now consider a line of cases (pre-Brexit) coming from England as further illustration of the rise in competitive-orientated balancing. I refer to the notorious

[156] All passages are drawn from my article Niglia, '"The Rules Dilemma"' (n 16).

[157] Joined Cases C-240/98 to C-244/98 *Océano Grupo Editorial SA v Roció Murciano Quintero and Salvat Editores SA v José M. Sánchez Alcón Prades, José Luis Copano Badillo, Mohammed Berroane and Emilio Viñas Feliú* ECLI:EU:C:2000:346.

[158] Case C-237/02 *Freiburger Kommunalbauten GmbH Baugesellschaft & Co KG v Hofstetter* ECLI:EU:C:2004:209, para 23.

line of cases where interest rates in a banking contract after a court's decision were at stake. Specifically, a loan agreement contained provisions which made interest payable, at the contractual rate, on the amount of principal advanced outstanding, together with accrued unpaid interest at the date of any judgment, during the period after judgment until finally discharged by payment. The High Court held that the term was not unfair since the consumer would not be surprised when told that interest at the contractual rate would continue to persist after a judgment.[159] In line with the trial judge's decision, in *National Bank* the House of Lords equally held that the term at stake is not 'unfair' as no surprise would occur on the part of the borrower.[160]

A dual shift away from certain customers' protectionist rules takes place here: judges turn their attention away from formal observance of consumer-friendly rules and instead decide on the basis of reasons of substance related to the circumstantial balancing of interests commanded by the Unfair Terms Directive.

Firstly, both the High Court and the House of Lords (now the Supreme Court) courts have downplayed certain relevant rules contained in the County Courts (Interest on Judgments Debt) Order 1991, which commands protection for the customer in the sense that it excludes regulated agreements under the Consumer Credit Act (1974) from the imposition of interest on a judgment debt: according to such legislative rules, no payment of post-judicial interests is allowed.[161]

Secondly, the House of Lords has given great weight to the substantive reasons that the term contemplates a risk that makes economic sense in the context of what the court considers 'the essential bargain'[162] – the lending of money in exchange for repayment with interest – and that the borrower was well aware of such a risk, having been informed by the bank about the term at stake.[163] Thus, a term deemed unfair under the traditional set of consumer protectionist rules has been considered to be fair due to circumstances peculiar to the transaction regarding the nature of the services *and* the risk awareness on the part of the consumer. One must no doubt recognise that the Court frames the substantive reason on which its judgment relies in relation to circumstances that the directive-based test

[159] See *Director General of Fair Trading v First National Bank plc* [2000] 1 WLR 98, 32. This is a decision based on the Regulations 1994 then in force, implementing Council Directive 93/13/EEC [1993] OJ L95/29.

[160] *National Bank* (n 159) 20–24.

[161] ibid 31–32, 42. For a middle-ground position, see the Court of Appeals decision in *First National Bank* [2000] 1 All ER (Comm) 371 (allowing the appeal on the basis that certain statutory rules – s 71 of the 1984 County Court Act and ss 129 and 136 of the 1974 Consumer Credit Act – would have enabled the bank to obtain judgment against the debtor under the regulated agreement and an instalment order under s 71, the court having not complied with such statutory rules; but also holding that to make the consumer pay interest after judgment is to create 'unfair surprise', thus clinging to the 'transparency' argument already adopted by the High Court, but, in contrast to the High Court's dicta, considering that the consumer would indeed be surprised had he had to pay).

[162] *National Bank* (n 159) 20.

[163] ibid 24.

of fairness is concerned with.[164] The UK Supreme Court adopts a reading which is remarkably market-orientated – it is balancing within a particular range of factors only, all of which are market orientated, rather than considering the broader range of potentially available non-market normative factors.

IV. Conclusion

The closest form of balancing to economised balancing, as developed by the jurisprudence of the CJEU and considered in the first part of this chapter, can be held to be the hermeneutics of teleological market-orientated balancing – in the sense of reflecting, and co-participating in, the hermeneutical structures entailed in that ideal type. *Freiburger* epitomises this process.[165] In *Freiburger*, the CJEU adopts a kind of economised balancing that, seen in the light of the hermeneutical material considered in the second part of this chapter, embodies the traits of market-orientated teleological balancing, effectively incorporating and re-elaborating a balancing test of unfairness thereto crafted in private law circles. That is, it is a balancing test that had been, according to my understanding of the legislative process, leading to the enactment of the Unfair Terms Directive, the template on the basis of which the EU legislator had chosen to frame the directive's key norms. The UK Supreme Court's judgment in *National Bank* equally epitomises a hermeneutics of teleological market-orientated balancing.[166]

Key tensions characterise the structure of scholarship and adjudication. First, the German side of the *Schulte* saga on the right of cancellation (the Doorstep

[164] See Council Directive 93/13/EEC on Unfair Terms in Consumer Contracts [1993] OJ L 95, Art 3(2), recitals 18–20.

[165] See F Snyder, 'The Effectiveness of European Community Law: Institutions, Processes, Tools and Techniques' (1993) 56 *MLR* 19 (on process).

[166] Here a critical parallelism emerges between the common law and the civil law that offers the ground for tackling from a newer perspective the ways in which the dilemma entailed in 'having to choose' between 'determinate rules' and 'indeterminate standards' is tackled both in the common law (on common law and balancing, see, eg n 142 above) and in the civil law (for discussion and literature, see Niglia, *The Transformation of Contract in Europe* (n 44); Niglia, '"The Rules Dilemma"' (n 16)). If both the civil law and the common law are post-axiomatic, that is, less about just 'legal science' and more about argumentation and reasoning (see, eg G Samuel, *Law of Obligations* (Cheltenham, Edward Elgar, 2010); G Samuel, *An Introduction to Comparative Law and Method* (Hart Publishing, 2014); G Samuel, *Rethinking Legal Reasoning* G Samuel, *Law of Obligations* (Cheltenham, Edward Elgar, 2018), then what is needed is to recount the structural ways in which post-axiomatic hermeneutics has been emerging. From this viewpoint, pursuing this dual line of analysis enables adding crucial arguments for strengthening the case for viewing the civil law and the English common law as much closer in structure than conventionalism might think, thereby contributing to scholarship that challenges the so-called 'civil law–common law divide' and that emphasises the close relationships between the civil law and the common law in Europe; see, eg the distinct perspectives on the meaning of such closeness between the civil law and the common law in the works of Samuel (*An Introduction to Comparative Law and Method*, ibid) and of Zimmermann (R Zimmermann, *Roman Law, Contemporary Law, European Law: The Civilian Tradition Today* (Oxford, Oxford University Press, 2001) and compare Niglia, *The Transformation of Contract in Europe* (n 44)).

Directive), considered in chapter two above, instead evidences exactly those traits of social balancing, broadly speaking, that fall in line with what I have labelled 'maximal balancing', which the CJEU (and the UK Supreme Court) has chosen to set aside with its new heteronomous jurisprudence. Second, the jurisprudence of interpretative obligation in its original version had started off as embedded in a kind of balancing teleologically orientated towards sociality that the Court chose to respect in the paradigmatic *Von Colson* decision (with regard to Council Directive 76/207/EEC, the Equal Treatment Directive).

It should also be noted that the jurisprudence of constitutional heteronomy engineered by the CJEU is grounded in a hermeneutics of economised balancing ideally suited for the strategy of the Court. It enables the Court to construct a European law that, in being heteronomously superimposed on national legal systems, is meant to be 'self-contained' in that it does not need to draw on the knowledges coming from national traditions of private law for it to exist.

In the next chapter, I argue that, on close inspection, a third transformation can be seen to be taking place that makes more intelligible the transformation from autonomy to heteronomy. The jurisprudence of constitutional heteronomy can be made intelligible not only as market-oriented (economised balancing), but also as 'total (constitutional) law', with the rising private order engineered towards replacing the EU constitutional order and, as a result, as a process aiming at totalising constitutional law material. This ongoing third structural transformation is a revolutionary change that now needs to be considered.

4

Absorption

I. Introduction

The jurisprudence of constitutional heteronomy analysed in the previous chapter is a hermeneutical architecture that produces a structural mutation of the relationship between, on the one hand, private law (statist private law) and, on the other hand, the integrationist constitutional order. It is a mutation around a heteronomous interface that sees the former being subjected to the latter as opposed to its previous autonomy – signifying a shift from autonomy to heteronomy. This is what I have argued in the previous chapter.

In the previous chapter I also explored the balancing technique, as it stands at the core of the jurisprudence of constitutional heteronomy. It consists of an economised type of balancing in that it is a balancing designed to be instrumental in facilitating market integration and accommodating market imperatives. It is a technique traceable to a private law discourse that actively participates in the making of market integration no longer from the 'outside' of state private law but from 'inside' a newly created European private law (EPL) discourse – a beyond-the-state private law discourse that develops away from, overcomes and transgresses nation-state boundaries, with a pretence to self-containment around the economised balancing formula.[1]

From this viewpoint, the previous chapter has unveiled a continuity pattern. One must recall the project of a European codification backed up by the claim of consisting of a set of self-standing norms and principles.[2] The demise of the codification project cannot be mistaken for the abandonment of its underpinning agenda, as many EPL scholars tend to believe. That project

[1] L Niglia, *The Struggle for European Private Law. A Critique of Codification* (Oxford, Hart Publishing, 2015). On EPL as scholarly discourse, see chs 2 and 3 (above); L Niglia, 'Taking Comparative Law Seriously – Europe's Private Law and the Poverty of the Orthodoxy (Instalment One)' (2006) 54 *American Journal of Comparative Law* 401; L Niglia, 'The Question Concerning the Common Frame of Reference' (2012) 18 *European Law Journal* 736; Niglia, *The Struggle for European Private Law* (ibid) (on genealogy).

[2] See Niglia, *The Struggle for European Private Law* (n 1) 38 et seq (discussing the code in its 'code corpus' characterisation as 'complete, coherent, self-standing, system', the project of a European codification as involving that conception and criticising this project in terms of jurisprudential material).

is still with us, albeit under a different form, that is, the form of constitutional heteronomy.

This chapter aims to delve deeper into the aspects addressed in the previous chapter. The jurisprudence of constitutional heteronomy is further characterised, this chapter argues, by the singling out of a range of privatistic freedom rights with a view to protecting them against state law. Constitutional absorption designates the strategy of expanding the structure of EU constitutional law (key sets of constitutional norms and principles) for that protectionist purpose. Through economised balancing, the privatistic freedom rights are incorporated and 'absorbed' into, and reshape, EU constitutional material. In turn, this amounts to a process aimed at 'totalising' (constitutional) law.[3]

In what follows, section II (constitutionalisation of rights) analyses the concrete ways in which constitutional material gets to be expanded with a view to achieving the objective of protecting certain private rights. Through an exploration of three worlds of privatistic praxis, this chapter proposes a rereading of the Court of Justice of the European Union (CJEU, the Court) case law in the light of this framework of analysis.[4]

Section III (constitutionalisation of orders) then considers that constitutional absorption is not just to be seen as a rights-based phenomenon that consists of incorporating and protecting certain private rights against the state. Deep down, I will argue that it is rather a complex phenomenon: as the CJEU chooses to erase from its jurisprudence the *state-based* hermeneutics of social balancing, as this can emerge at the level of the EU order through the co-normativising structures of the interpretative obligation, it draws entirely upon the *transnational* hermeneutics of private ordering. In so doing, it incorporates into the EU constitutional order juridical hermeneutical material that pertains to a *constructed* transnational privatistic praxis – a praxis, I also argue, that, as a result of such incorporation, becomes *constitutionally* jurisgenerative.[5] At the same time as constitutional absorption forecloses the state hermeneutics of private law, it opens up to the *transnational* hermeneutics of the private order, with the latter, in turn, being conceptualised at once as non-state, that is, as no longer coupled with the state, and as reliant only on its one-sided normative (economised) dictates.

I round off the chapter with a conclusion.

[3] On the meaning of constitutional absorption and of the totalising of law, see the rest of this chapter and ch 5.

[4] On the orientation of the EU Commission to take seriously 'practices' in terms of 'bettering' 'enforcement and modernisation of EU consumer protection rules', see the Proposal for a Directive amending Council Directive 93/13/EEC, Directive 98/6/EC, Directive 2005/29/EC and Directive 2011/83 as regards better enforcement and modernisation of EU consumer protection rules, https://eur-lex.europa.eu/legal-content/EN/TXT/?qid=1573719288581&uri=CELEX:52018PC0185.

[5] Contrast the constitutionally jurisgenerative processes considered in ch 2 above (jurisprudence of constitutional autonomy).

II. Absorption as New Constitutionalisation (Rights)

The jurisprudence of constitutional heteronomy is characterised, by its singling out, through the technique of balancing, a certain range of privatistic rights with a view to protecting them against the state – by expanding the structure of EU constitutional law (its norms and principles) so that it can be 'adapted' for the purpose of protecting those rights.

By working out a new reconstruction of the key constitutional norms and principles, as they had been crafted in the past by the Court itself, the Court ends up with absorbing a certain range of privatistic rights into EU constitutional material (constitutional absorption).

As a result of this, the EU constitutional order comes to constitutionally incorporate and immunise from state intervention a range of privatistic freedom rights that acquire a special status of absolute protection. They form an EU privatistic constitutional core against which states are not allowed to claim any sovereign control, as in classical constitutional absorption cases concerning integration in the past.[6]

As far as private law is concerned, one can hold that what Koen Lenaerts held 30 years ago – that 'There simply is no nucleus of sovereignty that the Member States can invoke, as such, against the Community'[7] – now applies equally to private law: with the qualification, however, that the quotation makes intelligible the *current* condition of national private law ('nucleus of sovereignty') now that the CJEU is adopting the new constitutionalising move under scrutiny in this chapter,

[6] See JHH Weiler, 'The Transformation of Europe' (1991) 100 *Yale Law Journal* 2405, 2435 (with regard to 'absorption' as erosion of jurisdictional demarcation between the Union and the Member States, in terms of 'strict enumeration', consisting of the erosion in the 1970s of the 'limited fields' as proclaimed in the jurisprudence of the CJEU since the early 1960s): in this chapter, by 'absorption' I mean instead a process of erosion of jurisdictional demarcation that pertains to an established set of EU constitutional doctrines being adjusted so as to accommodate a range of privatistic rights with a view to protecting them, rather than the issue of erosion of 'strict enumeration' of competences); on the need for overcoming the view of competences seen as self-standing EU doctrine, rather than as related to broader structural developments, see ch 5 below and see L Niglia, 'The European Judicial Saga on Law and Political Economy' (2022).For the restatement of the classical argument that in EU law competences (existence of) and proportionality (in the sense of the exercise of the conferred competences) are distinct, and for related criticism of the German Federal Constitutional Court, judgment of the Second Senate of 5 May 2020, 2 BvR 859/15, 2 BvR 1651/15, 2 BvR 2006/15, 2 BvR 980/16 (hereinafter *PSPP* judgment) for blurring that distinction, contrast, among others, M Wendel, 'Paradoxes of Ultra-Vires Review: A Critical Review of the PSPP Decision and Its Initial Reception' (2020) 21 *German Law Journal* 979, 985–86 (also drawing on P Craig and G de Burca *EU Law: Text, Cases and Materials*, 6th edn (Oxford, Oxford University Press, 2015) 96. 'Erosion' read in this way is part of the fuller argument I make in section III, where I explain that what gets 'absorbed' is not just the 'state order' (jurisdictional demarcation between the EU and its Member States), but 'private ordering' as a result made stateless.

[7] K Lenaerts, 'Constitutionalism and the Many Faces of Federalism' (1990) 38 *American Journal of Comparative Law* 205, 220, as cited in Weiler (n 6) 2407 (in relation to 'absorption' consisting of the erosion in the 1970s of the 'limited fields' as proclaimed in the jurisprudence of the CJEU in the 1960s).

whereas it could not capture the full condition of private law during the time of the jurisprudence of constitutional autonomy.[8]

In other words, in a climate in which the hermeneutics of national private law is set aside through the obliteration of the doctrine of interpretative obligation, and with the void left by that operation being filled by the hermeneutics of new balancing (the hermeneutics of economised balancing), one must note a deep dimension that connotes the jurisprudence of heteronomy. That is, the Court frames its heteronomous jurisprudence in constitutional terms not only through restructuring the constitutional doctrine of interpretative obligation (turning it into direct effect), an aspect considered in the previous chapter, but equally through re-engineering a further set of constitutional structures for the achievement of the chosen purpose in cases involving not a directive, but primary legislation. These are the key constitutional structures of the general principles of law, fundamental rights and proportionality. This chapter looks at the flip side of balancing. That is, it looks at the technique deployed in such a way that it neither tolerates nor operates through, but alters a variety of key EU constitutional structures: the interpretative obligation, the general principles of law, fundamental rights and proportionality.

I should preface this analysis with the consideration that I am conscious that the constitutional mutation that I am discussing here has been largely unnoticed, despite being willed so by the insiders (the legal and political actors) to the integration process. This is an irony (labelled 'cognitive dissonance') that repeats itself insofar as having characterised a previous distinct and, from the viewpoint of the analysis proposed in this book, more formal kind of mutation regarding the jurisdictional demarcation between the Union (then the Community) and the Member States in terms of strict enumeration of competences.[9]

***

In the paradigmatic judgments of *Freiburger*, *Laval* and *Viking*,[10] the Court rearranges constitutional material in two ways: negatively and positively. Negatively,

[8] Contrast the BVerfG judgment of *Lisbon* (BVerfG2 BvE 2/08 *Lisbon*, 30 June 2009) placing outer limits to the competences of the EU; it is remarkable how constitutional absorption takes place despite and against the grain of the line of jurisprudence that includes the *Maastricht* (BVerfG 89/155 *Maastricht*) and the *Lisbon* judgments of the BVerfG, and the *Taricco* judgment of the Italian Constitutional Court (the *Taricco* judgment of the Italian Constitutional Court, 115/2018, 10 April 2018). On federalism and private law, see L Niglia, 'Beyond Enchantment: The Possibility of a New European Private Law (Instalment Two)' (2009) 28 *Yearbook of European Law* 60.

[9] See Weiler (n 6) 2435 on 'cognitive dissonance'; see also n 6 above.

[10] Case C-237/02 *Freiburger Kommunalbauten GmbH Baugesellschaft and Co KG v Ludger Hofstetter and Ulrike Hofstetter* [2004] ECR I-3403; Case C-341/05 *Laval un Partneri Ltd v Svenska Byggnadsarbetareförbundet* ECLI:EU:C:2007:809; Case C-438/05 *International Transport Workers' Federation and Finnish Seamen's Union v Viking Line ABP and OÜ Viking Line EestiCase* ECLI:EU:C:2007:772. For further cases, see, as discussed in the rest of the book, also Case C-426/11 *Alemo-Herron and Others* ECLI:EU:C:2013:521, 31–32; Court of Justice, judgment of 11 December 2018, Case C-493/17 *Heinrich Weiss et al v ECB* ECLI:EU:C:2018:1000 (rearranging proportionality balancing: see ch 5 below); CJEU *Airb&b* 19 December 2019; *X, interveners: YA, Airbnb*

through suspending the interpretative obligation with a view to protect the privatistic right of entrepreneurs to provide for alternative combinations of quality/price offers rather than complying with state mandatory standards.[11] And positively, through framing the privatistic right of entrepreneurs to provide for terms and conditions of employment at their will, defending such right through a radical reconceptualisation of 'general principles of law' and also of 'fundamental rights' so as to serve that purpose, albeit at the sacrifice of an established understanding of both, whilst equally further protecting that right through arguments from proportionality that make a sham of proportionality (*Laval* and *Viking*). I will consider each case in turn.

(a) As I argued in the previous chapter, *Freiburger* is characterised by a 'suspension',[12] on the part of the CJEU, of the doctrine of the interpretative

Ireland UC, Hôtelière Turenne SAS, Association pour un hébergement et un tourisme professionnels (AHTOP), Valhotel ECLI:EU:C:2019:1112. This section focuses on rights; for duties and obligations, see section III below, arguing that not just rights but also obligations are encompassed by the jurisprudence of the CJEU under scrutiny (on the CJEU judgment of *ORF-Finance* as private ordering imposed upon state law through conjuring up certain duties – obliging, under indirect effect, the national courts to change the relevant national case law with a view to implementing a certain market regime for credit agreements). One consideration must be made at this point. The 'public law' counterpart of EU law and its order, and specifically decisions on contentious constitutional matters such as the CJEU's Case C-399/11 Judgment of the Court (Grand Chamber) 26 February 2013; *Stefano Melloni v Ministerio Fiscal* ECLI:EU:C:2013:107; the 'Taricco' decisions: European Court of Justice, Judgment of the Court (Grand Chamber) of 8 September 2015, Case C-105/1 *Criminal proceedings against Ivo Taricco and Others* ECLI:EU:C:2015:555 ('The national court must give full effect to Article 325(1) and (2) TFEU, if need be by disapplying the provisions of national law the effect of which would be to prevent the Member State concerned from fulfilling its obligations under Article 325(1) and (2) TFEU'); European Court of Justice Judgment of the Court (Grand Chamber) of 5 December 2017, Case C-42/17 *Criminal proceedings against MAS and MB* ECLI:EU:C:2017:936); European Court of Justice, Judgment of 16 June 2015, Case C-62/14 *Gauweiler and others v Deutscher Bundestag* ECLI:EU:C:2015:400; and CJEU *Weiss*, above (on which see below, as private–public development), all point to the CJEU taking a similar direction towards hierarchising and hegemonising EU law further in its relationship with national laws: the EU constitution is seen as an absolute that trumps national constitutional standards (*Melloni*, above), that places effectiveness above national constitutional principles (legality, as in the *Taricco* saga, above) and that equally places political and fiscal economy issues under the vigilance of market discipline through economised balancing (on market safeguards, see the CJEU's *Weiss* decision, above; *PSPP* judgment (n 6), as discussed in L Niglia, 'The European Judicial Saga on Law and Political Economy' (2022). The oxymoron of 'parallel convergence' can make sense of these developments as they take place in the proper constitutional realm, as well as in the private constitutional realms considered in this book. What this book considers is the 'private law' side of this story, signifying the impact of the hegemonising move on nation state laws as private law and, specifically, the decoupling of private order from state law and its acquiring autonomous force. There are intersections between the two processes; and voices at variance, including 'constitutional resistance', exist and point to critique and the potential for change: see ch 5 below.

[11] A first step towards altering the interpretative obligation by transforming it into a direct effect tool, an aspect considered in ch 2 above, and yet a defining way in which the CJEU alters constitutional material outright for the purpose of protecting the range of chosen privatistic freedom rights against the state.

[12] On the technique of 'suspension' in terms of (state of) 'exception', see L Niglia, 'The New Transformation of Europe. Arcana Imperii' (2020) 68 *American Journal of Comparative Law* 151; on 'state of exception' see ibid (referring to the 'state of exception' argument 'used in memoranda-related debates and in comparative assessments of judicial decisions in order to justify memoranda contracts' as 'self-contradictory', as 'false' and specifically: 'The state of exception argument implies the "necessity"

obligation, through omitting it from the judgment, with a view to pursuing its relentless juridification of any of the contractual terms of any entrepreneurial 'balancing' (economised).[13]

The decision mentions two 'law worlds', between which it chooses, opting for one over the other, without subjecting the chosen interpretation to the requirements of the interpretative obligation. Namely, whilst paragraph 16 belongs to the brave new world of economised balancing, paragraph 17 of the decision belongs to the hermeneutical world of social balancing:

> 16. Freiburger Kommunalbauten and the German Government submit that the disputed clause is not unfair. The disadvantages to which a consumer might be exposed as a result of the obligation to pay the price before performance of the contract are counterbalanced by the bank guarantee provided by the builder. It is true that this clause reverses the order for performance of the obligations under the contract laid down, in non-mandatory terms, in Paragraph 641 of the BGB [Bürgerliches Gesetzbuch]. However, as it reduces the need for the builder to finance the building work through use of borrowings, the price of that work may be reduced as a result. Furthermore, the bank guarantee provided by the builder limits the disadvantages faced by purchasers, as it guarantees repayment to them of sums paid in cases of both non-performance and defective performance of the contract, even if the builder were to become insolvent.
>
> 17. Mr and Mrs Hofstetter submit that the disputed clause is unfair and is a term of the kind referred to at point 1(b) and (o) of the Annex to the Directive. The fundamental principle, recognised in all systems of civil law, that mutual obligations must be performed contemporaneously, is contravened and the 'equality of arms' between the contracting parties is upset to the detriment of the consumer, whose position is significantly weakened, particularly where litigation arises in relation to defects in construction. They add that the clause is highly unusual, that it is unclear and that it was imposed by a builder who was in a monopoly situation.

At paragraphs 19–22, the Court goes on to accept in full the economised balancing kind of hermeneutics, based on the counterbalancing of the disadvantage to which consumers may be exposed by inter alia a bank guarantee, as opposed to the 'fundamental principle, recognised in all systems of civil law, that mutual obligations

of the austerity measures (and, by extension, the precondition of financial hardship for some countries). However, the austerity measures are not "necessary" according to those leading (although ultimately uninfluential in relation to the austerity orientation of EMU politics) economists who argue instead that adopting economic-political measures (including expansive monetary policies, issuing Euro bonds, or both) would be better, both in terms of economic output (resolution of the issue of financial hardship) and of avoidance of the social disintegration entailed in the implementation of the memoranda (see, eg, the work of Joseph Stiglitz, among others). Philosophically speaking, on the "fiction" of the "state of exception" argument including a critique of the positions of Carl Schmitt and Walter Benjamin, see the reconstruction in 2\1 Giorgio Agamben, *Homo Sacer: Stato di Eccezione* (2003).' The setting aside of the interpretative obligation on the part of the CJEU is particularly problematic insofar as the interpretative obligation is central to the jurisprudence of constitutional autonomy, with its ordering that revolves around a plural logic of constitutional respect towards state private laws, as argued above in ch 2 – it is this contingent kind of ordering that is set aside as a result.

[13] See CJEU *Freiburger* (n 10). See also the case-law of the CJEU on 'combined offers' under Art 34 TFEU.

must be performed contemporaneously', based on 'equality of arms', whilst then constitutionalising such economised balancing outright (with no mention of the interpretative obligation as conditional reasoning for any internalisation of such balancing in the body of national law) at paragraph 22, where it holds that:

> as the Advocate General has observed at point 25 of his Opinion, that in the context of its jurisdiction under Article 234 EC to interpret Community law, the Court may interpret general criteria used by the Community legislature in order to define the concept of unfair terms.

The Court grounds its hermeneutical position also through the constitutionalising deployment of Article 234 EC (now Article 267 TFEU) in the sense of indicating an interpretation of the relevant directive for the national court to adhere to, overcoming the distinction between fact and law in relation to preliminary references, that is, directly ruling on the facts of the dispute.

Interestingly, the Court pretends to present its interpretation as if it were an inevitable and apodictic consequence of the content of the Unfair Terms Directive – an approach also present in other judgments under scrutiny in this book.[14]

In choosing not to adopt the interpretative obligation, the Court is, at the same time, disregarding and unrecognising national law as applicable to unfair terms, as in the submissions of Mr and Mrs Hofstetter. Both moves are about deconstitutionalising (relative to national law), while, at the same time, reconstitutionalising the proposed economised balancing based on the preferred market factors. Once arguments from economic convenience (guarantee and price offsetting the condition of 'inequality of arms' through the imposition of contractual terms, apparently even by a market actor with a monopolistic position) are given centre stage in the judgment, then the principle is established apodictically, and not under the doctrine of interpretative obligation, that balancing arguments that make 'economic sense' fully belong to the structure of European constitutional law. Such 'economical sense' arguments are those adopted in *Freiburger* through a reading of the Unfair Terms Directive that mirrors its market orientated characterisation.[15]

Arguments (constitutionally coloured, in terms of national constitutional law) concerning exploitation by contract for lack of respect of the principle of reciprocity of obligations are not considered by the CJEU at all, and are in fact discarded.[16]

[14] See L Niglia, 'Eclipse of the Constitution' (2016) 22 *European Law Journal* 132 (on the CJEU judgments of *Laval* (n 10) and *Viking* (n 10)).

[15] See below for further discussion of this argument.

[16] On 'exploitation by contract', see L Niglia, *The Transformation of Contract in Europe* (The Hague, Kluwer Law International, 2003) (with relevant literature); on the extortionate or burdensome character of unilaterally imposed contracts, see Niglia, 'The New Transformation of Europe' (n 12). For analysis, see Niglia, *The Transformation of Contract in Europe* (ibid); the classical works on the subject of unilaterally imposed contracts include: L Raiser, *Das Recht der Allgemeinen Geschaftsbedingungen* (1961); R Saleilles, *Essai d'une théorie générale de l'obligation* (Paris, Librairie Cotillon, 1890); R Saleilles, *De la déclaration de volonté: Contribution á l'étude de l'acte juridique dans le code allemand (art. 116 á 144)* (Paris, 1901).

The lack of consideration of the doctrine of the interpretative obligation is a structural aspect of this move.

As a result of the above, constitutionally, market integration here is definitively about taking on the characterisation of a radical form of 'market without rules', as opposed to 'market with rules' (to put it in the vocabulary of one Advocate General).[17] This is so, however, only in the specific sense that economised balancing replaces the mandatory rules,[18] that is, those national mandatory rules that protect the weak contractor from any kind of exploitation through balancing operations parameterised after the public interest of the collective.[19]

On close inspection, *Freiburger* can be seen to be not just about the suspension of the interpretative obligation, in that the judgment also alters the architecture of the general principles of law (European private law).[20] The Court rejects the applicability of a 'fundamental principle' that flies in the face of economised balancing, that is: 'The fundamental principle, recognised in all systems of civil law, that mutual obligations must be performed contemporaneously.'

In other words, the protection of the privatistic right of the seller to provide for alternative (combinations of) offers through the technique of economised

[17] See Advocate General Tizzano in Judgment of the Court (Grand Chamber) of 5 October 2004 *CaixaBank France v Ministère de l'Économie, des Finances et de l'Industrie*, paras 62–63: 'that interpretation would permit economic operators – both national and foreign – to abuse Article 43 EC in order to oppose any national measure that, solely because it regulated the conditions for pursuing an economic activity, could in the final analysis narrow profit margins and hence reduce the attractiveness of pursuing that particular economic activity. However, that would be tantamount to bending the Treaty to a purpose for which it was not intended: that is to say, *not in order to create an internal market in which conditions are similar to those of a single market and where operators can move freely, but in order to establish a market without rules. Or rather, a market in which rules are prohibited as a matter of principle*, except for those necessary and proportionate to meeting imperative requirements in the public interest' (emphasis added). But on market *and* rules, see L Niglia, 'Standard Form Contracts in Europe and North America – One Hundred Years of Unfair Terms?' in C Rickett and T Telfer (eds), *International Perspectives on Consumers' Access to Justice* (Cambridge, Cambridge University Press, 2003) 101; L Niglia, '"The Rules Dilemma" – The Court of Justice and the Dilemma of the Regulation of Standard Form Contracts in Europe' (2006) 13 *Columbia Journal of European Law* 124; Niglia, *The Struggle for European Private Law* (n 1); Niglia, 'The New Transformation of Europe' (n 12); L Niglia, 'Comparative Jurisprudence' (unpublished manuscript on file with author, 2022).

[18] On the correspondence between mandatory norms and protection from exploitation in the history of private law in Europe, see Niglia, L, *The Transformation* (n 16); Niglia, 'Beyond Enchantment' (n 8); Niglia, *The Struggle for European Private Law* (n 1).

[19] See ch 3 above.

[20] On the general principles of civil law and Europeanisation, see MW Hesselink, 'The General Principles of Civil Law: Their Nature, Roles and Legitimacy' in D Leczykiewicz and S Weatheril (eds), *The Involvement of EU Law in Private Law Relationships* (Oxford, Hart Publishing, 2013) 131–80. For a confirmation of the economised balancing test, see Case C-226/12 *Constructora Principado SA v José Ignacio Menéndez Álvarez* ECLI:EU:C:2014:10: 'whether that significant imbalance exists cannot be limited to a quantitative economic evaluation based on a comparison between the total value of the transaction which is the subject of the contract and the costs charged to the consumer under that clause' and also including an assessment based on the banchmark of legal rules, default rules. On default rules, see Niglia, *The Struggle for European Private Law* (n 1); Case C-415/11 *Mohamed Aziz v Caixa d'Estalvis de Catalunya, Tarragona i Manresa (Catalunyacaixa)* ECLI:EU:C:2013:164 (on which see H Micklitz and N Reich, 'The Court and Sleeping Beauty: The Revival of the Unfair Contract Terms Directive' (2014) 51 *CML Rev* 771). Note that in *Aziz*, on statutory interest, the CJEU combines balancing and proportionality.

balancing is made prevalent over, and hermeneutically sealed vis-à-vis, the counterclaim put forward before the courts that a fundamental principle of European private law obliges the parties to perform simultaneously.

The Court takes a favourable position vis-à-vis the contractual clause that *reverses* the order for performance of the obligations under the contract by considering that this reversal is balanced by the other factors that the Court considers pre-eminent, and should be exclusively applied to the dispute at stake, rather than seeing the fundamental principle of simultaneous performance as a red line, and as such not to be derogated. This reversal is done by the Court's take of the principle of contemporary performance under paragraph 641 of the BGB as non-mandatory and in any case as not relevant to the resolution of the matter, thus frustrating that principle.

A double alteration of EU constitutional structures takes place here for the purpose of protecting privatistic rights against state law – with a view to protecting (through balancing) private rights against the state. First, a fundamental principle (contemporary performance) is subjected to balancing, and, second, the Court's determination to suspend the operation of the doctrine of indirect effect as applicable to the dispute insofar as pertaining to a horizontal relationship, in the sense of obliging the judges to interpret in conformity (if possible), *ex hypothesi* barring the setting aside of the principle of contemporary performance at least due to the *klare Wortlaut* (clear wording) of the relevant national norms (paragraph 641 BGB).[21]

(b) I now argue that a similar thesis must also apply to the two landmark cases of *Laval* and *Viking*[22] in the areas of labour law and of free movement of services and establishment.

The characterising mode of *Laval* and *Viking* is their positive grounding of economised balancing – that is, whilst, in *Freiburger*, the Court reconstitutionalised a range of EU law doctrines through negatively suspending the interpretative obligation, in *Laval* and *Viking* the Court – similarly to *ORF-Finance*, where the Court actively transformed the doctrine of the interpretative obligation in a direct effect tool – positively adopted arguments from the general principles of EU law, fundamental rights and proportionality with a view to protecting (through balancing) private rights against the state. Specifically, entrepreneurial rights are protected as fundamental rights whilst at the same time being balanced against other competing rights (labour), making the former prevail through a biased proportionality assessment.[23]

[21] For arguments from the *Klare Wortlaut* of national laws, and in any case suspending indirect effect despite the fact that the relevant 'principle' is not easily interpretable in the light of the Directive under any of the teleological reductionist methodologies adopted under national law, see ch 2 above; Niglia, 'Conforming Interpretation' (n 6).

[22] Above n 10. See also Case C-144/04 *Mangold* [2005] ECR I-9981; Case C-319/06 *Commission v Luxembourg* [2007] ECR I-4323; Case C-346/06 *Rechtsanwalt Dr Dirk Rüffert v Land Niedersachsen* [2008] ECR I-1989, as discussed in Niglia, 'Eclipse of the Constitution' (n 13).

[23] This argument draws on Niglia, 'Eclipse of the Constitution' (n 13), to which the reader should refer for further discussion. On *Viking*, see n 10 above.

That is: the Court in *Laval* chose to decouple the right to collective action and the right to strike from the right to collective bargaining. This somewhat counter-intuitive move[24] resulted in collective action and the right to strike being regarded as supranational 'fundamental rights',[25] and consequently (and decisively) being fully subject to review by reference to, in particular, freedom of establishment (Article 43 TFEU).[26] If, in previous rulings,[27] the CJEU had declared that the right to collective bargaining (and the resulting collective agreements) were exempted from review by reference to EU competition principles and norms, in *Laval* the right to strike was considered to be amenable to judicial scrutiny. In the view of the Court, the supranational right to strike can only hold as far as it can overcome balancing qua proportionality when conflicting with any of the economic freedoms.[28] From the national definition of the rights to collective bargaining and to strike not being open to be challenged even if in conflict with supranational constitutional standards, as, arguably, per *Albany*,[29] and from Member States enjoying a 'margin of appreciation', as per *Schmidberger*,[30] when solving conflicts between national fundamental rights and economic freedoms, the lawfulness of collective actions and strikes is now made dependent on their being consistent with European law. European law becomes in the process a tool with which trade unions, far from being protected, are disciplined. This is so because the 'proportionality test' of European constitutionality is manifestly biased against the right to collective action and the right to strike for two related reasons.[31]

First, the proportionality test, as now defined by the CJEU, places an almost insurmountable argumentative burden on trade unions. Once the exercise of collective rights creates obstacles to the exercise of economic freedoms, there is little actual chance of showing that collective rights should nonetheless be upheld. In *Laval*, the CJEU did not actually engage in any form of weighing and balancing whatsoever. Collective action by the unions, the CJEU stated, could not be justified

[24] C Barnard, '*Viking* and *Laval*: An Introduction' (2007) 10 *Cambridge Yearbook of European Law* 463, especially 470: 'Many trade unionists would argue that this misses the point: collective bargaining cannot exist without at least the threat of collective action. Trade unions need the possibility of calling their members out on strike to give themselves equality of arms with employers'. Barnard claims that the Court appears to acknowledge this point at para 36 of *Viking*.

[25] As the Court holds, remarkably, in *Laval* (n 10) para 90.

[26] ibid para 88; Barnard (n 24) 467.

[27] With respect to *Viking* (n 10) para 65, Barnard (n 24) notices (469–70) that 'while the Court is prepared to protect collective bargaining – and the resulting collective agreements – from the scope of Community law, it will not protect collective action in the same way'.

[28] *cf Viking* (n 10) para 44; Barnard (n 24) 468.

[29] Case C-67/96 *Albany International BV v Stichting Bedrijfspensioenfonds Textielindustrie* [1999] ECR I-05751. See B Bercusson, 'The Trade Union Movement and the European Union: Judgment Day' (2007) 13 *European Law Journal* 279; Barnard (n 24).

[30] Case C-112/00 *Eugen Schmidberger, Internationale Transporte und Planzüge v Republik Österreich* Judgment of the Court of 12 June 2003.

[31] Contrast its treatment in ibid: see S Weatherill, 'Viking Line and Laval: The EU Internal Market Perspective' in J Prassl and M Freedland (eds), *EU Law in the Member States: Viking, Laval, and Beyond* (Oxford, Hart Publishing, 2014) 23–40 (discussing the balancing exercise of the CJEU).

once the unions demanded compliance with rules and standards which were not mentioned in the Directive on Posted Workers. The CJEU added that the claims of the unions were not enshrined in 'provisions of any kind which are sufficiently precise and accessible'. The fact that their claims corresponded to the content of national collective agreements made them insufficiently 'transparent', so it was too much to ask the employer to abide by them.[32] In *Viking*, the CJEU went so far as to claim that collective actions creating obstacles to the exercise of economic freedoms could only be justified in extreme circumstances,[33] 'where jobs or conditions of employment were jeopardized or under serious threat'.[34]

Only in such exceptional circumstances does the right to strike (*Viking*) or the right to collective action (*Laval*) stand a chance.[35]

Second, the fact that proportionality is being applied to unions is, as such, irreversibly damaging of the unions' position. This is so because the specific breed of proportionality that the Court applies cannot but detract from the right to collective action. To quote from one acute comment on the case: 'industrial action is intended to cause sufficient disruption to extract concessions from an employer … to require unions to use means which are the "least restrictive of free movement" is, in such a context, rather curious'.[36] The greater the effectiveness of the strike, the harder it is to justify it under the CJEU's new understanding of proportionality, because the effectiveness stems from the restriction of the free movement rights of the employer.[37] Ultimately, despite being given the status of 'fundamental right', the right to strike is conceptualised as an obstacle to free movement rights as opposed to being acknowledged as belonging to the political and constitutional realm of the exercise of 'collective autonomy' in the deep sense of it being 'an original power of self-determination and production of rules', in the words of Silvana Sciarra.[38]

I will now explain how a transformed EU constitutional law – heteronomous, no longer autonomic in the sense of the jurisprudence of constitutional autonomy insofar as it has been reconstitutionalised through absorption in the ways just

[32] *Laval* (n 10) paras 108 and 110; Barnard (n 24) 484.

[33] *Viking* (n 10) para 83; Barnard (n 24) 486.

[34] For a full discussion, see Barnard (n 24) 479.

[35] *Laval* (n 10) para 10.

[36] T Novitz, 'A Human Rights Analysis of the Viking and Laval Judgments' (2007) 10 *Cambridge Yearbook of European Legal Studies* 541.

[37] A Davies, 'One Step Forward, Two Steps Back? The *Viking* and *Laval* Cases in the ECJ' (2008) 37 *Industrial Law Journal* 126, 143.

[38] On 'collective autonomy' as a key aspect of the social grammar of labour law from a historical and comparative perspective as 'original', see S Sciarra, '*Viking* and *Laval*: Collective Labour Rights and Market Freedoms in the Enlarged EU' (2007–08) 10 *Cambridge Yearbook of European Legal Studies* 563, 577–78. Sciarra emphasises that 'The Court ignores the fact that collective autonomy is vested with an original power of self-determination and production of rules' in the context of an analysis that denounces the 'limits in the grammar of social rights taken by the ECJ'. The argument about collective autonomy falls entirely within the paradigm of what I have called jurisprudence of constitutional autonomy insofar as referring to the autonomy of unions as self-determining units in the context of national realms whose laws are respected through the architecture of the interpretative obligation, understanding the interpretative obligation as hermeneutical openness towards the national realms' variety of voices qua interpretative patterns regarding the law: see ch 2 above.

described – comes to recognise (*carte blanche*) the autarkic self-normativisation of a constructed (post-state) private order, which, in turn, consists of what one might call privatistic balancing (a balancing that pertains only to privatistic determinations).[39]

III. Absorption as New Constitutionalisation of Orders

Constitutional absorption is not just about incorporating and protecting certain privatistic freedom rights against state law, as considered in section II; deep down, it is also an *inter-orderly* phenomenon of constitutional absorption. In singling out and protecting a range of privatistic rights independently of (and, indeed, against the dictates of) state law, the CJEU is far from a solitary actor. The Court takes a position that participates in the wider transnational legal consciousness whereby a private order would stand alone and generate its own 'normativity' independently of, and against the dictates of, state law. The Court is effectively constitutionalising (absorption) such private ordering. Below I argue that the Court is incorporating (absorption) a range of 'extra-orderly' (insofar as they are neither infra-EU order nor infra-state order) determinations of private parties – determinations that are assumed to be operating autonomously in the context of an autarkic private order (new constitutionalisation as inter-orderly).

The remainder of this section is organised as follows: first, I explain what I mean respectively by private ordering (subsection A(i)) and by new constitutionalisation through absorption of private ordering (subsection A(ii)), before then illustrating the new constitutionalisation thesis with three major exempla of privatistic praxis (*lex mercatoria*, *Kautelarpraxis* and techne) (subsection B).

A. Constitutionalising Private Ordering

(i) Private Ordering

Below a hermeneutics is recounted that consists of a 'transnational' privatistic praxis made out of usages and of contracting. The insiders choose to associate this

[39] 'Autarkic' is about stressing the perceived and pretended (in the literature that I will consider in the rest of this chapter: see *Rechtsordnung*), as a result of transnationalisation, 'originality' of private ordering in juridical terms as opposed to the composite structure of EU constitutional law and of national constitutional laws as ruling upon private law (rather than being ruled by it). And yet, as I argue in ch 5, one must note that the private order correlates to, and is a reflection of, certain decisions made from within the constitutional order, that is, the 'private order' self-constitutes itself because of the 'recognition' of the constitutional order – with a consequential 'taking over effect', given that internal constitutional requirements subside whilst private ordering ends up occupying the field. This should contribute to the quarrel over whether private ordering as *lex mercatoria* is a myth or 'real' – whether it has existed historically or not, whether it is imagined today or based on history and what this might mean (referred to through the argument from a middle-age *lex mercatoria*: for the debate, see P Zumbansen, 'Transnational Law, With and Beyond Jessup' (2020) TLI Think! Paper 23/2020).

hermeneutics with a constructed self-standing and self-regulating, and, I argue, 'self-balancing' private order. This is a trait of certain strands of 'transnational law' literature – a literature autonomus from, and yet intertwined with, European Private Law scholarship[40] – that this Part unearths through singling out three key 'transnational law' areas, that is, *lex mercatoria*, *Kautelarpraxis* and techne.

What is meant by the coextensive characterisation of a self-standing, self-regulating and 'self-balancing' private order can be split into three aspects.

First, a privatistic market order praxis is portrayed in contemporary 'transnational law' literature as key to a 'new law', 'beyond the state' (transnational, self-standing, self-regulating). It is a practice recounted and praised by the 'advocates of private ordering'.[41] In the words of one author:

> Advocates of private ordering have fallen in love with the Middle Ages. Scholars in fields ranging from domestic and international sales law, cyber law, law and economics, sports law, and aviation law, as well as judges and casebook authors have made the medieval law merchant into the archetypal sophisticated legal system that private groups can create when not impeded by the intermeddling of the state.

Second, strands of this transnational law literature, if looked at through the hermeneutical framework adopted in this book, have given rise to the complex phenomenon of 'alienation' of the traditional hermeneutics of private law. It is a phenomenon that one must label as 'alienation' as it consists of what I have referred to above as arguments from economic convenience – arguments that make 'economic' sense only. These arguments are, in the self-constructed discourse of (and about) private actors,[42] entirely about the legitimation (as internal discourse)

[40] See ch 3, s III on intertwining of scholarly and judicial discoursive patterns. On transnational law, see below. Note G Teubner, 'The Constitution of Non-monetary Surplus Value' [2020] *Social and Legal Theory* 1: 'SC turns against the claim that constitutions are bound exclusively to the nation-state. In its critique of methodological statism, SC sheds light on processes of global constitutionalisation, identifying constitutional phenomena in transnational regimes both in the public and in the private sector'; G Teubner, 'Societal Constitutionalism: Alternatives to State-Centred Constitutional Theory?' in C Joerges, I-J Sand and G Teubner (eds), *Transnational Governance and Constitutionalism* (Oxford, Hart Publishing, 2004) 3–28. On transnational law and European private law as 'trespassing', see below at *Lex Mercatoria*. Transnational law cannot be reduced to what certain, mainstream strands of private law thinking understands by it (as *lex mercatoria*): see, eg the alternative views contained in PC Jessup, *Transnational Law* (New Haven, CT, Yale University Press, 1956); C Joerges and J Falke (eds), *Karl Polanyi, Globalisation and the Potential of Law in Transnational Markets* (Oxford, Hart Publishing, 2011); HP Glenn, *The Cosmopolitan State* (Oxford, Oxford University Press, 2013); H Dedek (ed), *Cosmopolitan Jurisprudence Essays in Memory of H Patrick Glenn* (Cambridge, Cambridge University Press, 2021); H Muir Watt, 'Private International Law Beyond the Schism' (2011) 2 *Transnational Legal Theory* 347; Zumbansen (n 39).

[41] See eg E Kadens, 'The Myth of the Customary Law Merchant' (2012) 90 *Texas Law Review* 1153, 1153, criticising the recourse to the Middle Ages for justifying their arguments with this much cited statement (see also this quotation in Zumbansen (n 39)).

[42] In the sense that the jurists (transnational law scholarship, orthodoxy), in constructing the notions that I am about to discuss (juridification of facts), contribute to the formation of arguments from economised balancing/privatistic balancing: the convergence and mutual reinforcement between the 'inside' EPL discourse (see ch 3 above) and the 'international' private law discourse (transnational law) is evident (see, eg in the rest of the chapter the interface between European private law and *lex mercatoria*;

of the product of the selfish interests of the strongest party (eg through imposing their preferred standard form contracts) and, it should be stressed, are not at all 'juridical' in the sense of embodying any kind of 'law' – if 'law' is understood as orientated towards social principles, with social principles restraining property rights in the name of the public interest. In the view of these strands of transnational law discourse, market actors aim at the law's *recognition* of realms that are completely detached from the concrete public interest requirements of the affected concrete communities.[43] They are self-regulating 'business regulatory realms', in which market actors can do (post-hermeneutically)[44] as they wish, given that the law becomes a vocabulary reduced only to doing the minimal job of private power's enablement. These scholars even conceptualise private ordering as a *Rechtsordnung*, that is, as a legal (constitutional) order,[45] rather than related to, and as subjected to, (national) constitutional orders, entailing what might be called the great decoupling of private ordering from the state constitutional order.[46]

Third, the transnational juridical hermeneutics at bottom consists of juridifying 'facts' which, as I argue in the remainder of this chapter, in turn are the product of privatistic balancing (self-balancing). Whilst it is commonplace to argue that it is the special gift of the common law to undertake this role,[47] I am arguing here

see also H-W Micklitz, 'The Transformation of Private Law through Competition' (2016) 22 *European Law Journal* 627); on legitimation aspects regarding arguments from economised balancing in relation to EU law, see above at 'recognition'. Note alternative strands of transnational law scholarship, including those critical of scholarship on *lex mercatoria*, eg D Caruso, 'Non-Parties: The Negative Externalities of Regional Trade Agreements in a Private Law Perspective' (2018) 59(2) *Harvard International Law Journal* 389; see also n 39 above.

[43] This is by no means limited to the private law realms, but it is also related to the broader field of trade law. On private law and trade law, see the critical analysis of Caruso, 'Non-Parties' (n 42).

[44] In the sense of the negative process that I label 'trans-juridification': see below at n 102 (a law that, the moment it operates by shaping the world, negates law as 'juridical hermeneutical' material).

[45] See below at subsection B (*lex mercatoria*).

[46] On the one hand, I refer to the state constitutional order as it recognises the protection of property rights as constitutional liberties belonging to, and as subjected to (national), constitutional orders; on the other hand, one sees the current transformation, which sees private property rights implemented as private order unbound (rather than limited by constitutional law) and as even alternative to the constitutional order of the state (and of the EU understood as composite order, see above), given its being portrayed as *Rechtsordnung*.

[47] See the recent treatment of this position in M Reimann, 'The American Advantage in Global Lawyering' (2014) 78 *Rabels Zeitschrift* 1–36 (on the 'gift' of the American common law in terms of global lawyering); M Reimann, 'The European Advantage in Global Lawyering' (2018) 82 *Rabels Zeitschrift* 885. Here I am arguing that the (European) civil law mode of 'lawyering' seems to be corresponding less to Reimann's account of it (as non-business like: see below at n 114) given, inter alia, the structural transformation that the civil law discourse is undertaking as discussed in this book. Note multiple references to a 'global legal order' (ibid 892). Note F Gomez and J-J Ganuza, 'The Economics of Private Law Harmonised Law-making: Mechanisms, Modes and Standards' in R Brownsword, H Micklitz, L Niglia and S Weatherill (eds), *The Foundations of European Private Law* (Oxford, Hart Publishing, 2011) 115, 129: 'We personally, as many others, even within law and economics, remain strongly unconvinced about the broad statement that the common law is overall efficient as a set of legal rules (as we would also be unwilling to accept a similar claim over any other legal order at so broad and general a level of stating the proposition) … We are also equally unconvinced by the literature, of empirical bent, trying to show the superior economic performance of societies that possess a legal system of common law origin, with respect to those originating in the civil law tradition.'

that also the civil law presents itself as 'gifted' in this sense, insofar as it is transformed in the ways that I recount below.[48]

This triad of 'new' discoursive ways of the law can be mapped as happening in various areas at once. They point to the radical phenomenon of the traditional juridical hermeneutics of social balancing that becomes a sham. Its implosion leaves room for an empty exercise (emptied of the social meaning as reconstructed in chapter two) of the law being reduced to the administering of so-called 'facts' understood to be self-governing realms (the oxymoron of 'privatistic balancing')[49] in the presence of which the jurist gives up their conventional job as considered in chapter two above.[50] According to the transnational discourse, there are private subjects that have been creating 'their own' order 'transnationally',[51] as opposed to acting within and through the state constitutional order.[52]

(ii) A Constitutionalisation by Absorption of Private Ordering

It is submitted, with the three case studies that follow, that the CJEU participates in this transnational hermeneutics insofar as various of its judgments concerning the three areas articulate an understanding of law that echoes the construction of an imagined self-standing, self-regulating and self-balancing private order – assuming that 'out there are private parties' determinations with a juridical relevance of their own, that is, independently of state law and against any state-constitutional law determinations.[53] Instead of looking at these judgments as (just)

[48] See also Niglia, *The Transformation* (n 16); Niglia, *The Struggle for European Private Law* (n 1).

[49] 'Privatistic balancing' is an oxymoron, considering that balancing as conventionally understood (prior to the changes recounted in this book) is at odd with its 'privatisation' (see ch 3 above; Niglia, *The Transformation* (n 16); Niglia, *The Struggle for European Private Law* (n 1)). Yet, balancing re-emerges in a new way, estranged as a result of the juridification process entailed in private bodies held to be designing, autarkically, entire sets of 'relationships'.

[50] See ch 2 above.

[51] Note Kadens (n 41): 'the archetypal sophisticated legal system that private groups can create when not impeded by the intermeddling of the state'. See also G Teubner, *Constitutional Fragments. Societal Constitutionalism and Globalization* (Oxford, Oxford University Press, 2012). Note and compare the following critical definition of *lex mercatoria* by M Bussani,'Deglobalizing Rule of Law and Democracy: Hunting Down Rhetoric Through Comparative Law (December 1, 2019)' (2019) 67 *American Journal of Comparative Law* 701, 706–07: 'One may appreciate how processes of legal uniformization can take place without any driving force external to the concerned legal actors. These processes can be carried out through the spontaneous acceptance of the same body of rules by different groups of law users able to effectively enforce widespread, transnational compliance, with no imposition from above or outside. *Lex mercatoria*, the rules controlling the transnational diamond trade, as well as much of transnational financial law, are good examples in this respect.'

[52] See also N Walker, *Intimations of Global Law* (Cambridge, Cambridge University Press, 2015) (expanding on the relevant actors). The three case studies are exemplary cases insofar as they demonstrate the key thesis being advanced in this chapter. On the financial-political economic regimes, see ch 5 below.

[53] Compare the *Van Gend* (Case 26/62 *Van Gend en Loos* [1963] ECR 1) decision (individuals held to enjoy rights independently of state legislation) with the *Freiburger* (Case C-237/02 *Freiburger Kommunalbauten GmbH Baugesellschaft and Co KG v Ludger Hofstetter and Ulrike Hofstetter* [2004] ECR I-3403) and *Laval* (Case C-341/05 *Laval un Partneri Ltd v Svenska Byggnadsarbetareförbundet* ECLI:EU:C:2007:809) judgments as discussed in the rest of the chapter.

standard EU law cases,[54] this subsection looks at them comparatively as participating in, and sharing, that transnational hermeneutics – as comparative hermeneutical analysis of EU constitutional law, as articulated in the respective judgments of the CJEU in the three areas.

The constitutional side considered above, in section II, and the private ordering side that I discuss in this section, share this common hermeneutical ground of private ordering that needs to be unearthed. Below, I propose a reverse reading of a range of remarkable judgments of the CJEU. One can read them not only as the product of internal constitutional hermeneutics, that is, of the EU constitutional order, as considered in section II; one can and must also read them by taking the alternative route of the transnational discourse regarding the private order, so that then one can return to a re-reading of the CJEU decisions seen as incorporating, and as related to, that transnational discourse. I argue that, adopting economised balancing – that is, narrowing balancing to economised factors as opposed to including non-market normative considerations[55] – is the technique that the Court selectively chooses with a view to protecting the noted range of privatistic rights against the domain of, and the normative dictates of, state law (social balancing). On closer inspection, it can be seen that it is the dictates of privatistic praxis that get to be absorbed into economised balancing and as a result are protected. These are determinations that we can call 'privatistic balancing', in that the Court chooses to articulate balancing in the sense of absorbing and validating the 'balancing' that emerges from – or, rather, that is hermeneutically constructed as emerging from – the self-constructed privatistic praxis of balancing (private ordering as a *Rechtsordnung*).[56] What amounts to a constitutionalisation of rights process, as considered in section II, can be, and in my view must be, equally constructed as a constitutionalising jurisprudence both adhering to and internalising (by absorption) the transnational private ordering hermeneutics, that is, the hermeneutics concerning a privatistic praxis associated with the constructed private order as self-standing, self-regulating and self-balancing. At this conjuncture, the privatistic order's determinations praxis becomes constitutionalised.

Below, I map the ways in which the Court is effectively validating privatistic balancing through siding with the 'contractual' and the 'factual' balancing determinations of private actors. As the CJEU erases the hermeneutics of social balancing (state law), it draws upon this emerging transnational hermeneutics of private ordering thought of as privatistic balancing praxis – incorporating

[54] See above. The conventional treatment of the judgments of the CJEU under scrutiny in this book is blind to the transformational aspects concerning it as I unveil them in this book. I am conscious that my own treatment of them in section II concerns comparative constitutional (and private law) aspects, yet it goes further than conventional EU law scholarship, anticipating the analysis of section III. This new approach to the understanding of the CJEU decisions concretises the comparative hermeneutical methodology adopted in this book (see ch 1 above).

[55] See ch 3 above.

[56] See section B.

privatistic balancing praxis at the same time that this praxis is constructed as jurisgenerative and as *constitutionally* jurisgenerative. To put it otherwise: as the new jurisprudence forecloses the state hermeneutics of private law, at the same time it opens up to the transnational hermeneutics of the private order conceptualised as post-state, and no longer coupled with the state and its normative dictates. An exploration of three worlds of privatistic praxis allows a rereading of the CJEU case law in the light of this framework of analysis: as I argue in the remainder of this chapter, the CJEU has been constructing a hermeneutics that totalises private (non-state) order by making 'privatistic balancing' an absolute.

This kind of private ordering hermeneutics emerges both in the analysis of each of the three modes of constitutional absorption and in a reading of them in parallel. In other words, not just market order (economised balancing; see section II) but private ordering as juridical hermeneutics construction characterises the jurisprudence of the CJEU and the surrounding material that makes it intelligible.

I will now consider the three case studies and their interface with the jurisprudence of the CJEU.[57]

B. The Three Modes of Constitutional Absorption (Constitutionalisation of Orders)

(i) Lex Mercatoria

(a) *Lex Mercatoria*

In an extensive literature regarding private law matters seen as 'transnational',[58] one must single out the argument whereby certain phenomena, from *usages* to *contractual practices*, would as such enjoy the character of being 'legal', that is, they would attain 'the force of law'. This is what one can label by coining the oxymoron, 'juridification of facts'. According to the propounders of this opinion, the law only

[57] The new jurisprudence under scrutiny in this book has been happening despite, and against the grain of, the Constitutional Courts' stance towards attempting to limit the encroachment of EU law upon national legal systems by placing outer constitutional limits on the jurisdictional expansion of the EU, as in the BverfG's *Maastricht* and *Lisbon* judgments (above), and in the Corte Costituzionale's *Taricco* judgment (above).

[58] On transnational law, see, in a vast literature, the seminal work by PC Jessup, *Transnational Law* (New Haven, CT, Yale University Press, 1956); in the 1970s, W Friedmann, L Henkin and O Lissitzyn (eds), *Transnational Law in a Changing Society. Essays in Honor of Philip C Jessup* (New York, Columbia University Press, 1972); recently, P Zumbansen (ed), *The Many Lives of Transnational Law. Critical Engagements with Jessup's Bold Proposal* (Cambridge, Cambridge University Press, 2020); MB Likosky (ed), *Privatising Development. Transnational Law, Infrastructure and Human Rights* (The Hague, Brill, 2005); G-P Calliess (ed), *Transnationales Recht* (Tübingen, Siebeck Mohr, 2018); MW Reimann, JC Hathaway, TL Dickinson and JH Samuels, *Transnational Law. Cases and Materials* (St Paul, MN, West, 2013); AC Cutler, 'The Judicialization of Private Transnational Power and Authority' (2018) 25 *Indiana Journal of Global Legal Studies* 61.

plays the minimum role of 'registering' such mechanics believed to be 'out there' (mechanical juridification).

In the remainder of this section I argue instead that underlying this position is a 'hermeneutical' juridification through legitimating what is configured as mere 'facts' as embodying the force of law.[59] It is a development commented upon, and typically presented, as if it were a normal pattern in the history of private law, always existing from premodern times to today and now manifesting itself once more – so the argument goes, in authoritative legal historical literature.[60] The most notable area in which such a position – whereby usages and contractual practices get juridified per se through attaining the force of law – is being proposed is that of international-transnational contracts and *lex mercatoria*.[61] In turn, such juridification is, according to the propounders of this thesis, about *Rechtsordnung*. Let me discuss each argument in turn: juridification (of usages) and *Rechtsordnung*.

Juridification

Transnational contracting and *lex mercatoria* is an area in the context of which one court has made a statement that is representative of the current state of the law, that is:[62] 'commercial practice attains the force of law'.

This is at odds with conventional (national) private law, which recognises both the limited and the conditional relevance of customs (only validly relied upon insofar as referred to by legislation) and, in traditional vocabulary, the state monopoly of legal sources, including contracts having 'the force of law' in the sense of binding the parties under national law, as in the Code Napoleon. Here, the claim put forward is that (commercial) practice 'attains the force of law' among all of the transnational actors in the relevant market sectors, and not just among the contractual parties, that is, as privately generated material of general application across entire market sectors. This is a belief that is central to what the insiders to the field call 'transnational law'.[63]

[59] See below quotation from the US decision of *St Paul Guardian Ins, Co v Neuromed Medical Sys & Support GmbH, 2002* WL 465312, SDNY (26 March 2002).

[60] For a critical analysis of this belief, see Kadens (n 41); R Michaels, 'Legal Medievalism in Lex Mercatoria Scholarship' (2012) 90 *Texas Law Review* 259; R Michaels, 'The True Lex Mercatoria: Private Law Beyond the State' (2007) 14 *Indiana Journal of Global Legal Studies* 448.

[61] See n 58 above.

[62] See the US decision of *St Paul Guardian Ins* (n 59), as quoted in P Hellwege, 'Understanding Usage in International Contract Law Harmonization' (2018) 66 *American Journal of Comparative Law* 127. Contrast Art 1134 of the Code Napoleon (in force from 17 February 1804 until 1 February 2016): 'Les conventions légalement formées tiennent lieu de loi à ceux qui les ont faites. Elles ne peuvent être révoquées que de leur consentement mutuel, ou pour les causes que la loi autorise. Elles doivent être exécutées de bonne foi.' See now, for the persistence of the notion, Art 1103 of the French Code Civil (in force starting from 1 October 2016: see Ordonnance n 2016-131 of 10 February 2016, Art 2): 'Les contrats légalement formés tiennent lieu de loi à ceux qui les ont faits.' Note that EU directives impact upon this dogma by turning contracts in the direction of marketisation and of functionalisation: see Niglia, *The Transformation* (n 16); Niglia, *The Struggle for European Private Law* (n 1).

[63] See Jessup (n 58).

In international commerce, the belief in the relevance of usages as binding is commonplace as it is equally the argument that usages have legal force.[64] Scholars typically mention the Unidroit Principles of International Commercial Law (PICL – Unidroit Principles) as evidence of their claim. Their presentation of the topic is typically apodictic and, in the view of the propounders of this position, far from leaving any room for any uncertainty as to the legal standing of usages – which explains the almost automatic reference to the PICL (Unidroit Principles) in commentaries on international commerce as a way in which the commentators make their claim. The claim is one and the same thing as the argument regarding the 'harmonisation' of 'international contract law'. Here, notably, usages are relevant in matters of interpretation: Article 4.3(f) PICL (Unidroit Principles) states that, as far as interpretation is concerned: 'regard shall be had to all the circumstances, including: … (f) usages').

'Usages' are also binding on the parties: Article 1.9(2) PICL (Unidroit Principles) states that: 'The parties are bound by a usage that is *widely known* to and *regularly observed in international trade by parties in the particular trade* concerned *except where the application of such a usage would be unreasonable*' (emphasis added).[65]

Two opinions have been advanced in relation to the meaning and scope of usages, labelled the 'contractual' and the 'normative'.[66]

According to the contractual opinion, usages derive their binding force only from, and as a result of, the agreement. In contrast, the normative opinion holds that usages are applicable as binding upon the parties independently of the 'volition of the parties'.[67] Whilst here 'normative' only means bindingness, with no connotation of value-based argumentation, this long-term dispute in international commercial law only confirms the standing of usages as a major, prestigious source of law if, as is the case, they can get as far as acquiring a normative force even against the 'volition of the parties'.

At a further stage of analysis, one must note the role of the requirement of 'reasonableness' as of importance for understanding the relevance of the notion of usages as deployed in the above-noted texts. It is not by chance that such a general clause ('reasonableness') appears in international texts on contract law – it comes from, and is interrelated with, the tradition of private law and, more precisely, the hermeneutics of social balancing that is potentially available for limiting and countering the doings of market processes.

Yet, there emerges another shift away from conventional law that is crucial for the argument here being proposed: that is, the interpretation of reasonableness has given rise to a contested debate. Some authors[68] criticise the use of reasonableness, since in their view a normative understanding of usages makes any such

[64] See Hellwege (n 62) 127–28.
[65] ibid.
[66] ibid.
[67] ibid 131.
[68] See discussion in ibid 158.

interpretation obsolete – they argue that the binding nature of a norm means that it is as such reasonable, due to it being a 'norm'. Instead, and by contrast, others are open towards using reasonableness as a test for the credibility of usages, arguing that:

> In essence, the normative understanding of usage assigns to the relevant actors in a given sector the power to create binding rules through practice. It should be the binding rule as such that should pass a reasonableness test, not its application.[69]

Note how here practices become almost synonymous with binding rules and how, in order to strengthen this view, even reasonableness as a notion that might in principle lead to some limitation of this position is simply reduced to a sham when instead it should be the tool for protecting the collective's public interest. This is a consideration that descends from understanding reasonableness in the light of, and in relation to, the paradigm of conventional (social) balancing, as this is true both of the civil law and of the common law – as I have argued elsewhere, before the recent transformations under scrutiny in this book.[70] But once *lex mercatoria* scholars reduce the conventional meaning of 'reasonableness' to a sham, then evidently the privatistic practices must become (or pretend to be) 'self-legitimating', that is, far away from, and against the grain of, legitimation proper. For no private law-based reasonableness review, in the light of the public interest, will be exercised or will even be conceivable – that is, the conventional view of reasonableness in private law across the civil law and the common law is left behind in these strands of *lex mercatoria* writings.[71]

This is the real meaning of practices that are held to 'attain the role of law' as in the extract from the judgment quoted above – that law itself is represented as if it were somehow innocuous and neutral, rather than always open to contestation in each context,[72] and as if no longer concerned with exercising any public interest control over the practices themselves.

***

The position of usages as binding upon the parties and kept as far as possible away from the application of a reasonableness test, as conventionally understood, is one that has been trespassing into the wider European private law arena. After all, European private law has never been an autonomous and self-standing arena, but is deeply related to the debates on the harmonisation of (international) commercial law. This is due to the argument whereby the two areas of *lex mercatoria* and of European private law are seen as sharing common ground – in the internal market,

[69] ibid.

[70] I refer the reader to Niglia, *The Transformation* (n 16) for further discussion on reasonableness and good faith. On civil law and common law, see n 114 below (on Reimann's work).

[71] See Niglia, *The Transformation* (n 16).

[72] Contrast to the transnational law orthodoxy the criticism of Caruso (n 42).

whenever contracts trespass national boundaries. In this view, a 'consumer' is no longer just different from a business insofar as both engage with informed choices and are, and should be, treated as 'sovereign market actors'.[73] In other words, under this economic-law logic, by 'commercial' in EPL one may mean also 'private law', and vice versa. Here, the conventional distinction civil law/commercial law is put into question. The new narrative of economisation through economised balancing, such as was considered in the previous chapter, has been gaining ground and prestige, as opposed to remaining hidden under the cover of renditions that present EPL as if it were just about 'private law' or 'civil law' as strictly understood.[74] This logic is obviously far from objectively intelligible and tenable, as it tends to be portrayed by many of the insiders to EPL, but is part and parcel of the tensions, conflicts and struggles that this book and its companion volumes recount.[75]

The relevant texts need to be made intelligible in this light.

Article 1.9(2) PICL (Unidroit Principles), in the area of international contract law harmonisation, can be compared to Articles 1:105(2) of the Principles of European Contract Law (PECL) 11 and II. – 1:104(2) of the Draft Common Frame of Reference (DCFR), which deviate from Article 1.9(2) in minor points only: 'The parties are bound by a usage which would be considered generally applicable by persons in the same situation as the parties, except where the application of such usage would be unreasonable.'

The PECL and the DCFR still require that the application of the usage not be unreasonable. Yet, instead of the requirements that the usage be widely known and regularly observed, they only require that the usage be considered generally applicable by persons in the same situation as the parties.

Anything that falls under the notion of 'usage' is binding upon the parties according to two major texts of EPL common rules: that is, Articles 1:105(2) PECL and II. – 1:104(2) DCFR. This turns upside down the conventional hierarchies of laws in civil law settings, given the centrality of usages as opposed to their conventional subordinate status. This new status of usages entails that the parties are bound by practices in the relevant sectors, including competitive (or even non-competitive) market structures. It seems that here a normative view prevails whereby such bindingness applies to the parties regardingless of their wishes – in the sense that the parties to a standardised insurance contract would be bound by the prevailing practices in the sector without being able to alter them; this is particularly conforming with the competitive view of contracting that is at the core of the DCFR,[76] since in this view it will be competitive structures that determine how contract content is differentiated for consumers/customers' preferences.

[73] For this theoretical position, see H Micklitz, 'The Expulsion of the Concept of Protection from the Consumer Law and the Return of the Social Elements in the Civil Law: A Bittersweet Polemic' (European University Institute, 2012) EUI Working Papers 2012/03.

[74] ibid.

[75] On conflicts, see Niglia, *The Transformation* (n 16). On struggles as interpretative, see Niglia, *The Struggle for European Private Law* (n 1).

[76] See ch 3 above.

This is no less true when considering the provision contained in Articles 1:105(2) PECL and II. – 1:104(2) DCFR that usages are binding except where the application of such usage would be 'unreasonable'. This mirrors the above-noted dispute over the meaning of reasonableness: for example, an author[77] defends the view that usages enjoy 'a normative force',[78] yet with the qualification that Articles 1.9(2) PICL, 1:105(2) PECL and II. – 1:104(2) DCFR all state that the parties are bound by a usage 'except where the *application* of such usage would be unreasonable' (emphasis added).

Reasonableness, in turn, emerges as a central notion in the DCFR and it incorporates economised balancing considerations.[79]

***

Importantly, the above considerations (regarding both European Union law and European private law) also apply to national private laws. Here, one notes the shift towards expanding the scope of usages so as to make them normatively binding upon the contractual parties. At the same time, one must note the display of arguments against such normativity and the defence of a contractual view that is, deep down, about preserving the system of civil law and its social character from any such changes, that is, about resisting any attempt at replacing and setting aside the conventional set of intersubjective norms that incorporate the balancing of public interest normative considerations.[80] This is about resisting the turn towards the juridification of usages. In my view, these tensions emerge in two contexts: first is the defence of traditional law by an authoritative German private law scholar, Claus-Wilhelm Canaris, who argues that, as quoted in Hellwege's work:[81]

> The normative theory dominates the literature and case law, but it is not uncontested. One of the leading private lawyers, Claus-Wilhelm Canaris, writes in his textbook on

[77] Hellwege (n 62) 157–59.

[78] ibid 158.

[79] See L Niglia, 'The Question Concerning the Common Frame of Reference' (2012) 18 *European Law Journal* 736: 'not every "principle" matters to the (D)CFR, only a selected few. Principled reasoning is aimed at restructuring interpretation along the lines of the four "underlying principles" contained in the latest version of the DCFR, that is, freedom, security, justice and efficiency. An ideological matrix lurks behind the chosen four principles, for two reasons … the DCFR has dropped 11 principles that were contained in the previous edition, some being key "social principles" such as protection of human rights, solidarity and social responsibility; protection of consumers and others in need of protection; preservation of cultural and linguistic plurality; protection of reasonable reliance; and the proper allocation of responsibility for the creation of risks.' In fact, note the key role of 'costs' in the DCFR: Art IV.C.2:105 DCFR (providing for the obligation on the service provider to 'perform the service with the case and skill which *a reasonable service provider would exercise under the circumstances*' and, at Art IV.C.2:105(4)(b), that 'in determining the care and skill the client is entitled to expect, regard is to be had, among other things, to … if damage has occurred, the costs of any precautions which would have prevented that damage or similar damage from occurring') where by 'circumstances' is meant the following: Art II.7:205(3)(b) ('In determining whether good faith and fair dealing required a party to disclose particular information, regard should be had to all the circumstances, *including … the cost to the party of acquiring the relevant information*' (emphasis added)).

[80] On 'maximal balancing', see ch 3 above.

[81] Quoted in Hellwege (n 62).

> German commercial law that: [U]sage in the meaning of section 157 BGB and section 346 HGB is not legally binding per se and on its own terms, but only through the contract which is interpreted with the help of, and supplemented by, usage. Consequently, usage does not affect the contract from outwith as a legal norm would do, but from within by becoming part of the contract by way of interpretation.

In other words, here usages matter in terms of 'interpretation' of the contract and not as a matter of an external imposition of norms, that is, as external imposition of market norms upon state norms – 'market norms' being an oxymoron yet not considered as such by the insiders to the *lex mercatoria* fabric. Here what is rejected in my view is the idea that usages must matter as such, that is, independently of the private law rules on interpretation (of contracts). It is through the latter that traditional private law maintains its role.

The second context in which these tensions emerge in judicial settings is one 2019 decision of the Italian Court of Cassation (Corte di Cassazione).[82] According to the Italian Court of Cassation, a contractual term that refers to an Incoterms (International Commercial Terms) clause (considered to be customary contractual clauses) on transfer of risk cannot be the basis for also inferring a willingness of the parties to indicate the place of delivery as the jurisdiction of a court. Therefore, Incoterms as usages are held to be relevant but are subject to the interpretation of the parties, an approach that recalls Claus-Wilhelm Canaris's above-noted position. This is because the matter is seen through the lens of the contractual (interpretative) theory and not of the normative theory – the contractual theory is felt to be preferable since it allows avoidance of the mechanical and passive implication of an application of Infoterms/*lex mercatoria* terms to individual contractual situations. In other words, here is a confirmation that it is the interpretation of the contract that should matter above all and, as a result of this, conventional balancing and its crystallised social standards are kept in place.

Juridification as *Rechtsordnung*

The juridification of 'facts',[83] such as usages and contractual practices, is not just about their becoming juridically relevant. No less important is that juridification involves usages and contractual practices being treated as if giving rise to what is labelled in legal circles *Rechtsordnung*. This is what some scholars argue in their reading of *lex mercatoria*, thereby making readily intelligible the massive literature

[82] See Sentenza Cassazione Civile n 17566 del 28_06_2019.

[83] Contrast and compare 'juridification' (*Verrechtlichung*) as contingently used in this book with its conventional understanding: see Teubner, 'The Constitution of Non-monetary Surplus Value' (n 40); G Teubner, *Juridification: Concepts, Aspects, Limits, Solutions in Juridification of Social Spheres: A Comparative Analysis of the Area of Labour, Corporate Anti-Trust and Social Welfare Law* (Boston, MA, Walter De Gruyter, 1987) ('juridification' as consistent with the social welfare-state *Rechtsordnung*); LC Blichner and A Molander, 'What Is Juridification?' (Arena, 2005) Working Paper 14/2005 (however, one thesis is about 'juridification' understood as legal domination, on which see the rest of the chapter). Note the notion of 'jurisdomination' in Niglia, 'The New Transformation of Europe' (n 12).

on the topic in the sense of spelling out the radical implications of the movement towards what one may call the 'factualisation' of hermeneutical material.

These scholars argue that[84] at work is a true *sozial-faktische Akzeptanz in der Praxis* (that is, a social-factual acceptance in the praxis) of the PICL (Unidroit Principles), which, in turn, works as the basis for the applicable law qua 'new merchant law' – together with the customary contract clauses of Incoterms and arbitration norms – held to give rise to a *Rechtsordnung*. In this view, the factual[85] development of *lex mercatoria* norms by itself legitimises them to the extent that the *lex mercatoria*, seen as entailing a *Rechtsordnung* (recognised as a *Rechtsordnung*), is far from just a purely academic concern; rather, it is deployed as a precondition for the parties to be able to deploy their freedom to conclude *lex mercatoria* contracts and to use the PICL (Unidroit Principles) as applicable law.

To translate this in the hermeneutical framework of analysis deployed in this book: the automatic, mechanical understanding of *lex mercatoria* practices as entailing a kind of 'social-factual acceptance' and the assimilation between such 'social-factual acceptance' of norms and considerations pertaining to their qualification as *Rechtsordnung* are two trajectories through which the social-constitutional hermeneutics of private law can no longer sustain itself and it is in fact threatened, and increasingly overcome by, *lex mercatoria* thinking.

I must now note that the CJEU jurisprudence under scrutiny in this book is an articulation of this deeper process. This is due to the Court's playing a primary role in it through its deployment of economised balancing as prioritised over, and as setting aside, the social-constitutional hermeneutical material, as I have recounted in chapter two. It is this intersection that then precipitates the crisis of the social-constitutional hermeneutics of private law – in the sense that privatistic balancing is not just an interpretative technique, but is hermeneutical material out of which an alternative (to constitutional orders) *Rechtsordnung* takes shape whilst taking on the inter-orderly effects that I recount in section III.[86]

[84] On *lex mercatoria*, see, eg A Metzger, *Extra legem intra ius: Allegemeine Rechtsgrundsaetze im Europaeischen Privatrecht* (Tübingen, Mohr Siebeck, 2009) 543–44. On *lex mercatoria* as *ordinamento* ('vero e proprio ed originario ordinamento giuridico, separato dagli ordinamenti statuali'), see F Galgano, '*Lex mercatoria*' in *Enciclopedia del diritto V* (Milan, 2001) 721; see also B Pastore, 'Pluralismi giuridici e trasformazioni del diritto contemporaneo' [2021] *Quaderni Fiorentini* 399, 407 (who, inter alia, refers to Galgano, yet argues that '*lex mercatoria* … trova riconoscimento nell'ambito interno, *quasi come una fonte autonoma* proveniente da un ordinamento separato' (emphasis added), in my view critically distinguishing (note the 'quasi come una fonte autonoma') Galgano's argument, which automatically associates *lex mercatoria* with order).

[85] 'Factual' in the sense of being contractual or usage or customary based (see, eg Hellwege (n 62)) and not just a naked fact; in other words, it is still a juristic construction that sees the private sphere autarkically rule by itself and undisturbed (apart from some extreme boundaries such as *ordre public*).

[86] Contrast and compare 'juridification' as consistent with the social welfare state *Rechtsordnung* (Teubner, 'The Constitution of Non-monetary Surplus Value' (n 40); Teubner, *Juridification* (n 83) as opposed to being alternative to the latter, as in my view is the case today. This consciousness of the factual as *Rechtsordnung* may not be present everywhere, yet it is implicit in the writings that celebrate the 'innovativeness' of 'factual law'.

(b) An Inter-orderly Constitutionalisation (Usages): *Lex Mercatoria* and the Court of Justice of the European Union

To return to the argument about the intersection between the CJEU jurisprudence under scrutiny and the hermeneutics of transnational private ordering: section II above offers material that stresses the fact that the CJEU aims at hermeneutically 'recognising' (Europeanising) the alternative privatistic *Rechtsordnung*, which consists of the hybrid 'usage-like norms'; moreover, it consists of a 'constitutionalisation of orders' and not just isolated rights as in the logic of a 'constitutionalisation of rights'.

That is, the CJEU judgment in *Freiburger* is about 'recognising', in the sense of giving constitutional relevance within the EU constitutional order, not only a written contractual practice, as I argue below about *Kautelarpraxis*, but also a wider market-originated *norm-practice* (resembling 'usages').[87] This norm-practice consists of the sellers' marketing strategy of offering combinations of goods and price contractual terms and/or of goods and non-price contractual terms according to calculations of convenience. These are calculations that the Court validates outright rather than subjecting them to a balancing assessment that would also take into account normative considerations other than ones that are market-based.

According to this approach taken by the CJEU, the private parties' determinations matter as such. The parties' down-to-earth economic calculations regarding advantages and disadvantages in the contractual event (privatistic balancing), as made in the private realm, are what matters to the Court regardless of any of the determinations descending from the state order, such as the above-noted arguments from equality of arms invoked by one party. In fact, the argument from equality of arms relating to the principle of the contemporaneous performance of the relevant contractual obligations, as raised by one party to the dispute, is simply set aside. Secondly, the Court does not explain why the lowering of the price of the goods combined with a harsher term deviating from the background private law norms should be validated (it being at odds with the wider parameters of 'maximum balancing' noted in the previous chapter). Nor does the Court delve into any of the details regarding which specific private law norms are being derogated. Rather, it only refers to the argument from the general principle of the civil law that the parties have put forward, with the result that it constructs an interpretation whereby a lower price will be capable of derogating any private law norms without any qualification regarding the latter's content.

Note that not even 'freedom of contract' is deployed by the CJEU in order to justify its position, as in the classical balancing exposition *à la Lockner*,[88] whereby

[87] Norm-practice understood as an oxymoron, as in the transnational law vocabulary considered in this chapter that subverts conventional conceptions about the dichotomy of norm versus fact (see J Habermas, *Between Facts and Norms: Contribution to a Discourse Theory of Law and Democracy* (W Rehg trs, Cambridge, MA, MIT Press, 1996); Niglia, *The Transformation* (n 16); Niglia, *The Struggle for European Private Law* (n 1)).

[88] *Lochner v New York*, 198 US 45 (1905).

freedom of contract is held to prevail over any of the relevant conflicting normative considerations.[89] From this vantage point, the Court deploys a much narrower grammar than Lochner-like decisions would, in an attempt to thus avoid any of the controversiality entailed in openly clinging on to the language of freedom of contract – and having to justify its position in relation to the associated arguments from limits to that freedom. Similarly to the above-considered area of *lex mercatoria* and to techne (digitisation), which I discuss below, one can see how the Court is straightforwardly implementing a 'hermeneutical recognition' of private order material (privatistic balancing) rather than acting out of the conventional, normatively complex and multilayered structure of constitutional balancing.

(ii) Kautelarpraxis

(a) *Kautelarpraxis*

By *Kautelarpraxis* is meant, inter alia, any precautionary activity by lawyers towards minimising any of the relevant contractual risks for their clients. *Kautelarpraxis* is a contingent transnational private law praxis[90] associated with general conditions of contracts – that is, contractual practices that consist of standardised terms as conjured up by lawyers acting as advisors of clients, terms then packaged as contractual drafts typically imposed by the party who draws them (typically the strongest party) upon the counterparty. The (usually weaker) counterparty will typically be the consumer, albeit not necessarily so – as, for example, in the many accounts that look at the contracting that takes place between, on the one hand, small or medium-sized enterprises and, on the other hand, large businesses.

In transnational law writings, these kinds of contractual practices are held to belong to a constructed private order, which, in turn, generates its own norms that are held to be binding as such, rather than scrutinised as to their substantive content in terms of conformity or otherwise with the public interest. To put it in the language proposed in this book, these contractual practices amount to balancing decisions made unilaterally and imposed on the counterparty.[91] Note that the

[89] 'Prevailing' in the sense that, in substantively taking a 'freedom of contract' position, the CJEU alters EU constitutional material (fundamental rights): see the rest of the chapter. On the structure of freedom of contract in Europe, see Niglia, *The Transformation* (n 16).

[90] On *Kautelarpraxis* in relation to general conditions of business, see W Wurmnest, 'Kautelarpraxis und Allgemeine Geschäftsbedingungen' (2018) 82 *Rabels Zeitschrift* 346; see also H Fleischer, 'Kautelarpraxis und Privatrecht: Grundfragen und gesellschaftsrechtliche Illustrationen' (2018) 82(2) *Rabels Zeitschrift* 239; J Vetter, 'Kautelarpraxis und M&A-Verträge' (2018) 82(2) *Rabels Zeitschrift* 267; M Wenckstern, 'Kautelarpraxis und Erbrecht' (2018) 82(2) *Rabels Zeitschrift* 299; CS Rupp, 'Gestaltungsspielraum für die Kautelarpraxis im Sachenrecht? – Beispiele aus dem Wohnungseigentumsrecht' (2018) 82(2) *Rabels Zeitschrift* 315. On *Kautelarpraxis* as bound, and subjected to, state law (Britain, France, Germany, Italy), see Niglia, *The Transformation* (n 16), which also provides a comparative explanation of what legal actors mean by 'general conditions of contract' and 'standardised terms'.

[91] On standardised contracting and balancing, see Niglia, *The Transformation* (n 16).

contemporary dominant grammar denies that this is about 'imposition'. However, looking at the sociolegal features of these contractual practices,[92] one can hardly deny this unilateral imposition.

Therefore, it is not only usages such as *lex mercatoria* that entail the practice of juridifying facts; it is also stardardised terms as they emerge from contractual praxis, and equally representing a central dimension of *lex mercatoria*, that is, a further set of 'facts' to be (and being) juridified[93] – as they, subjectively speaking, trespass into the consumer and general private law arenas, considering the application of standardised terms in cases of contracts with small or medium-sized businesses.

With regard to the consumer, and to refer to the Unfair Terms Directive, as considered by the CJEU in the case *Freiburger*, contracts are coextensively (see above about usages) read as concerning contracts as 'fact', that is, contracts as the market 'product' of the parties' balancing – that is, the sellers' marketing strategy of offering combinations of goods and price contractual terms and/or of goods and non-price contractual terms according to calculations of convenience – as opposed to social balancing as the product of collective endeavour. In other words, they are the form of the decisions made by the relevant legal actors for and in lieu of the collective, as discussed in the previous chapters.

Juridification as *Rechtsordnung*

The privatistic *Rechtsordnung*[94] revolving around contractual practices gains ground from within the conventional realms of private law ordering as an imagined alternative to the state social-constitutional order. At the same time, it proceeds towards a deconstruction of the conventional state social-constitutional order, given that the drafting of combinations of terms that are, in the view of the drafters, 'balanced' (unfair terms 'balanced' by terms 'advantageous' to the other contractual party) implies market practices made out of clusters of standardised terms with different combinations of contractual terms/goods available as consumer choices. Some consumers are held to want a low-quality contract matched with a lower price, whilst others are held to prefer a high-quality contract with a higher price. Private parties (vendors, suppliers, manufacturers) would produce what they consider the best combinations of terms, whilst consumers interested in such

[92] On classical works on standardised contractual practices, see ibid. Even private autonomy as cherished in European civil law circles collapses under the praxis of standardised contracting, albeit remaining on hold in the arguments whereby, where 'negotiation' can be held to exist, standardised contracting norms (the Unfair Terms Directive) would not apply. For my response to these arguments, and for an anticipation of this position, see Niglia, *The Transformation* (n 16). I should add that 'private autonomy' as traditionally understood (hermeneutically) in civil law circles is radically different to private order as considered in this book: private autonomy stands for a conception of contractual liberty as part of an order (constitutional), whilst private ordering entails domination relations, as I argue in the rest of this chapter (see the Conclusion).

[93] On the intertwining of fact and contract, see the seminal work by R Sacco and G De Nova, *Il Contratto* (Turin, UTET, 1993).

[94] See the argument made earlier in this section.

a variety of terms/goods combinations are targeted to participate in the design of this *Rechtordnung*. This is an order in the making alternative to the conventional state order, which is made up from legislative, judicial and administrative standards on the basis of which certain contractual standardised terms end up being struck down once and for all for being unfair in any circumstances.[95] It should be pointed out that, in the scholarly literature, usages partly consist of the material, which then enables the making of standardised terms:[96] from this viewpoint, at work is another kind of *sozial-faktische Akzeptanz in der Praxis*, alongside the one regarding usages noted above.

The juridification here is also about validating facts understood as the work of lawyers advising their clients, who are typically those in the stronger contractual position relative to the counterparty, as to which terms to place in their contracts – as to what would be in their contractual interest. The underlying private ordering (competitiveness) conception would be to make lawyers knowledgeable about the market differentiation regarding consumer choices so as to formulate contracts that accommodate it. I will return to this aspect later in the chapter when considering the *Uber* saga, where one can note how the lawyers' drafting of standardised terms has gone as far as fictionalising contracts towards seeing (reifying) relations of subordination among entrepreneurs and workers as fictionally 'equal' relations among contractors, and, as a result, have ended up developing a new hermeneutics (symbolic) aimed at juridifying *techne* as fact. This is a major example of how the juridification process under scrutiny here shapes up as a naturalisation qua neutralisation of social conflicts, as I explain below.

Contrasting these practices with the early tradition of redaction of, and related control of, standardised form contractual terms, one must note how the early tradition presented us with clauses believed in legal circles to be clearly biased in the interest of the drafters (such as limitation of liability clauses and penalties) whilst here, according to strands of transnational law literature, what connotes the contemporary work of lawyers would be the characterisation of *Kautelarpraxis* as 'factualisation' seen as a new normal.

(b) An Inter-orderly Constitutionalisation (contracts): *Kautelarpraxis* and the Court of Justice of the European Union

The decisions in *Freiburger*, *Laval* and *Viking* are about 'incorporating' the grammar of privatistic balancing as *Kautelarpraxis* (as contractual praxis) in the EU constitutional order – about 'Europeanising' the privatistic *Rechtsordnung*. Here, entrepreneurs use standardised terms to regulate the contractual relationships that they wish to enter, with courts (the CJEU) validating the relevant terms.

[95] On the comparative history and contemporaneity of this contingent kind of law of standardised terms as developed under the conventional state order, see Niglia, *The Transformation* (n 16).

[96] See above.

Through actively setting aside any of the social elements that might go against its validating choice – such as the principle of the equivalence of the obligations' performance (*Freiburger*) or labour rights as protected under the (recognised by the CJEU as general principle of EU law) right to strike (*Viking*) – the CJEU ends up with implementing a narrow kind of balancing orientated to market discipline. That is, standardised contractual terms are 'contractual' in the sense of their being an instance of 'private legislation' that only matter to the Court as such in the above-noted decisions. Coextensively, the reduction of balancing to the mode of economised balancing means that no public interest requirement is taken into account since only the practical arguments from economic advantages and disadvantages traceable to the combinations of contractual offers, or to the lowered wages for the workers, matter to the Court. In singling out private ordering – an aspect that is connotative of the above-noted decisions of the Court – the Court is setting aside public interest normative considerations traceable to fundamental principles (contemporaneous performance, fundamental right to strike).[97]

As a result of this, the EU constitutional order ends up by incorporating ('constitutional absorption') the standards emerging from the contractual praxis under the reworked constitutional structure understood as a form of (articulation of) private ordering as *Rechtsordnung* – given the suspension of the interpretative obligation, of the right to strike as general principle of law and of the general civil law principle of contemporaneous performance.[98]

Note that contractual actors here are not treated, constitutionally, as 'citizens' (holders of rights and duties within a community) in the sense of being bound by solidarity obligations that counter economic rights, and in relation to which a balancing is required that takes also social rights into account. Rather, they are treated just as market actors subjected to the efficiency-bound discipline of the market. This is the result of the contingent hermeneutics of private ordering that connotes the CJEU jurisprudence, that is, the hermeneutics regarding, first, the drafters' practice of the writing of standardised terms and, second, contractual terms believed to be the best form of settlement of any conflicts among the parties through contractual risks' prevention (standardisation); and, third, it is the hermeneutics whereby standardised terms are believed to be the product of a *Rechtsordnung*.[99]

As rising forms of contractual practice, and of usages, eclipse the hermeneutics of social balancing, a European constitutional privatistic *Rechtsordnung* increasingly emerges as hermeneutics that mirrors the doings and choices of private actors and their balancing determinations – no longer a constitutional order that

[97] See the remainder of the chapter and ch 5.

[98] See ch 5.

[99] Scholarship tends to stress the denotation of Europeanisation through adjudication as neoliberal and/or ordoliberal and/or market orientated; however, whilst these theories remain key to understanding the relevant contexts and related structures and processes, reference to them should not mean playing down the role of juridical hermeneutics as discursive formations that shape and make intelligible Europeanisation.

acts out of 'constitutional respect' for the social regulation of Member States in matters of private law,[100] but one that stands away from them whilst countering them at the same time. From this viewpoint, *Freiburger*, *Laval* and *Viking* are about (re)constitutionalising Europe no less than *Van Gend* and *Costa Enel* did with the Court's first job of constitutionalisation of the early 1960s. It is a peculiar 'constitution of private ordering' that is being engineered here[101] – and in the techne realm that I am about to discuss.

(iii) Techne (Digitisation)

(a) Techne

Techne is one more instance of the phenomenon of factual juridification explained above.[102] I refer to the positions, discussed in a rich transnational literature, whereby technological developments, including digitisation, entail a new range of 'facts' that demand a new kind of law – a 'special law'. Standard qua ordinary rules would not be suitable for regulating technological developments.

This 'special law' thesis has significant implications for the law, if only considering that digitisation is portrayed as not just one sector of the economy and of society, but as omnipresent and central to the current modernisation processes through the impact of technology. One can read this everywhere, including in the whereas of the EU Data Regulation (Regulation 2016/679 of 27 April 2016):[103] 'Technology has transformed both the economy and social life'; 'The economic and social integration resulting from the functioning of the internal market has led to a substantial increase in cross-border flows of personal data.'

The special law thesis must imply that digitalisation is mostly a private phenomenon – massive experimentation taking place in private realms, even when publicly funded and/or enacted by states participating in the private enterprise. As such, it also takes place through private law – it is another range of 'facts' that would demand juridification through 'special' rules.

[100] See ch 2.

[101] See ch 5 (on 'taking over' and on 'totalising').

[102] On 'juridification', see Teubner, 'The Constitution of Non-monetary Surplus Value' (n 40) 1–22; however, in this book, 'juridification' is deployed as a contingent redescription of the law on the ground according to the legal comparative approach adopted (on methodology, see ch 1 above), as a law that in the private realms here considered, rather than transcending for then returning to itself (on this, see Teubner, 'The Constitution'), transcends 'without returning to itself', in that it gets hermeneutically transformed on the way – a phenomenon that I must label 'trans-juridification' as a law that, the moment it operates by shaping the world, negates law as 'juridical hermeneutical' material.

[103] See eg Regulation (EU) 2016/679 of the European Parliament and of the Council of 27 April 2016 on the protection of natural persons with regard to the processing of personal data and on the free movement of such data, and repealing Directive 95/46/EC (General Data Protection Regulation) [2016] OJ L119/1 (whereas 6 and 5, respectively).

At the same time, and regardless of one's position on the special law thesis, balancing is called for as a central tool for regulating digitisation. For example, the EU Data Regulation reads as follows:[104]

> The processing of personal data should be designed to serve mankind. The right to the protection of personal data is not an absolute right; it must be considered in relation to its function in society and be *balanced against other fundamental rights*, in accordance with the principle of proportionality. (emphasis added)

In other words, as technology impacts on both the economy and social life, legislators choose 'balancing' as the mode of settlement of the related social conflicts regarding personal data and its protection 'in relation to its function in society' with a view to it 'be[ing] balanced against other fundamental rights, in accordance with the principle of proportionality'.

This has been creating tensions within the structures of the hermeneutics of balancing, regarding how to balance conflicts related to digitisation, which, in turn, embody transformational aspects as I am recounting them in this chapter. Two types of such tensions can be detected in the case law of the CJEU that imply the Court's own deployment of the transnational hermeneutics of private ordering as it concerns us in this chapter.

First are tensions regarding how to balance interests in relation to digital matters. Here, courts confront conflicts regarding challenges that go deep into changing the basic terms of the law, relative to traditional law – as in the *Uber* saga (discussed below), where a dispute among workers and employers is recast as one concerning relations among allegedly independent businesses, thus framing the dispute in terms of the balancing of the interests of parties on equal arms. Platforms are considered to be implicitly capable of generating their own rules whilst the Court places itself in a position of having to then justify whether or not general (constitutional, internal market) law should apply to the relevant disputes. Here, the hermeneutics of private order sidesteps the public–private divide. The *Schrems* saga (also considered below)[105] is another illustration of this point.

Second are tensions regarding 'delegation' in relation to digital matters, concerning both the issue of the delegation not just of economised balancing, but of broader balancing powers regarding the extent of the respect of fundamental rights, and the issue of which institutions or private entities should be given the power to decide and balance with regard to the relevant conflicts.

I will discuss each in turn.

[104] ibid (whereas 4).

[105] See the *Schrems* saga Judgment of the Court (Grand Chamber) of 6 October 2015, Case C-362/14 *Maximillian Schrems v Data Protection Commissioner* ECLI:EU:C:2015:650 (*Schrems I*); Judgment of the Court (Grand Chamber) of 16 July 2020, Case C-311/18 *Data Protection Commissioner v Facebook Ireland Limited and Maximillian Schrems* (*Schrems II*) as discussed in the rest of the chapter.

1. The Hermeneutics of Private Ordering as Background to the Issue of How to Balance Interests in Relation to Digital Matters

In *Uber*,[106] a professional taxi drivers' association sought a court declaration that the activities of Uber Systems Spain, a company related to Uber Technologies, amounted to misleading practices and acts of unfair competition, arguing that 'neither Uber Systems Spain, nor the non-professional drivers of the vehicles concerned have the licences and authorisations required under the Regulation on taxi services in the metropolitan area of Barcelona'.[107]

The question revolved around whether or not Uber was subjected to a prior administrative authorisation for it to exercise its economic activities, an issue that the CJEU addressed as it follows:

> In order to determine whether the practices of Uber can be classified as unfair practices that infringe the Spanish rules on competition, the Juzgado de lo Mercantil No 3 de Barcelona considers it necessary to ascertain whether or not Uber requires prior administrative authorisation. To that end, the court considers that it should be determined whether the services provided by Uber are to be regarded as transport services, information society services or a combination of both. Indeed, whether or not prior administrative authorisation may be required depends on the classification adopted. In particular, if the service at issue were covered by the directive on services in the internal market or the directive on electronic commerce, Uber's practices could not be regarded as unfair practices.

Here, to 'translate' in the light of the framework of analysis adopted in this chapter, (EU) private law norms are ready-made for justifying the claims of Uber that it operates as just an 'information society' company, and therefore as such immunised from the public interest requirements of holding an administrative authorisation to undertake its activities. Put the other way around, the claims of Uber are substantiated by the argument that theirs is an 'information society service' covered by the relevant private law directives. Here, Uber is arguing that their work is about offering an electronic service, and that it is 'transnational' and not 'local', so is therefore beyond the reach of conventional law.

Before the CJEU, Uber was not articulating an 'original' position, but an interpretation of the legal situation of it as operating within an order of its own ('private order') and claiming 'supremacy' over and above the competing constitutional order of local laws comprising the provision of administrative authorisations for the exercise of transport services.

The decision of the CJEU is only formalistic in its holding that Uber must obtain an authorisation before undertaking its activities, activities that the Court understands to be about 'transport' rather than the 'information society'. Whilst the

[106] Judgment of the Grand Chamber of the Court of Justice of the European Union, 20 December 2017, Case C-434/15 *Asociación Profesional élite Taxi v Uber Systems Spain SL* ECLI:EU:C:2017:981 (a professional taxi drivers' association in Barcelona (Spain) had brought an action in 2014 before the Juzgado de lo Mercantil No 3 de Barcelona (Commercial Court No 3, Barcelona, Spain).

[107] ibid.

Court stopped short of defending the public interest on stronger, more substantive grounds that would pertain directly to the underlying theme of the adverse effects of Uber's business on the transport market in Barcelona, there are, in contrast (in terms of output), CJEU decisions that instead favour the position of the stronger party in the area of electronic platforms.[108] The latter decisions signify a more radical departure from the conventional hermeneutics centred on the defence of the public interest as typical of social private law (applied to special contracts such as transports). One such CJEU decision is *Airbnb*,[109] where the Court distinguishes the precedent *Uber* decisions.[110]

Here, having established that 'Under Article 1(1)(b) of Directive 2015/1535, the concept of an "information society service" covers any service normally provided for remuneration, at a distance, by electronic means and at the individual request of a recipient of services', the Court goes on to deny that a substantial service is offered by Airbnb: 'an intermediation service such as the one provided by Airbnb Ireland cannot be regarded as forming an integral part of an overall service, the main component of which is the provision of accommodation'.

And, distinguishing the previous CJEU judgment of *Uber France*:[111]

> [T]he services, optional or otherwise, provided by Airbnb Ireland and referred to in paragraphs 59 to 63 above, do not call into question the separate nature of the intermediation service provided by that company and therefore its classification as an 'information society service', since they do not substantially modify the specific characteristics of that service. In that regard, it is also paradoxical that such added-value ancillary services provided by an electronic platform to its customers, in particular to distinguish itself from its competitors, may, in the absence of additional elements, result in the nature and therefore the legal classification of that platform's activity being modified, as was observed by the Advocate General in point 46 of his Opinion.
>
> Furthermore, and contrary to what AHTOP and the French Government maintain, the rules for the functioning of an intermediation service such as the one provided by Airbnb cannot be equated to those of the intermediation service which gave rise to the judgments of 20 December 2017, *Asociación Profesional Elite Taxi* (C-434/15,ECLI:EU:C:2017:981, paragraph 39), and of 10 April 2018, *Uber France* (C-320/16, ECLI:EU:C:2018:221, paragraph 21). Apart from the fact that those judgments were given in the specific context of urban passenger transport to which Article 58(1) TFEU applies and that the services provided by Airbnb Ireland are not comparable to those that were at issue in the cases giving rise to the judgments referred to in the previous paragraph, the ancillary services referred to in paragraphs 59 to 63 above do not provide evidence for the same level of control found by the Court in those judgments.

[108] CJEU judgment of 19 December 2019, Case C-390/18 *X, interveners: YA, Airbnb Ireland UC, Hôtelière Turenne SAS, Association pour un hébergement et un tourisme professionnels (AHTOP), Valhotel* ECLI:EU:C:2019:1112.

[109] ibid.

[110] C-434/15 *Asociación Profesional élite Taxi* ECLI:EU:C:2017:981, para 39 and C-320/16 *Uber France* ECLI:EU:C:2018:221, para 21.

[111] C-320/16 *Uber France* ECLI:EU:C:2018:221.

> Thus, the Court stated in those judgments that Uber *exercised decisive influence over* the conditions under which transport services were provided by the non-professional drivers using the application made available to them by that company (judgments of 20 December 2017, *Asociación Profesional Elite Taxi*, C-434/15, ECLI:EU:C:2017:981, paragraph 39, and of 10 April 2018, *Uber France*, C-320/16, ECLI:EU:C:2018:221, paragraph 21).
>
> The matters mentioned by the referring court and recalled in paragraph 19 above do not establish that Airbnb Ireland exercises such a decisive influence over the conditions for the provision of the accommodation services to which its intermediation service relates, particularly since Airbnb Ireland does not determine, directly or indirectly, the rental price charged, as was established in paragraphs 56 and 62 above, still less does it select the hosts or the accommodation put up for rent on its platform. (emphasis added)

It then concludes:

> The matters mentioned by the referring court and recalled in paragraph 19 above do not establish that Airbnb Ireland exercises such a decisive influence over the conditions for the provision of the accommodation services to which its intermediation service relates, particularly since Airbnb Ireland does not determine, directly or indirectly, the rental price charged, as was established in paragraphs 56 and 62 above, still less does it select the hosts or the accommodation put up for rent on its platform.

The Court here addresses the issue of the 'decisive influence' in terms deferential to private ordering, considering that what matters to the Court are the private parties' determinations concerning the rental terms and the terms regarding selection of the host and of the accommodation, rather than the unequal bargaining position of the two parties as underlying the contractual terms in the online platform economy. Similarly to the *Freiburger*, *Laval* and *Viking* judgments, it is the privatistic arrangements that matter (private ordering) above any public interest consideration pertaining to reversing inequalities of power (state constitutional ordering). The hermeneutics of contract as fictionally equal, with balancing reduced to a mere consideration of economised factors, prevails over a social hermeneutical perspective that would look at unequal relations of bargaining power among the parties,[112] and that would adopt balancing as comprising both market and non-market considerations.[113]

Overall, the hermeneutical struggles here pertain to the qualification of the subjects and of their activities and functionalities, each actor defending their own view insofar as positioning their claims in a given orderly perimeter (private ordering versus state constitutional ordering). It seems that here it all depends on the actual internal hermeneutics that develops in each dispute, albeit all moving significantly towards a post-conventional hermeneutics of balancing considerations revolving around the monologics of market-efficiency objectives.

[112] See eg BVerfG 19 October 1993, BVerfGE 89, 214.
[113] See chs 1 and 2 above.

The 'fictional' character of the 'contract among equals' concluded through online platforms – that is, a key structure at the basis of the new rising hermeneutics with its claim to self-legitimating privatistic balancing – has been effectively criticised and rejected in a major decision on Uber in the UK, whose passages are worth being repeated here. Here, the potential for a conventional private law hermeneutics, from within the English common law,[114] to resist arguments from the fictionality of contractual situations emerges:[115]

> 70. In the circumstances, the ET concluded any supposed driver/passenger contract was a 'pure fiction', bearing no relation to the real dealings and relationships between the parties. It further rejected any suggestion that Uber was working for the drivers – the only sensible interpretation was that the relationship was the other way around
>
> …
>
> 92. … The drivers provide the skilled labour through which the organisation delivers its services and earns its profits. We base our assessment … in particular on the following considerations.
>
> (1) The contradiction in the Rider Terms between the fact that ULL purports to be the drivers' agent and its assertion of 'sole and absolute discretion' to accept or decline bookings.
> (2) The fact that Uber interviews and recruits drivers.
> (3) The fact that Uber controls the key information (in particular the passenger's surname, contact details and intended destination) and excludes the driver from it.
> (4) The fact that Uber requires drivers to accept trips and/or not to cancel trips, and enforces the requirement by logging off drivers who breach those requirements.
> (5) The fact that Uber sets the (default) route and the driver departs from it at his peril.
> (6) The fact that UBV fixes the fare and the driver cannot agree a higher sum with the passenger. (The supposed freedom to agree a lower fare is obviously nugatory.)

[114] Signifying, inter alia, the difficulty of seeing the common law as business-like, in contrast to the civil law, which is seen as less business-like. For further discussion of this perception of the (American) common law, see Reimann, 'The European Advantage in Global Lawyering' (n 47); and, Reimann, 'The American Advantage in Global Lawyering' (n 47). Note that Reimann, 'The European Advantage in Global Lawyering' (n 47) rereads the findings of Hans Micklitz on a 'European advantage' in legal scholarship (H-W Micklitz, 'A European Advantage in Legal Scholarship?' in R van Gestel, H-W Micklitz and EL Rubin, *Rethinking Legal Scholarship* (2017) 262) as only applicable to the EU, whilst in this book I consider 'private lawyering' as being everywhere – at the CJEU and at the national courts, and at the national, EU and transnational scholarship levels, insofar as it is about juridical hermeneutics. Reimann focuses on global lawyering and on European lawyering in the two articles noted above, whilst Micklitz focuses on the EU lawyering (Micklitz, A European Advantage' (ibid)); instead, I talk here of hermeneutics as it matters in national, European and global (transnational) legal realms in its trespassing on each and all of these levels of analysis. Here, the continental civil law mind features as less non-business-like than typically portrayed, and indeed it is very much matching its common law counterpart as described in Reimann's above-noted contribution on global lawyering; in order to capture this perspective, one must look at both private law and EU law through a 'post-classical' lens.

[115] Employment Appeal Tribunal judgment of Judge Eady on 10 November 2017 *Uber BV and Others v Mr Y Aslam and Others* UKEAT/0056/17/DA, www.gov.uk/employment-appeal-tribunal-decisions/uber-b-v-and-others-v-mr-y-aslam-and-others-ukeat-0056–17-da.

(7) The fact that Uber imposes numerous conditions on drivers (such as the limited choice of acceptable vehicles), instructs drivers as to how to do their work and, in numerous ways, controls them in the performance of their duties.
(8) The fact that Uber subjects drivers through the rating system to what amounts to a performance management/disciplinary procedure.
(9) The fact that Uber determines issues about rebates, sometimes without even involving the driver whose remuneration is liable to be affected.
(10) The guaranteed earnings scheme (albeit now discontinued).
(11) The fact that Uber accepts the risk of loss which, if the drivers were genuinely in business on their own account, would fall upon them.
(12) The fact that Uber handles complaints by passengers, including complaints about the driver.
(13) The fact that Uber reserves the power to amend the drivers' terms unilaterally.

Here, one must contrast the arguments of the company before the court, as it aims to portray itself as if operating in the context of a contractual relationship among equals,[116] with the court's own portrait of the whole contractual situation as 'fictional'; to which the court then adds:

> 73. Having found that the terms on which Uber relied did not correspond with the reality of its relationship with the drivers, the ET considered itself free to disregard them; noting the unequal bargaining positions of the parties (in particular, many Uber drivers – a substantial proportion of whom did not speak English as their first language – would be unused to reading and interpreting dense legal documents couched in impenetrable prose), the ET saw this as:
>
> …
>
> 96. … an excellent illustration of the phenomenon of which Elias J warned in the *Kalwak* case of *'armies of lawyers' contriving documents in their clients' interests which simply misrepresent the true rights and obligations on both sides*. (emphasis added)

Note how here *Kautelarpraxis* is seen as being far from neutral and objective, in that it is presented less as if it concerns lawyers' drafting of contractual terms with the mere objective of decreasing and preventing contractual risks for the benefit of all parties involved, and more as biased towards drafting a set of contractual conditions engineered so as to be superimposed upon the drivers to the advantage of Uber. One must note how the English *Uber* saga shows how similar tensions between social protection and market objectives characterise the English common law – similarly to the civil law, the common law no doubt presents a parallel history of social protectionist standards understood as balancing.[117]

[116] Here the claim is that the company would be 'working for' the drivers, a vocabulary that effectively embodies the claim, articulated in terms of a 'fact', whereby structural relations of labour would be reversed in that the worker, traditionally (as per conventional social private law) seen as the 'weak party' in the contractual relation, would become just a business-like contractual party, with the result that, following this claim, labour law collapses into commercial law (see Micklitz, 'The Expulsion of the Concept of Protection' (n 73)). Compare 'freedom of contract' in the CJEU judgment of 18 July 2013 in Case C-426/11 *Alemo-Herron and Others* ECLI:EU:C:2013:521, as discussed in ch 5 below.

[117] On such parallelism between the English common law and the civil law, see Niglia, *The Transformation* (n 16).

2. The Hermeneutics of Private Ordering as Background to 'Delegation' in Relation to Digital Matters

The *Google* saga concerning the 'right to be forgotten' brings to light further dimensions that underly the CJEU strategy of crafting a hermeneutics of private ordering through, and congenial to, economised balancing. Here, one sees how the balancing regarding sensitive private data and involving the potential breach of fundamental rights, in the form of the striking of a balancing among the various factors, including fundamental rights, is delegated to the private operator rather than kept in the exclusive domain of the courts (and of legislators), namely, in the words of the Court:[118]

> The provisions of Directive 95/46 must be interpreted as meaning that, where the operator of a search engine has received a request for de-referencing relating to a link to a web page on which personal data falling within the special categories referred to in Article 8(1) or (5) of Directive 95/46 are published, the operator must, on the basis of all the relevant factors of the particular case and taking into account the seriousness of the interference with the data subject's fundamental rights to privacy and protection of personal data laid down in Articles 7 and 8 of the [EU Charter of Fundamental Rights], ascertain, having regard to the reasons of substantial public interest referred to in Article 8(4) of the directive and in compliance with the conditions laid down in that provision, whether the inclusion of that link in the list of results displayed following a search on the basis of the data subject's name is strictly necessary for protecting the freedom of information of internet users potentially interested in accessing that web page by means of such a search, protected by Article 11 of the Charter.

The Court (CJEU) decided that, as name-based searching through the Google search machine algorithmically brings to light past events of one's life, any claim by individuals about any perceived infringement of fundamental rights should in the first instance be weighed and balanced by the operator.[119]

In a subsequent case, the Court has also held that, among the factors to be considered (in relation to the relevant regulation) in the balancing regarding

> whether the inclusion of that link in the list of results displayed following a search on the basis of the data subject's name is strictly necessary for protecting the freedom of information of internet users potentially interested in accessing that web page by means of such a search, protected by Article 11 of the Charter [are] the *contractual clauses* agreed between the controller or processor established in the European Union and the recipient of the transfer established in the third country concerned (emphasis added).

In other words, such contractual clauses, apportioning risks relative to the bargaining position of each party, can be relied upon in deciding *ex hypothesi* about the 'strict necessity' of referencing unfavourably the past life events of an individual claiming that her or his rights have been infringed. This is another major

[118] Case C-136/17 *GC and Others v CNIL* 24 September 2019 (Google, dereferencing), para 69.
[119] See above.

deferential move towards private ordering through consideration of the terms of the contracts as relevant in a judgment regarding the protection of individuals' fundamental rights.[120] In a fictional reading of the phenomenon of contract,[121] this might sound just as if it were a reasonable kind of balancing. However, in the more realistic and powerful reading of contract as a phenomenon involving situations of unequal bargaining power, this is one more case of narrow balancing geared to promote the flow of market forces regardless of the need to take seriously, in the balancing act, any of the non-market normative considerations as relevant. In addition, in delegating such powers to online operators, balancing also means endangering the protection of any relevant fundamental rights other than the fundamental rights to privacy and protection of personal data laid down in Articles 7 and 8 of the Charter of Fundamental Rights of the European Union, rights which should be protected through balancing where relevant. In fact, the argument against delegation goes hand in hand with the need to ensure that courts make this broader kind of balancing, given that any balancing detached from its complex of normative considerations as such endangers the overall objective of protecting fundamental rights.[122]

To be sure, nothing bars a subsequent judicial review of the operators' determinations,[123] yet the fact is that to enable the online private operators to make that kind of balancing – as the CJEU chooses to do[124] – is, at least partly and yet

[120] I am referring to *Schrems II* (n 105), as discussed in the rest of the chapter.

[121] For critical discussion of fictional readings of the phenomenon of contracting, see Techne and *Lex Mercatoria* above.

[122] On balancing understood in this way in the history of European private law, see ch 2.

[123] Even Directive 95/46 provides, in Art 22, that: 'Remedies: Without prejudice to any administrative remedy for which provision may be made, inter alia before the supervisory authority referred to in Article 28, prior to referral to the judicial authority, Member States shall provide for the right of every person to a judicial remedy for any breach of the rights guaranteed him by the national law applicable to the processing in question.' See now Regulation (EU) 2016/679 of the European Parliament and of the Council of 27 April 2016 on the protection of natural persons with regard to the processing of personal data and on the free movement of such data, and repealing Directive 95/46/EC (General Data Protection Regulation) [2016] OJ L119/1.

[124] See *Schrems I* and *Schrems II* (n 105), commented on below at ch 5. Note https://www.europarl.europa.eu/RegData/etudes/ATAG/2020/652073/EPRS_ATA(2020)652073_EN.pdf on standard contract clauses. At paras 132–35, the Court in *Schrems II* explicitly adopts a delegation approach (note also 'or, failing that …'): 'the standard data protection clauses adopted by the Commission on the basis of Article 46(2)(c) of the GDPR are solely intended to provide contractual guarantees that apply uniformly in all third countries to controllers and processors established in the European Union and, consequently, independently of the level of protection guaranteed in each third country. In so far as those standard data protection clauses cannot, having regard to their very nature, provide guarantees beyond a contractual obligation to ensure compliance with the level of protection required under EU law, they may require, depending on the prevailing position in a particular third country, the adoption of supplementary measures by the controller in order to ensure compliance with that level of protection. In that regard, as the Advocate General stated in point 126 of his Opinion, the contractual mechanism provided for in Article 46(2)(c) of the GDPR is based on the responsibility of the controller or his or her subcontractor established in the European Union and, in the alternative, of the competent

significantly, about delegating key sovereign powers to private actors themselves. The operator possesses powers and responsibilities[125] that must be interpreted in the sense of it being entitled to, and obliged to, make decisions about sensitive issues as the first port of call for the affected individuals. The sovereign power to decide over fundamental rights as protected supranationally and nationally is, to say the least, somehow shared with the operator: the operator will set the stage for framing the issues and will decide in the first instance, with judicial review only following eventually, with obvious implications in terms of the quality of any subsequent[126] judicial review that cannot be disregarded or underestimated.

In fact, one must contrast with the above the more conventional position of the 2019 'right to be forgotten' Order of the Bundesverfassungsgericht (BVerfG) on the principle that it is 'primarily' a task of ordinary courts to exercise the relevant balancing:[127]

> It is primarily incumbent upon the ordinary courts to decide which detailed requirements operators of online archives must meet to protect persons affected by an article from the burdens that arise over time. The aim is to strike a balance that preserves unrestricted access to the original texts to the greatest extent possible, while also ensuring that where protection is merited in the individual case – especially in relation to name-based searches via search engines – sufficient limitations are put in place.

Here, the BVerfG stresses that it is 'primarily incumbent upon the ordinary courts' to decide the requirements regarding the protection of the affected persons, rather than holding that it should be primarily incumbent upon the private operator to exercise such balancing powers, in consideration of biases that inform private power over data as structurally tending to sacrifice and to disrespect fundamental

supervisory authority. It is therefore, above all, for that controller or processor to verify, on a case-by-case basis and, where appropriate, in collaboration with the recipient of the data, whether the law of the third country of destination ensures adequate protection, under EU law, of personal data transferred pursuant to standard data protection clauses, by providing, where necessary, additional safeguards to those offered by those clauses. Where the controller or a processor established in the European Union is not able to take adequate additional measures to guarantee such protection, the controller or processor or, failing that, the competent supervisory authority, are required to suspend or end the transfer of personal data to the third country concerned. That is the case, in particular, where the law of that third country imposes on the recipient of personal data from the European Union obligations which are contrary to those clauses and are, therefore, capable of impinging on the contractual guarantee of an adequate level of protection against access by the public authorities of that third country to that data.' Apparently in this area there is little or no litigation involving the relevant standard contract clauses (a confirmation of the contemporary power of the praxis of privatistic balancing).

[125] See *Schrems I* and *Schrems II* (n 105 and n 124 above).

[126] See n 133 below ('The role of judicial review, which also serves as a dynamic feedback loop for lawmakers, is furthermore undermined': M Finck, 'Automated Decision-Making and Administrative Law' in P Cane et al (eds), *Oxford Handbook of Comparative Administrative Law* (Oxford, Oxford University Press, 2020) ch 32).

[127] BverfG Order of 6 November 2019–1 BvR 16/13, para 141 (and para 148), at www.bundesverfassungsgericht.de/SharedDocs/Entscheidungen/EN/2019/11/rs20191106_1bvr001613en.html.

rights, biases that are in turn recognised in a wide literature regarding the sensitivity of data collected by online private operators.[128] In the view of the BverfG, public structures (the courts) are 'primarily' required to establish for operators of online archives the requirements of public interest that they must apply.

The delegation of balancing powers to private parties, and the inclusion of contractual clauses among the factors relevant for the operators' balancing exercise, adds to the phenomenon of the use of the transnational hermeneutics regarding usages and *Kautelarpraxis* in the light of the arguments from *Rechtsordnung*. Delegation is a position that confirms the background consideration of an imagined private order rendered capable of regulating itself independently of the state, and independently of the corresponding supranational constitutional authority structures, notwithstanding the structural issues of unequal bargaining power underlying the relations involved in such matters. Economised balancing as part of this kind of hermeneutics entails the 'recognition' of the determinations of the private realm; and in an idealised mode, that is, as if such determinations belonged to a private realm primarily believed to be credible in relation to its making them rather than determinations primarily to be assessed with regard to public interest considerations.[129]

***

If one looks at the increasingly important practice of using algorithms in relation to the making of administrative decisions, one must recognise the further dilemmas that characterise this delegation strategy as pursued by the CJEU in similar situations of administering through artificial intelligence (AI) (involving data or for similar applications). In this scenario, administrators would delegate to private parties the task of organising the AI/algorithmic calculations for the public administration under contracts that provide for their terms of service. It is private parties that are given the power to fully control decisions that pertain to public authorities (administrative), given the centrality of AI in relation to the given determinations.

In stipulating contracts with AI operators, public administrations increasingly rely on decisions made by the AI and must face the dilemma of combining the efficiency of AI with the overarching objective of acting according to reasonableness (public interest) standards.[130] Yet here, equally, the balancing decisions are made by private operators under the cloak of the 'form' of technique, that is, as if they were neutral decisions. Such balancing decisions may, however, be found

[128] On biases see, eg n 131 below.

[129] 'Idealised' since it is doubtful that a private order exists 'out there' as autarkic praxis other than as a result of the singular acts of 'recognition' through the relevant judgments (as conditional praxis insofar as dependent on recognition acts) – it is such 'recognition' that makes order-regimes come into existence: see above at s. III (A) (i) on historical and critical views on private ordering.

[130] On reasonableness, see section (i) above on *Lex Mercatoria* (reasonableness understood as public interest requirement).

to be biased, and frequently are, as the judges considered them in the remarkable judgments of *Compas/Loomis* and *Deliveroo*.[131]

This implies that, under the logic of delegation as defended by the CJEU in the above-noted decisions and as a reference point (adhered to or criticised) in a number of important decisions inter alia concerning the 2016 EU General Data Protection Regulation (GDPR),[132] a hybrid of public–private forces has emerged that is reshaping the relationships between the EU order and constitutional orders. For attributed to the private order are key powers that normally belong in the public domain (the public administration). What is particularly worrying, insofar as they subvert the allocation of responsibility and liabilities across public administration versus the citizenry, are issues regarding the constraints that the underlying contract (between the provider of AI and the public administration) places on the work of public officials. Note the following considerations on the open issues regarding the intertwinement of contracting and public administration in such situations in which AI/algorithms are deployed in administration, all of which confirm the thesis of this book that at work are structural imbalances entailed in the delegation of public power to private entities:[133]

> Where models are developed in-house, administrations need to ensure that public servants are trained properly to stimulate awareness of these issues and take possible precautions … Due to expertise and budget limitations, public authorities have, however, often outsourced the development of ADM systems. Such outsourcing to external private providers often entails *contractual clauses that prevent them from accessing the training data, algorithm and model.* Through such procedures, *private companies may become participants in the public administrative process and administrations may forfeit their ability to exercise meaningful control.* This can be controversial, such as in relation to smart city data, which is generated through the interplay of many different actors but *subsequent subject to the sole control of a given corporate entity* … It has, furthermore, been highlighted that where profiling is used to develop predictive knowledge from data through profiles subsequently applied as a basis for decision-making, *citizens oftentimes 'do not have access to the procedure behind the construction and application of*

[131] See the recent judgments regarding issues related to artificial intelligence: in the USA, the *Loomis* judgment of the Supreme Court of Wisconsin, *State of Wisconsin v Eric. Loomis*, Case no 2015AP157-CR, 5 April–13 July 2016 (software *Compas*, artificial intelligence, indicating high risks concerning the conduct of the individual and deciding on the basis of this); in Italy, see the *ordinanza* (*Deliveroo*) of the Tribunal (labour) of Bologna no 2949 of 2019, 31 December 2020 (workers, bookings of work sessions based on algorithms, digital platform, judged as discriminatory). On algorithms and exploitation, note G Wagner and HGM Eidenmueller, 'Down by Algorithms? Siphoning Rents, Exploiting Biases and Shaping Preferences – The Dark Side of Personalized Transactions (March 30, 2018)' [2019] *University of Chicago Law Review* 581: 'a common underlying theme: the exploitation of consumers or at least an impoverishment of their lives by firms that apply novel and sophisticated technological means to maximize profits. Hence, the dark side of personalized B2C transactions may be characterized as consumers being "brought down by algorithms," losing transaction surplus, engaging in welfare-reducing transactions, and increasingly being trapped in a narrower life.'

[132] EU Regulation 2016/679 (n 103).

[133] M Finck, 'Automated Decision-Making and Administrative Law' in P Cane et al (eds), *Oxford Handbook of Comparative Administrative Law* (Oxford, Oxford University Press, 2020) ch 32.

> *profiles* … Consequently, given that a data-analysis system is only as good as the data on which it depends, administrations planning to rely on such systems should accordingly carefully think about questions of data provenance and access. This is especially the case *when administrations enter into agreements with external third parties, as these may impact on the future ability to ensure the legally mandated transparency of administrative decision-making processes.* This is a particular concern as the well-documented *power-asymmetries between those that develop AI systems and those that deploy them also affect the State.* Similar transparency concerns can be identified in relation to the algorithms and models used to analyze such data. (emphases added)

The outsourcing of computational intelligence applied to administrative matters comes at a further risk, which is that[134] 'those breaching legal principles are no longer held responsible, and the role of judicial review, which also serves as a dynamic feedback loop for lawmakers, is furthermore undermined'.

The requirement of transparency that courts deploy in disputes concerning the use of AI, with implications in terms of discrimination and inequalities, is intertwined with all of the above issues:[135] the observance of high standards of

[134] ibid.

[135] On transparency as a public requirement applied to disputes regarding the relationship between the public administration and AI operators, see the Italian Consiglio di Stato judgment nos 8472, 8473, 8474/2019: '(12.) In tale contesto, premessa la generale ammissibilità di tali strumenti … assumono rilievo fondamentale, anche alla luce della disciplina di origine sovranazionale, due aspetti preminenti, quali elementi di minima garanzia per ogni ipotesi di utilizzo di algoritmi in sede decisoria pubblica: a) la piena conoscibilità a monte del modulo utilizzato e dei criteri applicati; b) l'imputabilità della decisione all'organo titolare del potere, il quale deve poter svolgere la necessaria verifica di logicità e legittimità della scelta e degli esiti affidati all'algoritmo. (13.1) Sul versante della piena conoscibilità, rilievo preminente ha il principio della trasparenza, da intendersi sia per la stessa p.a. titolare del potere per il cui esercizio viene previsto il ricorso allo strumento dell'algoritmo, sia per i soggetti incisi e coinvolti dal potere stesso. In relazione alla stessa p.a., nel precedente richiamato la sezione ha già chiarito come il meccanismo attraverso il quale si concretizza la decisione robotizzata (ovvero l'algoritmo) debba essere 'conoscibile', secondo una declinazione rafforzata del principio di trasparenza, che implica anche quello della piena conoscibilità di una regola espressa in un linguaggio differente da quello giuridico. Tale conoscibilità dell'algoritmo deve essere garantita in tutti gli aspetti: dai suoi autori al procedimento usato per la sua elaborazione, al meccanismo di decisione, comprensivo delle priorità assegnate nella procedura valutativa e decisionale e dei dati selezionati come rilevanti. Ciò al fine di poter verificare che i criteri, i presupposti e gli esiti del procedimento robotizzato siano conformi alle prescrizioni e alle finalità stabilite dalla legge o dalla stessa amministrazione a monte di tale procedimento e affinché siano chiare – e conseguentemente sindacabili – le modalità e le regole in base alle quali esso è stato impostato. In proposito, va ribadito che, la 'caratterizzazione multidisciplinare' dell'algoritmo (costruzione che certo non richiede solo competenze giuridiche, ma tecniche, informatiche, statistiche, amministrative) non esime dalla necessità che la 'formula tecnica', che di fatto rappresenta l'algoritmo, sia corredata da spiegazioni che la traducano nella 'regola giuridica' ad essa sottesa e che la rendano leggibile e comprensibile. Con le già individuate conseguenze in termini di conoscenza e di sindacabilità.' Contrast the situation in France in the light of the 2018 judgment of the Conseil Constitutionel (12 December 12 June 2018, No 2018-765 DC): L Cluzel-Métayer, 'The Judicial Review of the Automated Administrative Act' [2020] *European Review of Digital Administration & Law* 101: 'In France, the constitutional judge has thus prohibited the use of self-learning algorithms to make individual administrative decisions exclusively based on algorithms (CC dec. 12 June 2018, n°2018–765 DC), because the judge is aware of the fact that the administration cannot explain how these algorithms work. Also, in accordance with the GDPR, if the judge has validated the possibility of taking individual administrative decisions exclusively based on an algorithm, it is only because he

transparency would not necessarily mean adequately resolving the issues regarding the contractual imbalances, issues that would remain in place.

Juridification as *Rechtsordnung*

Scholars consider platforms and further technological artifacts, insofar as they structure the rising realm of digitisation, to constitute a self-regulated private order – that is, a private order explicitly taken to be a 'constitutional' order (the 'digital constitution').[136] There is even no distinction in their accounts of digital matters between the constitutional order and the realm of digitisation insofar as the latter constitutes an autonomous 'digital constitutional' order. This indistinction marks a new ground whereby the resolution of key constitutional dilemmas regarding social conflicts entailed in digitisation takes place through hermeneutical structures that stand outside constitutionalism as conventionally understood – which is the very negation of constitutionalism from within.[137] Whenever subscribing to this view by participating in the work of fictionalising contractual situations, the CJEU judgments re-enact, and contribute to the making of, the phenomenon of factual juridification.[138] At work is once more a *sozial-faktische Akzeptanz in der Praxis*[139] that this time pertains to the phenomenon of technological innovation.

(b) An Inter-orderly Constitutionalisation (Platforms): Techne and the Court of Justice of the European Union

A hybridised juridical version of usages and contracts – 'platforms' as technological artifacts – emerges in the relevant judgments of the CJEU in the realm of digitisation, involving and being determined by algorithms (*Uber*, *Google*, *Schrems*).[140]

considers that the legislator provides sufficient guarantees: in particular being about when it obliges data controllers to master the algorithm and its evolutions and to be able to explain the algorithm (CC dec. 12 June 2018). But isn't this injunction illusory? Making the algorithm intelligible to citizens is a real challenge, essentially for two reasons: firstly, because translating lines of code into human language is a complex task; and secondly, because it is difficult to identify the perimeter of the code's opening, integrating the elements necessary for a global understanding of the system, while excluding modules that present security risks.'

[136] See Teubner, 'The Constitution of Non-monetary Surplus Value' (n 40) 1–22. Note H Micklitz, 'The COVID-19 Threat: An Opportunity to Rethink the European Economic Constitution and European Private Law' (2020) 11 *European Journal of Risk Regulation* 249, who draws on Teubner's notion of digital constitution: 'In the scholarly debate on digitisation and the impact of economic and private law, there seems to be agreement that red lines are needed that cannot be crossed by anyone and that should not be submitted to a balancing test. The digital constitution is supposed to set benchmarks for all sorts of European, national and private regulation that governs private relations in the digital society and economy': classifying digital structures both as order and as constitutional order, yet at the same time taking it as 'constitutional order', which I understand in this book to be 'private' insofar as 'setting benchmarks' for any kind of other private regulation, and as a result empowering the private order to regulate, through impacting on any other kind of constitutional orders.

[137] See above and ch 5.

[138] On 'resistance patterns' from within the CJEU jurisprudence, see ch 5 below.

[139] See the section on *lex mercatoria* above.

[140] That is, the practice of determining contractual content through using artificial intelligence algorithms.

What is somehow only implicit in *Freiburger* and *Laval* becomes more explicit. As a matter of fact, the above-noted *Schrems* saga illustrates how the privatistic determinations take centre stage in the CJEU judgments, here articulated in the vocabulary of the juridical justification of the delegation to private parties of the power to scrutinise the extent of protection of the relevant fundamental rights. The *Rechtsordnung* that is being recognised as a result by the CJEU decisions is meant to include technologically 'innovative' material coming out of the productionist private realms as 'platforms'.[141] This, in turn, is one more instance of inter-orderly constitutionalisation insofar as constitutional absorption takes place also in the techne realm.

IV. Conclusion

Comparing the three case studies (*lex mercatoria*, *Kautelarpraxis* and techne) allows a conclusion to be drawn that applies to all of them. Constructing the privatistic *Rechtsordnung*, understood as usages, contracts and hybridised usages/contracts (platforms), means to the relevant legal actors that they not only 'recognise' it, but emancipate it from (the constraints of) both state law and EU law. The state constitutional orders and the EU 'new order', once upon a time the output of 'learning mutually' and 'co-determining' norms and principles in matters of private relationships under the jurisprudence of constitutional autonomy,[142] now make room for the determinations of the privatistic *Rechtsordnung*, which, in turn, are implemented unboundedly.

[141] On networks, see, eg KH Ladeur, '"We, the European People …" – Relâche?' [2008] *European Law Journal* 14.

[142] See ch 3 above.

5

Epilogue: Transformations, Critique

The structural transformation from autonomy (chapter two) to heteronomy (chapter three) is intertwined with a third, coextensive, transformation process which chapter four understands as 'constitutional absorption', that is, Europe's new constitutional constellation as enabler of privatistic freedom rights at the sacrifice of the once established social rights. At the same time, I have argued in chapter four that the transformation through absorption is an *inter-order* phenomenon of private ordering's constitutionalisation. I will now emphasise certain critical aspects of this transformation through absorption in terms of the totalising of orders (i–iv), then critically consider certain dilemmas associated with such totalising (v–vii).

(i) Due to the Court of Justice of the European Union (CJEU)'s strategy at the ongoing incorporation, constitutionalisation and legitimation[1] of the contingent set of privatistic materials considered above, one assists in the remaking of the constitutional orders.

The privatistic material is no longer constitutionally parameterised after the once only relevant constitutional orders (the national constitutional orders; the EU order) and their relations,[2] but is rearranged in the image of another (constructed) order – private ordering.

[1] I should stress the point that 'constitutional absorption', understood as incorporation and constitutionalisation, is far from a definite process, and it should not be reified either, in that it is the reflection of a positioning of the CJEU (in terms of incorporation, constitutionalisation and legitimation, strategic attempt at), the impact of whose decisions is contingent on the reactions of the other legal actors, from judges to scholars and beyond. Only a positivistic reading would content itself with the appearance of a reordering process as if somehow sheltered from the underlying hermeneutical struggles (for this approach, see L Niglia, *The Struggle for European Private Law. A Critique of Codification* (Oxford, Hart Publishing, 2015); the resulting legitimation drawn on constitutional incorporation and emerging as new constitutionalisation must therefore be seen as both contested and contestable (ibid; see also ch 3 above on contestation patterns within the hermeneutics of balancing, whether maximal or minimal, and economised; see also the rest of this chapter).

[2] See ch 2 above. Contrast the conception of the EU order as embodying acts parameterised according to its own autonomous constitutional standards (see the progression of cases, including, CJEU, Case 26/62 *Van Gend en Loos* [1963] ECR 1; Case 6/64 *Costa Enel* 15 July 1964; Case 106/77 *Symmenthal* [1978] ECR 629; Case T-315/01 *Yassin Abdullah Kadi v Council of the European Union & Commission of the European Communities* [2005] ECR II-3649; Opinion 2/13, EU Accession to ECHR, ECLI:EU:C:2014:2454 (18 December 2014); see also, from the vantage point of national constitutional orders through the decisions of the constitutional courts, eg Constitutional Court (Italy) no 183 of 1973 (*Frontini*); Constitutional Court (Italy) no 170 of 1984 (*Granital*); BVerfG 89/155 *Maastricht*; BVerfG BVerfG2 BvE 2/08 *Lisbon*, 30 June 2009 judgments).

A converging double movement can be noted.

From the viewpoint of private ordering, at work is the reshaping of the EU and national constitutional orders after contingent privatistic (economised) balancing parameters.

From the constitutionalist viewpoint, conventional EU constitutional doctrines and principles are re-engineered (suspended and/or altered) for the purpose of absorption, thus creating a 'special' constitutional realm 'from within' that is treated as insulated from, and unaffected by, the otherwise 'normal' operation of the norms and principles of EU constitutional law.[3] In fact, in the CJEU judgments concerning private dimensions noted in the previous chapters, the following sets of constitutional requirements are set aside, suspended, rearranged, replaced:[4]

- The interpretative obligation suspended/replaced by direct effect (*Freiburger*, *OPR-Finance*); relatedly, private law traditions (national) set aside by direct effect (*Freiburger, OPR-Finance*):
- Fundamental rights set aside by economic freedoms (*Laval*);
- The principle of contemporary performance through good faith as general principle of (civil) law set aside by economic freedoms (*Freiburger*);
- Proportionality rearranged as economised balancing (*Laval, Viking*);

[3] See the rest of the chapter.

[4] The hermeneutics of private ordering is intertwined with economic and law theories such as the 'law market' (see EA O'Hara and LE Ribstein, *The Law Market* (Oxford, Oxford University Press, 2009), the market state (see, eg H Micklitz, 'The Expulsion of the Concept of Protection from the Consumer Law and the Return of the Social Elements in the Civil Law: A Bittersweet Polemic' (European University Institute, 2012) EUI Working Papers 2012/03) and the conception of a 'market without rules' (see, critically, Opinion of Advocate General Tizzano in Judgment of the Court (Grand Chamber) of 5 October 2004 *CaixaBank France v Ministère de l'Économie, des Finances et de l'Industrie*, paras 62–63: 'that interpretation would permit economic operators – both national and foreign – to abuse Article 43 EC in order to oppose any national measure that, solely because it regulated the conditions for pursuing an economic activity, could in the final analysis narrow profit margins and hence reduce the attractiveness of pursuing that particular economic activity. However, that would be tantamount to bending the Treaty to a purpose for which it was not intended: that is to say, *not in order to create an internal market in which conditions are similar to those of a single market and where operators can move freely, but in order to establish a market without rules. Or rather, a market in which rules are prohibited as a matter of principle*, except for those necessary and proportionate to meeting imperative requirements in the public interest' (emphasis added)). I am proposing an interpretation of the CJEU jurisprudence less as a manifestation and application of a 'theory' to which the judges would subject themselves (see, eg Judge Vosskhule, 2020), a matter that deserves autonomous consideration, given the centrality of 'theory' in the work of understanding the development of the law (L Niglia, 'The Political Foundations' in R Brownsword, H Micklitz, L Niglia and S Weatherill (eds), *The Foundations of European Private Law* (Oxford, Hart Publishing, 2011); L Niglia (ed), *Pluralism and European Private Law* (Oxford, Hart Publishing, 2013); Niglia, *The Struggle for European Private Law* (n 1); S Grundmann, H Micklitz and M Renner, *New Private Law Theory* in *New Private Law Theory: A Pluralist Approach* (Cambridge, Cambridge University Press, 2021)), and more as being about re(in) stating a broader juridical hermeneutics – 'restating' in the sense of participating in a broader hermeneutical space as recounted in this book; 'reinstating' in the sense of redeploying this hermeneutics and constructing it actively.

- Solidarity as entailed in collective actions in labour set aside and replaced by economised balancing (*Laval, Viking*);
- Rule of law (jurisdiction) suspended/rearranged/replaced by delegation to private power (*Google, Schrems*);
- Rule of law (administrative law) suspended/rearranged/replaced by unlicensed private power (*Uber*);
- Rules on unequal bargaining power (contract law) suspended/rearranged/replaced by the hermeneutics of contract fictionally seen as entailing equality among the parties (*Airbnb*);
- Fundamental rights of workers – employees' protected rights in situations of transfer of a business (*Alemo-Herron, Facility Services*)[5] – set aside by 'freedom of contract';
- Privatistic (associational) social rights elevated to the rank of fundamental rights and sacrificed at the same time (the right to strike in *Laval, Viking*) – balancing replaces fundamental rights;
- Fundamental rights suspended/set aside in the politico-economical realm of the Economic and Monetary Union (*Florescu*);[6]
- Proportionality set aside/replaced by balancing (economised) in relation to the European Central Bank (ECB) asset purchase programme (CJEU *Weiss*; BVerfG *PSPP*);[7]
- Competences, attributed (Article 5 TEU), set aside/suspended by proportionality balancing (BVerfG *PSPP*; BVerfG 2021 order of 15 April 2021).[8]

This sequence of judgments indicates that the constitutional autonomy of EU law (*sensu stricto*) is now under siege. I refer to constitutional autonomy (*sensu stricto*) as written in stone in such various judgments as *Van Gend*, *Symmenthal* and *Kadi* (CJEU), *Frontini* and *Granital* (Italian Constitutional Court), and *Solange I* and *II* (BVerfG),[9] and consisting of the EU order possessing its own decisional parameters

[5] See the rest of this chapter; as to the *Uber* saga, see ch 4 above (the claims of the private company before the Employment Appeal Tribunal: judgment of 10 November 2017 *Uber BV and Others v Mr Y Aslam and Others* UKEAT/0056/17/DA); as to the others cases, see the previous chapters.

[6] See Case C-258/14 *Florescu v Casa Județeană de Pensii Sibiu*, 2017 EUR-Lex CELEX LEXIS 448 (13 June 2017) (as discussed in L Niglia, 'The New Transformation of Europe. Arcana Imperii' (2020) 68 *American Journal of Comparative Law* 151).

[7] Court of Justice, judgment of 11 December 2018, Case C-493/17 *Heinrich Weiss et al v ECB* ECLI:EU:C:2018:1000; German Federal Constitutional Court, judgment of the Second Senate of 5 May 2020, 2 BvR 859/15, 2 BvR 1651/15, 2 BvR 2006/15, 2 BvR 980/16 (hereinafter *PSPP* judgment). See also the rest of the chapter.

[8] See respectively BVerfG *PSPP* (n 7); BverfG Order of 15 April 2021, 2 BvR 547/21. See also the rest of the chapter.

[9] See Case 26/62 *Van Gend en Loos* [1963] ECR 1; BVerfGE 37 (*Solange* I); BVerfGE 73 (*Solange II*); It Corte Costituzionale *Frontini* 183/1973; It Corte Costituzionale *Granital* 170/1984; Case 106/77 *Symmenthal* [1978] ECR 629; and the Grand Chamber judgment of 3 September 2008, Joined Cases C-402/05 P and Case C-415/05 P *Yassin Abdullah Kadi and Al Barakaat International Foundation v*

as deserving constitutional respect from the state constitutional orders (including from the national constitutional courts), within the limits of the attributed competences. A shift 'internal' to the EU constitutional order is taking place: from the EU order having its own established constitutional parameters to creating a new set of autonomous parameters from within the EU order through the deployment of the hermeneutics of private ordering.

This kind of balancing corrodes the EU order from within: in the above-considered decisions it gives rise to a kind of implosion of the CJEU-constructed constitutional 'coherence' of EU law insofar as it is replaced by the technicality of (economised) balancing. As a result, we are presented with a scenario in which social rights (in *Viking*) are elevated to the rank of fundamental rights under the EU order and yet they are contemporaneously emptied of any substantial constitutional force through a balancing exercise that sees the competing economic parameters prevail.[10] In turn, this process entails a double disintegration – not only does it set aside key EU constitutional requirements, but it equally, and coextensively, sets aside national constitutional private law hermeneutics.[11] The new jurisprudence entails a change that affects key areas of national private law and

Council of the European Union and Commission of the European Communities [2008] ECR I-06351, ECLI:EU:C:2008:461, para 282: 'It is also to be recalled that an international agreement cannot affect the allocation of powers fixed by the Treaties or, consequently, the autonomy of the Community legal system, observance of which is ensured by the Court by virtue of the exclusive jurisdiction conferred on it by Article 220 EC, jurisdiction that the Court has, moreover, already held to form part of the very foundations of the Community (see, to that effect, Opinion 1/91 [1991] ECR I-6079, paragraphs 35 and 71, and Case C-459/03 *Commission v Ireland* [2006] ECR I-4635, paragraph 123 and case-law cited)'; and see Constitutional Court (Italy) *Granital* judgment 170 of 1984, www.cortecostituzionale.it/actionSchedaPronuncia.do?anno=1984&numero=170: 'l'ordinamento della Comunità e quello dello Stato – ed i rispettivi processi di produzione normativa – ... per quanto coordinati, sono distinti e reciprocamente autonomi. Proprio in ragione, dunque, della distinzione fra i due *ordinamenti*, la prevalenza del regolamento adottato dalla CEE va intesa come si è con la presente pronunzia ritenuto: nel senso, vale a dire, che la legge interna non interferisce *nella sfera occupata da tale atto*, la quale è *interamente attratta sotto il diritto comunitario*' (emphasis added). From the viewpoint of the paradigm of the jurisprudence of 'constitutional autonomy' (see ch 2 above), the respect for the autonomy of national legal systems of private law is distinct from, and parallels, the conception of the internal autonomy of European law (as illustrated by the position of the Italian Constitutional Court in *Granital* at 'occupied sphere', as the 'internal law' is meant 'not to interfere with the sphere occupied' by the EU Regulation in that it is 'entirely absorbed into Community law': my translation), whilst today it is exactly this overall architecture that is being put in danger by the new jurisprudence, due to its disintegrationist effects in relation to both national private laws and the autonomy of EU constitutional law itself: as I argue in the rest of the chapter, there is a shift from distinct orders to a symbiotic constitutionalism that sees private ordering 'taking over' and trespassing the autonomy of constitutional orders, national and EU.

[10] This is far from an isolated process. In fact, in the area of migration, rights are, on the one hand, recognised as worthy of protection as fundamental and human rights but, on the other hand, are equally frustrated: see, critically, L Niglia, 'Europe and "Crisis" (First Part)' (2018) 3 *European Papers – A Journal on Law and Integration* 601. In section (i), balancing is not just limited to proportionality as a third-step assessment of proportionality, in that one sees it operating across a variety of norms and principles, from interpretative obligation to fundamental rights and to solidarity to rule of law – from this viewpoint, comparatively speaking, balancing is a formant (R Sacco, 'Legal Formants' (1991) 39 *American Journal of Comparative Law* 1; on formants and Europeanisation, see L Niglia, *The Transformation of Contract in Europe* (The Hague, Kluwer Law International, 2003) that operates across the EU and national orders by rearranging constitutionality.

[11] See ch 4 above.

that adversely reaches deep into key structures (hermeneutical) of traditional private law.[12]

(ii) The range of privatistic rights that are being protected constitutionally by the CJEU in the above-noted decisions are grounded in the hermeneutics of (private) ordering, mirroring the earlier constitutionalisation (the 'new legal order') but with the qualification that here it is order that establishes rights and not the other way around.[13]

Recall that in *Van Gend* the CJEU is held to have established a 'new legal order' as constitutional through the explicit argument that individuals are subjects of the law (subjectivisation), including as EU citizens understood as (what would become the legacy of the) EU market citizenship.[14]

In the subject area under consideration in this book, the grounding is primarily about ordering: this grounding emerges in the deployment of a range of hermeneutical private ordering constructs that envisage a private realm with its own attributes and specificities in relation to which the arguments from rights are put forward.

The key notions noted above indicate: the praxis of alternative market offers (combinations) as a privatistic mechanism capable of 'protecting' weak contractual parties, reputed not to be in need of protection as would be the case under national (social) standards, with the right of the seller to use combinations of offers justified in the vocabulary of the alleged necessity of unbound market ordering (*Freiburger*); similarly, labour contracts are interpreted by recognising the privatistic power of contractors to allocate contractual risks as they think best (*Laval*); and, delegating balancing powers to private parties such as online/data operators means determining fundamental rights in relation to private data, depending, in the first instance, on the operator's own privatistic balancing rather than seeing fundamental rights as a primary public good to be protected as such by the courts in the first instance (*Schrems I* and *II*).[15]

Moreover, the primary role of (private) ordering in the case law of the Court is constructed by imposing certain market-orientated requirements on private parties with a view to establishing a competitive market process. Three such requirements must be noted in turn:

First, the *Weiss* judgment of the CJEU in 2018 and the *PSPP* judgment of the BVerfG in 2020, where the judges conjured up an obligatory standard of market

[12] Contrast the arguments typical of what I label 'conventional constitutional private law' as critically recounted in Niglia, *The Transformation of Contract in Europe* (n 10); Niglia, *The Struggle for European Private Law* (n 1) (with relevant literature).

[13] On this aspect, see the rest of the chapter.

[14] Ever since *Van Gend* (n 2) on subjectivisation of individuals. On citizenship as relevant to subjectivisation in terms of the 'market citizen', see M Everson, 'The Legacy of the Market Citizen' in J Shaw and G More (eds), *New Legal Dynamics of the European Union* (Oxford, Clarendon Press, 1995) 73–89.

[15] See Judgment of the Court (Grand Chamber) of 6 October 2015, Case C-362/14 *Maximillian Schrems v Data Protection Commissioner* ECLI:EU:C:2015:650 (*Schrems I*); Judgment of the Court (Grand Chamber) of 16 July 2020, Case C-311/18 *Data Protection Commissioner v Facebook Ireland Limited and Maximillian Schrems* ECLI:EU:C:2020:559 (*Schrems II*).

'uncertainty' as opposed to 'certainty' as defining the contractual regime regarding the European Central Bank's buying of bonds on the secondary market.

Second, the provision of an obligation on the part of private parties to perform according to certain market standards as a condition for enjoying the relevant directive rights – as in the CJEU's *OPR-Finance* case, where the stronger contractual party (one bank) is held to be under the duty to assess creditworthiness if it wants to get back all of the credit in case of default of the mortgage.

Third, the provision of an obligation on digital (internet) operators (namely, eg Google) to weigh interests at stake in relation to a request for de-referencing (the CJEU data saga).

All of this entails a new constitutionalisation of duties and obligations, and not just rights, towards constructing and legitimating a rearranged private 'order'.[16]

Note also how more than just freedom of contract is at work here, given the construction of an order of contractual freedoms descending from the privatistic balancing determinations. In choosing no longer to deploy the argument from freedom of contract, after *Alemo-Herron*,[17] the CJEU has not given up on pursuing the normative commitments enshrined in that freedom. On the contrary, it has been establishing the normativity of contractual freedoms in greater scope, in the mode of an unbound privatistic order rather than just freedom rights. And the Court has done this subtly, by avoiding the talk of freedom of contract and the limitations attached to it, as they result from the conventional rendition of freedom of contract.[18] In other words, here is a 'recognition' of an alternative order that aims at debunking the conventional constitutional order (both EU and nation-state).[19]

(iii) There is a third characterisation of the phenomenon under consideration. The emergence of 'self-standing' private regimes in Europe has been noted through the lens of pluralism or of regulatory studies (the silos thesis) or, from another perspective, through reliance on the EU *acquis* (private law) pillar thesis (pragmatic).[20]

The preceding analysis allows a new synthesis that is founded upon previous work on pluralism by the author. Seen in this pluralist light, the CJEU, irrespective of any alleged 'coherence' of the *acquis*, has been adapting the *acquis* (contractual rights such as the right to withdrawal; the test of unfairness; labour rights)[21] to the requirements of the 'regulatory' regimes by constitutionalising them. It is a constitutionalisation that revolves around the hermeneutics of private order, that is, the hermeneutics regarding the constructed self-balancing of the regimes, which I would label 'order-regimes', given that here I adopt a hermeneutical perspective

[16] Legitimation here refers to the construction of a hermeneutics that 'constitutionalises' by means of what is represented as an act of 'recognition' of private ordering as an-other ordering, and that 'recognises' through 'constitutionalisation'.

[17] CJEU, 18 July 2013, Case C-426/11 *Alemo-Herron and Others* ECLI:EU:C:2013:521.

[18] For this argument, see Niglia, *The Transformation of Contract in Europe* (n 10).

[19] See n 16 above.

[20] See respectively the readings of Niglia, *Pluralism and European Private Law* (n 4); H-W Micklitz, 'The Transformation of Private Law through Competition' (2016) 22 *European Law Journal* 627; MW Hesselink, 'Private Law, Regulation, and Justice' (2016) 22 *European Law Journal* 681.

[21] See Niglia, *The Struggle for European Private Law* (n 1).

that matters more than has hitherto been thought. The privatistic regimes that are 'emerging' are those that the CJEU contributes to creating as a result of its chosen hermeneutics of 'recognition' (of private ordering as an*other* order).

One can also try and look at the privatistic regimes sociologically, by understanding them as 'silos' and/or networks.[22] However, this perspective and its background methodology in my view needs more elaboration and refinement. Privatistic regimes can be made really intelligible by retaining the hermeneutics of private ordering insofar as emphasising the legal relevance of 'networks' in terms of the above-considered phenomenon of 'factual juridification'.[23] Rather than taking for granted the argument that these networks would somehow exist pre-eminently as a matter of functionality 'out there', and that they should be considered to be 'making law' as much as state law does, I argue that we are presented with the more complex contingency of the creation of a *hermeneutics* – the hermeneutics of private ordering – that *constitutionalises* certain market developments in the language of self-standing regimes (order-regimes).

The juridical hermeneutical perspective adopted here really matters in two more respects: Teubner has recently written about 'surplus', understood as the functional systems' own destructiveness.[24] In the phenomena under scrutiny in this book, there is a surplus qua destructiveness in the sense of hermeneutical ordering articulated as setting aside, and ultimately annihilating, key constitutional structures such as those noted above – for the purpose of enhancing economisation. I understand Teubner's choice here as suggesting ways for recovering constitutionality by other means (its own theoretical framework of analysis), and therefore lending itself to be reconstructed as part of a broader range of writings attempting to redeem the constitutional as annihilated through economisation.

Moreover, and also rethinking Hans Micklitz's thesis that the European Regulatory Private Law would be a 'counter-project', I surmise that we are

[22] Micklitz, 'The Transformation of Private Law' (n 20); for criticism of the 'silos' thesis, see Hesselink (n 20).

[23] On 'factual juridification', see ch 4 above.

[24] G Teubner, 'The Constitution of Non-monetary Surplus Value' [2020] *Social and Legal Theory* 1, 1: 'Similar to the monetary profit pressure in the economy (auto- and hetero-) destructive tendencies of non-monetary surplus pressures have multiplied in the law and in other areas of life … an excessive ambivalence: immense productivity and its destructive dark side.' I adapt this position here and propose a distinct reading in that I consider the relevance of orders and not just functional systems – in other words, I look at aggregation of functional systems around and through order(s) and not singular 'function systems'. On 'economisation', I must refer the reader to L Niglia, 'Law or Economics – Some Thoughts on Transnational Private Law' in K Purnhgen et al (eds), *Varieties of European Economic Law and Regulation* 93 (2014) (critically discussing 'economization' as both economic efficiency and as reducing the redistributional scope of nation-states' policies, that is: '"Economization", described as the phenomenon of "the growing importance of the economic efficiency doctrine" and as "a process that reduces the scope of Member States' redistributive interventions to that of providing a fair chance to benefit from the Internal Market", can be taken to mean both things at once, as I argue in this chapter in which I call this perspective "economics-that-replaces-law" or "law-economized"' (the two quotations are from H Micklitz, 'The Visible Hand of European Regulatory Private Law' (2009) 28 *Yearbook of European Law* 3). Here, by 'the growing importance of the economic efficiency doctrine' I mean economised balancing.

confronting another kind of 'codification', both substantively speaking, given its material agenda, and formally speaking, in terms of the 'reordering' of orders. This is so because the same private law project (typically labelled as 'individualism')[25] stands at the core of the ongoing private order constitutionalisation that I am discussing here. I have been considering the order-regimes, the product of a hermeneutics through judicial intervention (through 'balancing'), as an apparently fragmentary process that deep down embodies a shared logic around private ordering. Private relations are constitutionalised through the intrumentalisation of a range of established constitutional principles and norms for the purpose of protecting freedom of contract and associated rights – balancing as protecting freedom of contract, in the language of the *Alemo-Herron* judgment. Balancing (economised) is deployed where the Court chooses to pursue this strategy – in these cases, the technique of balancing (economised), and freedom of contract and the associated rights/freedoms as considered above, are two sides of the same coin.

***

Seen in the light of the above analysis, the 2013 CJEU judgment of *Alemo-Herron* emerges not just as a one-off aberration, as has been argued;[26] rather, it explicitly represents the broader hermeneutics of private ordering in the vocabulary of freedom of contract as allegedly implied in the Charter of Fundamental Rights of the European Union. To paraphrase Stephen Weatherill's view on *Alemo-Herron*: it is about institutionalising an 'abuse' in that it is about instantiating the subversion of both freedom of contract as understood in the sociality tradition of private law and legal thought and in the Charter of Fundamental Rights itself.[27]

[25] On the relationships between the European codification project and individualism, see critically Niglia, *The Struggle for European Private Law* (n 1).

[26] *Alemo-Herron* (n 17) 31–32 (Art 16 CFREU understood as 'the freedom to conduct a business, a fundamental right [which] covers, inter alia, freedom of contract'; for criticism, see Hesselink (n 19): 'the CJEU's radically libertarian *Alemo-Herron* ruling, that seemed to constitutionalise a right to freedom of contract (as an aspect of the 'fundamental' right to conduct a business, itself hardly a human right), but which the Court has not repeated since, is perhaps best read as a one-off aberration'; S Weatherill, 'Use and Abuse of the EU's Charter of Fundamental Rights: On the Improper Veneration of "Freedom of Contract"' (2014) 10 *European Review of Contract Law* 167. On freedom of contract, see Niglia, *The Transformation of Contract in Europe* (n 10); Niglia, *The Struggle for European Private Law* (n 1). Balancing as deployed in the *Alemo-Herron* judgment has been confirmed in the Judgment of the Court (Fourth Chamber) of 26 March 2020 Case C-344/18 *ISS Facility Services NV v Sonia Govaerts and Atalian NV, formerly Euroclean NV* ECLI:EU:C:2020:239, para 26: 'Directive 2001/23 *does not aim solely to safeguard the interests of employees* in the event of transfer of an undertaking, *but seeks to ensure a fair balance between the interests of those employees, on the one hand, and those of the transferee, on the other* (see, to that effect, judgment of 18 July 2013, *Alemo-Herron and Others*, C-426/11, ECLI:EU:C:2013:521, paragraph 25)' (emphasis added).

[27] See Niglia, *The Struggle for European Private Law* (n 1) (on balancing freedom of contract with social normative considerations; on fundamental rights as ethical and moral (as to private law), see ibid. and L Niglia, 'Between "Institutionalizing Reason" and Private Law. A Comparative Map of Influences' in M La Torre, L Niglia and M Susi (eds), *The Quest for Rights* (Cheltenham, Edward Elgar, 2019).

This phenomenon, in turn, is but one manifestation of that kind of hermeneutics that emerges out of the CJEU jurisprudence and that this book singles out – considering the deployment of the further, altered, constitutional principles noted above. In order to understand critically the CJEU jurisprudence further, one must acknowledge a deeper dimension to the *Alemo-Herron* judgment.The mosaic of the hermeneutics of private order as presented in this chapter can be articulated in its relationship with the notion of 'freedom of contract' in the following terms: balancing is the key constitutional technique of the repertoire of the hermeneutics of private order (*Laval, Viking, Freiburger, Alemo-Herron*), although not always made explicit; the hermeneutics of private order that characterises the jurisprudence of the CJEU is about freedom of contract, although it is not always made explicit as such; the Court has chosen not to make 'freedom of contract' explicitly the centre of its case law, arguably to avoid open contestation, as happened when it explicitly referred to freedom of contract in *Alemo-Herron*, and has chosen a more subtle way to constitutionalise private relations with a view to promoting market interests above non-market interests; and the hermeneutics of private order constitutionalises private relations by altering, hermeneutically, a diverse set of doctrines and principles from fundamental rights to proportionality and the interpretative obligation; the broader, contentious implication of this hermeneutics is the valuing of market over society.

This mosaic of the hermeneutics of private order through balancing is a ready-made material that the Court can use widely, as in the judgment of *Facility Services* in 2020,[28] where the Court refers back to *Alemo-Herron*, and, recently, with the re-engineering of proportionality in a market-orientated sense that enables the Court to place market above society, and governance over society, in the context of crisis management governance (financial-political economic regimes) – in the paradigmatic judgment *Weiss* in 2018.[29] Here, proportionality, from pursuing social objectives and functions (as in the *Kokopelli* judgment),[30] becomes

[28] *ISS Facility Services* (n 26): as discussed at n 26.

[29] See CJEU *Weiss* (n 7); see also L Niglia, 'The European Judicial Saga on Law and Political Economy' (unpublished manuscript on file with author, 2022) (on German Federal Constitutional Court, judgment of the Second Senate of 5 May 2020, 2 BvR 859/15, 2 BvR 1651/15, 2 BvR 2006/15, 2 BvR 980/16, on the ECB asset purchase programme, through bonds bought by the ECB on the secondary market, for the purpose of financing states; under market conditions of 'uncertainty' as to their buying as required by the *Weiss* (n 7) and by the BVerfG 5 May 2020 judgments; states in need of financial support can finance their public debt; on BverfG Order of 15 April 2021, 2 BvR 547/21); and, on the memoranda of understanding and the EMU, and on the CJEU's *Florescu* (n 6), see Niglia, 'The New Transformation of Europe' (n 6).

[30] See Case C-59/11 *Association Kokopelli v Graines Baumaux SAS* ECLI:EU:C:2012:447, para 77: 'It is clear from settled case-law that the freedom to pursue an economic activity forms part of the general principles of EU law. Those principles are, however, not absolute, but must be viewed in relation to their social function. Consequently, the exercise of the freedom to pursue an economic activity may be restricted, provided that any restrictions in fact correspond to objectives of general interest pursued by the European Union and do not constitute in relation to the aim pursued a disproportionate and intolerable interference, impairing the very substance of the rights guaranteed (see, in particular, Case 265/87 *Schräder HS Kraftfutter* [1989] ECR 2237, paragraph 15, and Joined Cases C-154/04 and C-155/04

instrumental to market discipline, first in *Gauweiler* and then in *Weiss*, which refers back to *Gauweiler* on this point.[31] The hermeneutics of the private order expands further towards a deeper strategy aimed at the structural transformation of the EU constitutional order from composite order[32] to recognising private ordering as absolute and, coextensively, from sociality to marketisation.

(iv) Effectively, out of the juridical hermeneutical patterns under scrutiny in this book as redescribed in chapter four, private ordering considerations (typically associated with individualism)[33] are 'taking over' public interest considerations as enshrined in Europe's constitutional composite structure and as articulated in the hermeneutical terms of social balancing.[34]

As a result, a range of privatistic regimes, as 'self-standing' and yet as the newer articulation of the hermeneutics of private ordering, emerge in which unbounded private power holds sway. They are the contractual, usage and hybrid-digital regimes recounted in chapter four above. To these must be added the politico-financial economic regimes consisting of the ECB asset-buying programme and aspects of the Next Generation EU-RRF (Recovery and Resilience Facility) arrangements.[35]

An area of indistinction is generated by the new CJEU jurisprudence, where the relevant issues are held to belong neither to state order nor to EU order, and

Alliance for Natural Health and Others [2005] ECR I-6451, paragraph 126).' And at paras 78–79: 'In the present case, it is true that the acceptance regime for vegetable seed laid down by Directive 2002/55 and 2009/145 is capable of restricting the freedom of traders in old seed, such as Kokopelli, to pursue their professional activity.' 'However, the rules set out in Articles 3 to 5 of Directive 2002/55 are intended to secure improved productivity in vegetable cultivation in the European Union, the establishment of the internal market for vegetable seed by ensuring its free movement within the European Union, and the conservation of plant genetic resources, which are objectives of general interest. As is apparent from the grounds of the present judgment relating to the alleged breach of the principle of proportionality, those rules and the measures laid down by them are not inappropriate to the attainment of those objectives, and the obstacle to the freedom to pursue an economic activity which such measures represent cannot, in the light of the aims pursued, be regarded as disproportionately impairing the right to exercise that freedom.'

[31] See *Weiss* (n 7); European Court of Justice, Judgment of 16 June 2015, Case C-62/14 *Gauweiler and others v Deutscher Bundestag* ECLI:EU:C:2015:400; Case C-438/05 *International Transport Workers' Federation and Finnish Seamen's Union v Viking Line ABP and OÜ Viking Line EestiCase* ECLI:EU:C:2007:772.

[32] See ch 2 above.

[33] On individualism in private law, see Niglia, *The Struggle for European Private Law* (n 1) 39 (113), 67, 84, 97, 101; D Kennedy, 'A Transnational Genealogy of Proportionality in Private Law' in Brownsword et al (n 4); M Auer, *Materialisierung, Flexibilisierung, Richterfreiheit* (Tübingen, Mohr Siebeck, 2005).

[34] See ch 2; L Niglia, 'Eclipse of the Constitution' (2016) 22 *European Law Journal* 132 (on composite constitutionalism in Europe). On both private and public interest concerns, see Niglia, *The Struggle for European Private Law* (n 1); Niglia, 'Eclipse of the Constitution' (ibid); in the area of (EU) law and regulation, see F Snyder, 'Better Regulation in EU Law: Variations on a Theme' in N Rubio and F Peraldi-Leneuf (eds), *La fabrication du droit de l'Union europénne dans le context du Mieux Légiférer: Du modèle ã la réalité* (Aix-en-Provence, Presses de l'Université Aix-Marseille, 2017); P Drahos (ed), *Regulatory Theory: Foundations and Applications* (Canberra, Australian National University Press, 2017) http://press-files.anu.edu.au/downloads/press/n2304/pdf/book.pdf?referer=2304.

[35] See (iii)above. On the ECB asset-buying programme, see CJEU *Weiss* (n 7); BVerfG *PSPP* (n 7). On the Next Generation EU-RRF (Recovery and Resilience Facility), see https://ec.europa.eu/info/strategy/recovery-plan-europe_en#nextgenerationeu.

where the once openness of orders that used to ensure the disciplining of private relations according to the constitutional registers of both orders cooperatively (under the paradigm of 'constitutional autonomy') fades away. In the midst of this area of indistinction, private regimes can flourish untamed with their destructive potential of sociality material and relations.

One can also put this argument in the following terms, considering the critical methodological perspective adopted through this book's focus on orders' relations and transformations.[36] That is, at work is a *totalising* of the hermeneutics of private ordering insofar as its requirements, insulated from both EU constitutional and national constitutional constraints, constitute the shared ground of the distinct regimes. In other words, the apparent plurality of the regimes (consumer, labour, digital, commercial, politico-economical)[37] is effectively grounded in this dimension of totality.

Were the CJEU to pursue its totalising jurisprudence further, constitutional absorption would be bound, in ever greater areas and with greater intensity and scale, to make EU law and its constitutional order dependent on privatistic determinations derived from private ordering – according to a logic of reordering through constitutional appropriation of one order's determinations by another's. This process is not just an inversion of the public–private distinction, as rightly argued by Alain Supiot in relation to that area of EU law and policy that I label here as financial-political economic regimes.[38] Rather, it is a subversion of it towards totalising the private order's law: a constitutionally engineered subversion that, in Europe, both adds to and complexifies Supiot's noted 'inversion'.

One could then, and one should, articulate all of this in terms of reconstructing the emerging private order as a constellation of order-regimes[39] that have been 'taking over' the (once) new legal order and, correspondingly and coextensively, the national private legal orders – a reordering of Europe's constellation of orders through an internal 'takeover' among orders (as a new constitutional symbiotic paradigm).

And yet, this phenomenon is far from a definite process in that it is down to the contingency of the relevant hermeneutical struggles, as I am about to argue below in section (vi).

[36] See ch 1 above.

[37] See ch 4 above.

[38] See (iii) above; see also A Supiot, 'The Public–Private Relations in the Context of Today's Refeudalization' (2013) 11 *International Journal of Constitutional Law* 129, 141 (discussing an inversion of the private–public interface also in relation to the EMU; on the EMU, see Niglia, 'The New Transformation of Europe' (n 6)).

[39] Talking of 'order-regimes' means discussing 'pluralisation' (the anarchic and arbitrary ways of the private power regimes, given the unilaterality entailed in self-balancing: see below and ch 4 above), a notion to be contrasted with the phenomenon of 'pluralism' as characterising the paradigm of the jurisprudence of constitutional autonomy both as historically developed (see ch 2) and as a contemporary reference point, as I am about to argue. See Niglia, *Pluralism and European Private Law* (n 4).

(v) The implications of this totalising 'take over' are dilemmatic.[40] Constitutional absorption entails the shifting away from the previous state of jurisprudence, with its protecting equality and self-determination deriving from state laws as part of the constitutional paradigm of 'constitutional autonomy', to the new constitutional paradigm of a European constitutional law that totalises. Here, totalising renders the European constitutional order no longer connected to, or deriving meaning from, state laws while, at the same time, state (private) laws become negated insofar as they constitute difference and plurality.

This amounts, in turn, to a grammar of disciplination that institutionalises conditions of unfreedom and of unequal relations, as one can decode them under a critical reading that defies the mystification of arguments from the fictionality of contract represented as if necessarily entailing equality among the parties.

Such conditions include: the unfreedom of individuals and groups subjected to the contractual determinations of the stronger party; the unequal relations entailed in the EU regimes dictating conditionalities for states in need of funding (the Economic and Monetary Union (EMU)-related memoranda of understanding and the ECB buying bonds programmes);[41] and the complex conditions entailed in the use of digital instruments, placing individuals and groups at the mercy of private bodies' (sometimes monopolising) power whilst taking it away from legislators and courts.[42]

[40] *cf* the debate between H Lindhal, 'Authority and the Globalisation of Inclusion and Exclusion: Conceptual and Normative Considerations' (2019) 29 *Duke Journal of Comparative & International Law* 437 and R Michaels, 'A Symmetry of Asymmetries? A Private-International-Law Reconstruction of Lindahl's Work on Boundaries' (2019) 29 *Duke Journal of Comparative & International Law* 405. 'Totalising' through the 'taking over' among orders, as per the reading that I propose in this chapter, is a contingent process that I believe must be taken seriously. Compare Lindhal (ibid), who argues at 459 that 'no legal order is or can become universal because no legal order can include without excluding' and at 450 criticises pluralist views of legal orders, whilst equally referring to 'entwinements' (459: 'a condition of entwinement of orders and worlds') and to 'a "we" global'; compare Michaels (ibid), who discusses private international law as enabling a making room for otherness, talking of 'symmetrical asymmetry'. I am describing critically a contingent process of an-other order (an order other than the constitutional order, both EU and nation-state – the private order) becoming incorporated and absorbed, and transforming from within, the EU constitutional order through suspending and setting aside the latter's key requirements. I should stress that a comparative juridical hermeneutics not only includes but is composed of the study of these interdependent processes of taking over and absorption as hermeneutical situatedness (see ch 1 above).

[41] See on the financial-political economic regimes the *PSPP* decision of the BVerfG 2020 (n 7 above) and Niglia, 'The New Transformation of Europe' (n 6).

[42] See, respectively, *Kautelarpraxis*, *lex mercatoria* and digitisation (techne), in ch 4 above; as to the financial/political economic regimes, see (iii) above, and note that the 'conditionalities' are unequal in themselves (see Niglia, 'The New Transformation of Europe' (n 6), on the memoranda of understanding) and insofar as they are implemented through the market disciplinary (financial-fiscal) ECB 'buying bonds' programme(s) regime as envisaged by the CJEU and by the BVerfG in the remarkable judgments, respectively, of *Weiss* (n 7) and *PSPP* (7) (both on the ECB asset buying programme), as well as in the 15 April 2021 order of the BVerfG (on the Own Resources Decision 2020: BverfG Order of 15 April 2021, 2 BvR 547/21). For this reading, see Niglia, 'The European Judicial Saga' (n 29). On exploitation in contexts of digitisation (algorithms), see G Wagner and HGM Eidenmueller, 'Down by Algorithms? Siphoning Rents, Exploiting Biases and Shaping Preferences – The Dark Side of Personalized Transactions (March 30, 2018)'[2019] *University of Chicago Law Review* 581 (also discussed in ch 4). The perspective of private ordering adopted in this book enables one to understand

In other words, the associated exploitative and domination effects constructed and legitimated through the 'monistic' logic of economised balancing, as the hermeneutics of private order, includes imbalances as exploitation in a variety of areas (consumer contracting, labour contracting and digital contracting), as well as imbalances as unequal relations of 'jurisdomination' among states under the EU/EMU/ECB financial-political economic regimes.[43]

As a result, the CJEU jurisprudence promotes more than just the convergence of common norms, according to the template of reading it all as *harmonisation* or in terms of the more intensive form of convergence of private law's *unification*.[44] It also promotes, critically, the superimposition on the living law, as previously arranged under the jurisprudence of 'constitutional autonomy', of the hermeneutics of the economised type of balancing – which, in turn, must be understood as disciplination.[45]

further the analogy with the *Grossraum* (qua 'zone of influence') proposed in two writings that have gone against the grain of EU law scholarship on the EMU: D Chalmers, 'The European Redistributive State and a European Law of Struggle' (2012) 18 *European Law Journal* 667, 668, which draws on, and with the author explicitly mentioning his indebtedness for this point, C Joerges, 'Europe as Großraum?' in C Joerges and NS Ghaleigh (eds), *Darker Legacies of Law in Europe* (Oxford, Hart Publishing, 2003) 167: '[T]he euro area slips unwittingly into a form of Grossraum. A zone of influence dominated by the Commission and ECOFIN is established, with political conflicts taking place within these, but the atrophying of local democracy leads to a hollowing out of domestic processes so that these become little more than administrative containers. Conflicts will take place within these, but these will take place either only within the narrow parameters set for local discretion by the Union or over execution of policy.' I have argued in Niglia, 'The New Transformation of Europe' (n 6) that: 'it is not just the structures of public law (the EMU surveillance mechanisms), but also the structures of private law, though with greater force, which contribute to the worrying renewal of a European *Grossraum*. In other words, as the 'normalization' of governance by contract increases, integration through law as an anti-hegemonic project of equal respect for all members states regresses to a condition in which state orders, under a transformed EU law, gravitate around unequal relations of subordination.'

[43] On the first three typologies of imbalances, see ch 4 above; on imbalances as unequal relations of jurisdomination, see Niglia, 'The New Transformation of Europe' (n 6). On competences in relation to proportionality and balancing in both the CJEU and BVerfG jurisprudence, see Niglia, 'The European Judicial Saga' (n 29). The saga of the buying bonds programme (CJEU *Weiss* (n 7); BVerfG PSPP 2020 (n 7)) is telling in this regard whenever the courts choose to apply economised balancing to sensitive and contentious issues such as monetary politics and political economy. Here, the courts choose to take the path of exercising their power unconstrained by certain constitutional standards as conventionally applied (proportionality, fundamental rights, competences) and implement an order-regime based on the balancing of a variety of market factors at the sacrifice of non-market standards. This technique is deployed by the BVerfG as much as by the CJEU in the *Weiss* decision (n 7): see Niglia, 'The European Judicial Saga' (n 29). On issues regarding power as it underlies plural relations among orders, see R Michaels, 'Why We Have No Theory of European Private Law Pluralism' in Niglia, *Pluralism and European Private Law* (n 4); Michaels, 'A Symmetry of Asymmetries?' (n 40); Niglia, *Pluralism* (ibid); Niglia, 'The New Transformation' (n 6) (on 'jurisdomination').

[44] For relevant literature and for critique of the mystificatory meanings attached to these notions, see Niglia, *The Transformation of Contract in Europe* (n 10) (on harmonisation); Niglia, *The Struggle for European Private Law* (n 1) (on unification).

[45] This process counters, insofar as it aims at regimenting, the phenomenon of plurality and of constitutional pluralism (see Niglia, *Pluralism and European Private Law* (n 4)). Here, the plurality of 'private orders' are each being given the power to decide according to the economising determinations of the stronger party, turning orders' relations in 'pluralisation', far away from the 'pluralism' characterising the age of constitutional autonomy.

(vi) Totalisation, despite its inner pretence at obliterating any alternative positions, is far from a one-sided process that would somehow automatically exclude other normative dimensions uncontestedly.

There remains what we can call resistance patterns,[46] as evidenced by the ongoing hermeneutical struggles concerning, among others: first, *lex mercatoria*, as in the controversy between the contractual versus the normative views; second, standardised contracts, whenever seen as entailing unequal relations as opposed to just adopting arguments from market efficiency and competitiveness; third, digitisation, as in the controversies that have arisen in the context of the *Airbnb*, *Uber* and *Schrems* sagas; and fourth, the disputes concerning the EU financial-political economic regimes.[47]

Whether the resistance patterns will be able to obstruct and counter the operations of the new jurisprudence remains to be seen. What we know from the history of integration, as read through the lenses of critical comparativism and economic sociology, is that resistance patterns have never been and cannot be eliminated.[48] The question is also hermeneutical: will resistance patterns develop hermeneutically or will private law take a turn towards more intensively conforming to the emerging totalising hermeneutics?

Overall, the jurisprudence of constitutional autonomy itself remains a hermeneutical reference point never entirely given up or annihilated, that is, it is a discursive basis for the ongoing struggles over the law in Europe whenever actors wish to resist the turn towards totalising law around market ordering.[49]

[46] L Niglia, 'The Non-Europeanization of Private Law' (2001) 4 *European Review of Private Law* 575; Niglia, *The Struggle for European Private Law* (n 1); Niglia, 'Eclipse of the Constitution' (n 34); Niglia, 'The New Transformation of Europe' (n 6).

[47] Seech 4 and (iii) above; see also Niglia, *The Struggle for European Private Law* (n 1); Niglia, 'The New Transformation' (n 6). On the financial-political economic regime of the ECB buying bonds programme, see, eg J Basedow et al, 'European Integration: Quo Vadis? A Critical Commentary on the PSPP Judgment of the German Federal Constitutional Court of 5 May 2020' (2021) 19 *International Journal of Constitutional Law* 188; M Dani et al, 'It's the Political Economy …' (2021) 19 *International Journal of Constitutional Law* 309. Note how resistance patterns can be found even within the body of decisions of the CJEU: see the *Uber* saga (ch 4 above), signifying the complexity of the new symbiotic constitutional paradigm concerning constitutional orders and private ordering.

[48] L Niglia, 'The Non-Europeanization of Private Law' (2001) 4 *European Review of Private Law* 575; L Niglia, 'Diritto giurisprudenziale e direttive comunitarie in materia di diritto privato: note critiche' [1998] *Rivista critica di diritto privato* 459; Niglia, *The Struggle for European Private Law* (n 1). See C Joerges and J Falke (eds), *Karl Polanyi, Globalisation and the Potential of Law in Transnational Markets* (Oxford, Hart Publishing, 2011).

[49] See Niglia, *The Struggle for European Private Law* (n 1) 65 et seq (with further discussion and relevant judgments); see also ch 2 above. Authors take this stance of criticism and resistance by drawing on part of the material that I have labelled in this book 'jurisprudence of constitutional autonomy' in the sense of a criticism that can also be made intelligible with the vocabulary of what I call in this book 'heteronomy' and 'absorbtion': eg KH Ladeur, 'The State in International Law' in Joerges and Falke (n 48) 397, 402 (critically referring to 'an initially productive, but, more recently, increasingly disruptive, indiscriminating option for the implementation of the supremacy of European law with the assistance of a systematic penetration into national law', with the example of an expansive interpretation of product liability by the CJEU in its jurisprudence on the Product Liability Directive as entailing that 'the application of all possible national laws fulfilling or extending liability in any scenario touched

What is urgently needed is the expansion of the potential for a renovated jurisprudence of containment: that is, the pursuit of the strategy of containing the totalising of the law by returning to, with a view to revivifying and reinvigorating, the plural forms of co-normativising, hermeneutically, according to the structures of constitutional autonomy, as discussed above in chapter two. The fact that the jurisprudence of constitutional autonomy, despite being increasingly left behind, remains a reference point is a factor that goes towards making a jurisprudence of containment possible.

(vii) In the face of the totalising of law around private ordering, can law still be regarded as a 'safe place' (to paraphrase a recent journal's editorial[50]) ? To refer to a critical line of writings about Europeanisation seen as the product of modernism and rationalism,[51] with its new jurisprudence the CJEU insists in positing the EU as a structure that keeps recreating itself, confident in its doings, under its own self-perception (constructed) of a rational and modernist enterprise[52] that gives rise to a 'new' 'new socio-economic order'[53] in the sense, I am arguing in this book, of becoming a *juridical* order represented as if it were 'immune to its … radical conflicts, and power-based relationships' – through the characterisation of both neutralising conflicts, as entailed in the noted domination and exploitation dynamics, and enabling certain forces to gain prominence over others (dynamics of private ordering *vis-à-vis* constitutional orderings).[54]

upon by European law is excluded', and referring inter alia to C Joerges, 'The Impact of European Integration on Private law: Reductionist Perceptions' [1997] *European Law Journal* 374); and Ladeur (ibid) (referring to CU Schmid, 'The ECJ as a Constitutional and a Private Law Court', ZERP-DO 4/2006), arguing that 'The EU can, upon the basis of its size and the plurality of its experience, and its political, cultural and legal traditions never meaningfully strive to become a European "superstate". The ECJ seems to ignore this in its over-estimation of the meaning of the unity of law as an interpretive tool, which threatens the boundaries of the division of competences'; C Joerges, 'A New Type of Conflicts of Law as the Legal Paradigm of the Postnational Constellation' in Joerges and Falke (n 48) 465 et seq (on conflicts of law as legal paradigm) – which exemplify the kind of patterns of argumentation that go towards defending what I am calling jurisprudence of constitutional autonomy, arguments that in turn amount to a reference point for criticism of the new paradigm of constitutional absorption); see Advocate General P Mengozzi's Opinion in *Laval*, as discussed in Niglia, 'Eclipse of the Constitution' (n 34).

[50] See L Azoulai, 'Editorial. Europe Is Trembling. Looking for a Safe Place in EU Law' [2020] *CML Rev* ('We may be shaken by what is happening to Europe. True, we are eagerly seeking a safe place and a "survival unit," one that is responsible for taking care of us, protecting us from our own vulnerable condition, supporting the welfare State, keeping us in employment, maintaining our standard of living, and controlling the spread of the virus').

[51] See JHH Weiler, *The Constitution of Europe; 'Do the New Clothes Have an Emperor?' and Other Essays on European Integration* (Cambridge, Cambridge University Press, 1999). See also Azoulai (n 50): 'European integration posited Europe as the creation of a new socio-economic order, immune to its past, radical conflicts, and power-based relationships.'

[52] JHH Weiler, 'To Be a European Citizen – Eros and Civilization' (University of Wisconsin – Madison International Institute, 1998) http://aei.pitt.edu/8990/1/weiler.pdf: 'The very transnationalism of the Community, which earlier on was celebrated as a reinvention of Enlightenment idealism, is just that: Universal, rational, transcendent, and wholly modernist.'

[53] Azoulai (n 50).

[54] See above at ch 4 on contract as 'fiction', and note the argument from 'taking over'.

If it is true (and it is) that 'This crisis has exposed our dependency on external infrastructures, understood as a complex of global supply value chains, digital equipment, essential industries, and world trade patterns',[55] then it is the new jurisprudence, read through the hermeneutical reading adopted in this book, that creates the framework (in the logic of European integration as subjectivity that 'creates' its own condition) for those dependences to take shape and to rule upon us – making Europe even more the servant of, and legitimising, the unbound privatistic determinations that come out of the underlying and pervasive digital, industrial trade complexes.

From this viewpoint, recounting the ways of Europe's reordering patterns enables one to see into the material to which the 'anxiety, anger, fear'[56] that connote the integration project are traceable, for such anxiety flourishes as symptomatic of deep structural inequalities – the noted exploitation and domination patterns – whose matrix must be intercepted. The 'structural transformations' presented in this book aim to bring to light that matrix with a view to making possible any project of real emancipation towards overcoming the ongoing collapse of constitutional orderings.

To put it differently: a jurisprudence of containment is needed that recovers the logic of co-normativisation, as discussed in chapter two, and that can offer support for social demands related to the anxieties regarding the deep structural inequalities and towards emancipation from them.

This should start, I argue, with adopting and engaging with critical comparative hermeneutical readings. One illustration of such a reading is the *Google Spain* saga: I have offered an interpretation of this saga that is less optimistic than others suggest.[57] The comparative analysis of this saga and of the other sagas considered

[55] Azoulai (n 50) at p. 1677. See also Niglia, 'Europe and "Crisis"' (n 10).

[56] Azoulai (n 50): 'While the European Community, and then the European Union, worked hard to establish itself and its law as a "structured network of principles, rules, and mutually interdependent relations," it is now prey to amorphous social passions – anxiety, anger, fear.' On 'the deep modern and postmodern anxiety of European belongingness', see Weiler, 'To Be a European Citizen' (n 52).

[57] On the Judgment of the CJEU C-136/17 *GC and Others v CNIL* 24 September 2019 (Google, dereferencing), see ch 4above and above in this chapter. On my reading, it seems that it is not the case here that, in the area of data protection, 'The Court has chosen this area to develop in its case law the highest standards of protection offered to individuals', as in the opinion of Azoulai (n 50), also referring on this point to K Lenaerts, 'Limits on Limitations: The Essence of Fundamental Rights in the EU' (2019) 20 *German Law Journal* 779. Here, 'cognitive dissonance' applies. In fact, in the CJEU's judgment in *Schrems II* (n 15), the Court confirmed its approach, labelled 'delegation of sovereign powers' (see ch 4 above), in two senses. First, the assessment regarding the adequacy of the level of protection is made dependent (also) on the contractual clauses, and therefore on the actual arrangements made by the private parties. See at paras 102 and 103: 'The referring court also seeks to ascertain what factors should be taken into consideration for the purposes of determining the adequacy of the level of protection where personal data is transferred to a third country pursuant to standard data protection clauses adopted under Article 46(2)(c) of the GDPR. In that regard, although that provision does not list the various factors which must be taken into consideration for the purposes of assessing the adequacy of the level of protection to be observed in such a transfer, Article 46(1) of that regulation states that data subjects must be afforded appropriate safeguards, enforceable rights and effective legal remedies'; and at para 104: 'The assessment required for that purpose in the context of such a transfer must, in particular, take into consideration both the *contractual clauses* agreed between the controller or processor

above indicates that such less enchanted readings[58] are highly needed – if one is to take seriously real-life developments and, above all, the urgent need for restoring and relaunching co-normativisation. Cases in other areas not directly pertaining to private law confirm the view of a CJEU jurisprudence that chooses, counterintuitively, to not protect fundamental and human rights in certain critical situations (migration),[59] pointing to a distinct yet connected set of problems. As key components of the constitutional cathedral are emptied of their once established meaning, given the direction taken by the jurisprudence under scrutiny in this book, there remains a weakened constitutional architecture which, in turn, negatively impacts on all areas. The space of indistinction, created as a result of a jurisprudence that keeps crafting a law no longer belonging to the state or to the EU order as in the composite ways of the past, is an ideal condition for such de-constitutionalising (in the sense of setting aside key constitutional standards of the once composite constitutional order as considered in chapter two above) spillover effects across areas.

established in the European Union and the recipient of the transfer established in the third country concerned and, as regards any access by the public authorities of that third country to the personal data transferred, the relevant aspects of the legal system of that third country. As regards the latter, the factors to be taken into consideration in the context of Article 46 of that regulation correspond to those set out, in a non-exhaustive manner, in Article 45(2) of that regulation' (emphasis added). Second, the operators are called upon to exercise the assessment regarding the level of 'appropriateness' of the protection required by EU law relative to the relevant third country (confirming the point about delegation of sovereign powers; note Azoulai (n 50): 'by subjecting data exporters to the duty to verify whether the level of protection required by EU law is respected in the third country concerned'), that is, at paras 140 and 141: 'Clause 5(a) and (b), in both cases to which it refers, confers on the controller established in the European Union the right to suspend the transfer of data and/or to terminate the contract. In the light of the requirements of Article 46(1) and (2)(c) of the GDPR, read in the light of Articles 7 and 8 of the Charter, the controller is bound to suspend the transfer of data and/or to terminate the contract where the recipient is not, or is no longer, able to comply with the standard data protection clauses. Unless the controller does so, it will be in breach of its obligations under Clause 4(a) in the annex to the SCC Decision as interpreted in the light of the GDPR and of the Charter. It follows that Clause 4(a) and Clause 5(a) and (b) in that annex oblige the controller established in the European Union and the recipient of personal data to satisfy themselves that the legislation of the third country of destination enables the recipient to comply with the standard data protection clauses in the annex to the SCC Decision, before transferring personal data to that third country. As regards that verification, the footnote to Clause 5 states that mandatory requirements of that legislation which do not go beyond what is necessary in a democratic society to safeguard, inter alia, national security, defence and public security are not in contradiction with those standard data protection clauses. Conversely, as stated by the Advocate General in point 131 of his Opinion, compliance with an obligation prescribed by the law of the third country of destination which goes beyond what is necessary for those purposes must be treated as a breach of those clauses. *Operators' assessments* of the necessity of such an obligation must, where relevant, take into account a finding that the level of protection ensured by the third country in a Commission adequacy decision, adopted under Article 45(3) of the GDPR, is appropriate' (emphasis added).

[58] On disenchantment and European private law, see L Niglia, 'Beyond Enchantment: The Possibility of a New European Private Law (Instalment Two)' (2009) 28 *Yearbook of European Law* 60.

[59] For this critical argument see Niglia, 'Europe and "Crisis"' (n 10) (General Court, order of 28 February 2017, Case T-192/16 *NF v European Council* ECLI:EU:T:2017:128; and CJEU, order of 12 September 2018, Joined Cases C-208/17 P to C-210/17 P *NF and Others v European Council* ECLI:EU:C:2018:705: appeal dismissed as 'manifestly inadmissible', pursuant to Art 181 of the Rules of Procedure of the Court of Justice).

Moreover, as the CJEU juridifies private ordering as an absolute, the rule of law and solidarity are increasingly not only suspended and set aside, as seen above, but also made altogether preposterous. This is because the premises upon which they are predicated collapse as a result of the fragmentation of the EU constitutional order around order-regimes and the related 'taking over' effects.[60]

In fact, the preconditions upon which both the rule of law and solidarity rest[61] recede. What solidarity is possible, after all, if the very material upon which solidarity stands – orders orientated towards mutual learning and support, as in the paradigm of constitutional autonomy[62] – is replaced by a clashing of orders? And what solidarity is possible if private ordering is conceptualised, internally, as a range of competing individualistic positions without any bond of solidarity – as in the judicial construction of the relations among the contractors and the workers respectively in the *Freiburger* and the *Laval*/*Viking* sagas – whilst, externally, private ordering is conceived of as a kind of absolutising ordering, that is, rendered free from (*solutus*) the conventional constitutional constraints, under the spell of a reordering through 'constitutional subversion'?

We are left with a caricature of constitutionalism, that is, the making of a quasi-constitutional order of privatistic relations where exploitation and domination can take place unchecked. This is far away from the long-term commitment to the constitutionally designed principles of equality and liberties that has characterised

[60] With regard to the EU financial-political economic regimes (in particular, the ECB asset buying programmes), see the reaction of scholarship to the German Federal Constitutional Court, Second Senate's judgment of 5 May 2020, 2 BvR 859/15, 2 BvR 1651/15, 2 BvR 2006/15, 2 BvR 980/16 on the ECB asset purchase programme, eg J Basedow et al, 'European Integration: *Quo vadis*? A Critical Commentary on the *PSPP* Judgment of the German Federal Constitutional Court of May 5, 2020' (2021) 19 *International Journal of Constitutional Law* 188.

[61] Note Advocate General Sharpston's Opinion in Joined Cases C-715/17, C-718/17 and C-719/17 *European Commission v Republic of Poland and Others* ECLI:EU:C:2019:917, para 241: 'The rule of law has many important sub-components, such as respect for the proper balance of power between the different branches of government and ensuring the independence of the judiciary by protecting their tenure in office. At a deeper level, respect for the rule of law implies compliance with one's legal obligations. Disregarding those obligations because, in a particular instance, they are unwelcome or unpopular is a dangerous first step towards the breakdown of the orderly and structured society governed by the rule of law which, as citizens, we enjoy both for its comfort and its safety. The bad example is particularly pernicious if it is set by a Member State.' And at paras 253–54: '253. Solidarity is the lifeblood of the European project. Through their participation in that project and their citizenship of European Union, Member States and their nationals have obligations as well as benefits, duties as well as rights. Sharing in the European "demos" is not a matter of looking through the Treaties and the secondary legislation to see what one can claim. It also requires one to shoulder collective responsibilities and (yes) burdens to further the common good. 254. Respecting the 'rules of the club' and playing one's proper part in solidarity with fellow Europeans cannot be based on a penny-pinching cost–benefit analysis along the lines (familiar, alas, from Brexiteer rhetoric) of 'what precisely does the EU cost me per week and what exactly do I personally get out of it?' Such self-centredness is a betrayal of the founding fathers' vision for a peaceful and prosperous continent. It is the antithesis of being a loyal Member State and being worthy, as an individual, of shared European citizenship. If the European project is to prosper and go forward, we must all do better than that.'

[62] See ch 2 on the jurisprudence of constitutional autonomy (on mutual learning and co-normativisation).

the march of constitutionalism towards progress since post-war times – principles that are now increasingly being left behind by a cadre of jurists that have been silently turning juridical hermeneutics against itself.[63]

This predicament no doubt calls for the responsibility of the wider community of jurists to reverse this process – whether they be jurists specialising in European law, private law, comparative law, constitutional law, legal history or jurisprudence. As woven into constitutional structures are cracks that result from the above-noted powerful tendencies towards law's totalising, which intersects wider concerns regarding the condition of Europe ('Europe is trembling'),[64] only a return to juridical hermeneutics, in the sense of reclaiming what has been left behind of that heritage, can redeem the constitutional cathedral and rescue our polities.

[63] According to the 'trans-juridification' reading above proposed: see ch 4 above.

[64] See Azoulai (n 50). On Europe and crisis, see Niglia, 'The New Transformation of Europe' (n 6); Niglia, 'Europe and "Crisis"' (n 10).

BIBLIOGRAPHY

Ackermann, T, 'Public Supply of Optional Standardized Consumer Contracts: A Rationale for the Common European Sales Law?' (2013) 50 *CML Rev* 11.

Adams, M and Heirbaut, D (eds), *The Method and Culture of Comparative Law: Essays in Honour of Mark Van Hoecke* (Oxford, Hart Publishing, 2014).

Adorno, TW, *Vorlesung über Negative Dialektik* (R Tiedemann ed, Suhrkamp, 2007).

Aleinikoff, TA, 'Constitutional Law in the Age of Balancing' (1987) 96 *Yale Law Journal* 943.

Alexy, R, 'Constitutional Rights, Balancing and Rationality' (2003) 16(2) *Ratio Juris* 131.

Alpa, G, *La cultura delle regole. Storia del diritto civile italiano* (Rome, Laterza, 2000) 307).

Alpa, G and Andenas, M, *I Fondamenti del Diritto Privato Europeo* (Milan, Giuffrè, 2005).

Amato, G, Barbisan, B and Pinelli, C (eds.) *Rule of Law vs Authoritarian Democracy* (Oxford, Hart Publishing, 2021).

Amstuz, M, 'In-Between Worlds: Marleasing and the Emergence of Interlegality in Legal Reasoning' (2005) 11 *European Law Journal* 766.

Ascarelli, T, 'L'idea di codice nel diritto privato e la funzione dell'interpretazione (1945)' in T Ascarelli, *Saggi Giuridici* (Milan, Giuffrè, 1949) 48.

Asquini, A, 'Codice di commercio' in F Calasso (ed), *Enciclopedia del Diritto*, vol VII (Milan, Giuffrè, 1960).

Aubry, C and Rau, C, *Cours de droit civil français* (1869–71).

Auer, M, *Zum Erkenntnissziel Der Rechtstheorie* (Baden-Baden, Nomos, 2018).

Auer, M, *Materialisierung, Flexibilisierung, Richterfreiheit* (Tübingen, Mohr Siebeck, 2005).

Azoulai, L, 'Editorial. Europe Is Trembling. Looking for a Safe Place in EU Law' (2020) 57 *CML Rev* 1675, https://hal-sciencespo.archives-ouvertes.fr/hal-03230201/document.

Azzariti, G (ed), *Interpretazione Costituzionale* (Turin, Giappichelli, 2007).

Baquero Cruz, J, *What's Left of the Law of Integration? Decay and Resistance in European Union Law* (Oxford, Oxford University Press, 2018).

Bar-Gill, O and Ben-Shahar, O, 'Regulatory Techniques in Consumer Protections: A Critique of European Consumer Contract Law' (2013) 50 *CML Rev* 109.

Barkhuysen, T and Lindenbergh S (eds), *Constitutionalisation of Private Law* (Leiden, Martinus Nijhoff, 2006).

Barnard, C, '*Viking* and *Laval*: An Introduction' (2007) 10 *Cambridge Yearbook of European Law* 463.

Basedow, J, 'Codification of Private Law in the European Union: The Making of a Hybrid' (2001) 9(1) *European Review of Private Law* 35.

Basedow, J, 'The State's Private Law and the Economy: Commercial Law as an Amalgam of Public and Private Rule-Making' (2008) 56 *American Journal of Comparative Law* 703.

Basedow, J, 'Transjurisdictional Codifications' (2009) 83 *Tulane Law Review* 973.

Basedow, J, 'The Optional Instrument of European Contract Law: Opting-in through Standard Terms – A Reply to Simon Whittaker' (2012) 8 *European Review of Contract Law* 82.

Basedow, J, Hopt, K and Zimmermann, R, 'Preface' in J Basedow, K Hopt and R Zimmermann (eds), *Max Planck Encyclopedia of European Private Law* (Oxford, Oxford University Press, 2012).

Basedow, J, Fleischer, H and Zimmermann, R, *Legislators, Judges and Professors* (Tübingen, Mohr Siebeck, 2016).

Basedow, J et al, 'European Integration: *Quo vadis*? A Critical Commentary on the *PSPP* Judgment of the German Federal Constitutional Court of May 5, 2020' (2021) 19 *International Journal of Constitutional Law* 188.

Bauer, H, Czybulka, D and Kahl, W, *Wirtschaft im offenen Verfassungsstaat, FS für Reiner Schmidt* (Munich, Verlag CH Beck, 2006).

Beach, D, 'EU Institutions and ICG Negotiations – How the Negotiation Process Affects Their Ability to Gain Influence in ICGs' in P Meertz and F Cede (eds), *Negotiating European Union* (Basingstoke, Palgrave Macmillan, 2004).

Beach, D, *The Dynamics of European Integration* (Basingstoke, Palgrave Macmillan, 2005).

Beale, H, 'The European Commission's Common Frame of Reference: A Progress Report' (2006) 2 *European Review of Contract Law* 303.

Beaumont, P and Weatherill, S, *EU Law* (Harmondsworth, Penguin, 1999).

Belleau, M-C, 'The "Juristes Inquiets": Legal Classicism and Criticism in Early Twentieth-Century France' (1987) 2 *Utah Law Review* 379.

Bellomo, M, *L'Europa del Diritto Comune*, 8th edn (Rome, Il Cigno Galileo Galilei Edizioni di Arte e Scienza, 1998).

Bentham, J, 'Papers Relative to Codification and Public Instruction' in J Bowring (ed), *The Works of Jeremy Bentham*, vol IV (Edinburgh, Tait, 1843) 518.

Bentham, J, 'Letter to the President of the United States, 1811' in P Schoefield and J Harris (eds), *Jeremy Bentham, 'Legislator of the World': Writings on Codification, Law, and Education* (Oxford, Clarendon Press, 1998).

Bercusson, B, 'The Trade Union Movement and the European Union: Judgment Day' (2007) 13 *European Law Journal* 279.

Berman, PS, 'Jurisgenerative Constitutionalism: Procedural Principles for Managing Global Legal Pluralism' (2013) 20 *Indiana Journal of Global Legal Studies.*

Besselink, LFM, *A Composite European Constitution. Een Samengestelde Europese Constitutie* (Groningen, Europa Law Publishing, 2007).

Betti, E, *General Theory of Interpretation* (Teoria Generale dell'Interpretazione), 1st edn (Milan, Giuffré, 1955).

Blichner, LC and Molander, A, 'What Is Juridification?' (Arena, 2005) Working Paper 14/2005.

Block, F, 'Towards a New Understanding of Economic Modernity' in C Joerges, B Strath and P Wagner (eds), *The Economic as a Polity: The Political Construction of Modern Capitalism – An Interdisciplinary Perspective* (London, UCL Press, 2005).

Bomhoff, J, *Balancing Constitutional Rights: The Origins and Meanings of Postwar Legal Discourse*, Cambridge Studies in Constitutional Law (Cambridge, Cambridge University Press, 2013).

Bomhoff, J, 'Review of Alec Stone Sweet & Jud Mathews, *Proportionality Balancing and Global Governance: A Comparative and Global Approach* (Oxford University Press, 2019)' (2021) 69 *American Journal of Comparative Law* 168.

Brechmann, W, *Die Richtlinienkonforme Auslegung: Zugleich ein Beitrag zur Dogmatik der EG-Richtlinie* (Munich, CH Beck, 1994).

Brownsword, R, 'The Theoretical Foundations of European Private Law: A Time to Stand and Stare' in R Brownsword, H Micklitz, L Niglia and S Weatherill (eds), *The Foundations of European Private Law* (Oxford, Hart Publishing, 2011) 171.

Brownsword, R, Micklitz, H, Niglia, L and Weatherill, S (eds), *The Foundations of European Private Law* (Oxford, Hart Publishing, 2011).

Brandner, HE and Ulmer, P, 'EG-Richtlinie über missbräuchliche Klauseln in Verbraucherverträgen. Kritische Bemerkungen zum Vorschlag der EG-Kommission' [1991] *Betriebs Berater* 701.

Brüggemeier, G, 'Constitutionalisation of Private Law – The German Perspective' in T Barkhuysen and S Lindenbergh (eds), *Constitutionalisation of Private Law* (Leiden, Martinus Nijhoff, 2006) 59.

Brüggemeier, G, Colombi Ciacchi, A and Comandé, G (eds), *Fundamental Rights and Private Law in the European Union*, vol I, *A Comparative Overview* (Cambridge, Cambridge University Press, 2010).

Buchanan, JM, *Constitutional Economics* (Oxford, Blackwell, 1991).

Burgess, JP, 'Culture and the Rationality of Law from Weimar to Maastricht' in C Joerges and NS Ghaleigh (eds), *Darker Legacies of Law in Europe* (Oxford, Hart Publishing, 2003) 143.

Bürge, A, *Das franzosische Privatrecht im 19. Jahrhundert zwischen Tradition und Pandektenwissenschaft, Liberalismus und Etatismus*, 2nd edn (Frankfurt, Klostermann 1995).

Bussani, M, 'Deglobalizing Rule of Law and Democracy: Hunting Down Rhetoric Through Comparative Law (December 1, 2019)' (2019) 67 *American Journal of Comparative Law* 701.
Calabresi, G and Melamed, AD, 'Property Rules, Liability Rules, and Inalienability: One View of the Cathedral' (1972) 85 *Harvard Law Review* 1089.
Calliess, G-P (ed), *Transnationales Recht* (Tübingen, Mohr Siebeck, 2018).
Canaris, C-W, *Systemdenken and Systembegriff in der Jurisprudenz* (Berlin, Dunckler und Humblot, 1983).
Canaris, C-W, 'Grundrechte und Privatrecht' (1984) 184 *Archiv für die civilistische Praxis* 201.
Canaris, C-W, 'Die richtlinienkonforme Auslegung und Rechtsfortbildung im System der juristischen Methodenlehre' in H Koziol and P Rummel (eds), *Im Dienste der Gerechtigkeit: Festschrift für Franz Bydlinski* (Berlin, Springer, 2002).
Canaris, C-W, 'Gemeinsamkeiten zwischen verfassungs- und richtlinienkonformer Rechtsfindung' in *Wirtschaft im offenen Verfassungsstaat, Festschrift für Reiner Schmidt* (Munich, Verlag CH Beck, 2006) s 53.
Cannizzaro, E, *Il Diritto dell'Integrazione Europea. L'Ordinamento dell'Unione* (Turin, Giappichelli, 2020).
Cannizzaro, E, 'Preface' in E Cannizzaro (ed), *The Present and Future of Jus Cogens* (2015) vi, vii.
Cappellini, P and Sordi, B (eds), *Codici. Una riflessione di fine millennio* (Milan, Giuffrè, 2002).
Carbonnier, J, 'Le Code civil' in P Nora (ed), *Les Lieux de mémoire*, vol 1(Paris, Éditions Gallimard, 1997).
Caroni, P, 'Kodifikation' in A Erler and E Kaufmann (eds), *Handwoerterbuch zur Deutchen Rechtsgeschichte* (Berlin, Erich Schmidt Verlag, 1978) 907.
Caroni, P, 'Il codice rinviato. Resistenze europee all'elaborazione e alla diffusione del modello codicistico' in P Cappellini and B Sordi (eds), *Codici. Una riflessione di fine millennio* (Milan, Giuffrè, 2002).
Caroni, P, 'Codificare su due versanti: quello civile e quello penale. Riflessioni sul mito del codice-guida' in E Tavilla (ed), *Giuseppe Luosi, giurista italiano ed europeo. Traduzioni, tradizioni e tradimenti della codificazione. A 200 anni dalla traduzione in italiano del Code Napoléon (1806–2006)*, Atti del Convegno Internazionale di Studi, Mirandola-Modena, 19–20 October 2006 (Carpi, APM Edizioni, 2009) 347.
Cartabia, M and Weiler, JH, *L' Italia in Europa. Profili istituzionali e costituzionali* (Bologna, Il Mulino, 2000).
Caruso, D, 'The Missing View of the Cathedral: The Private Law Paradigm of European Legal Integration' (1997) 3 *European Law Journal* 3.
Caruso, D, 'Non-Parties: The Negative Externalities of Regional Trade Agreements in a Private Law Perspective' (2018) 59(2) *Harvard International Law Journal* 389.
Chalmers, D, 'Constituent Power and the Pluralistic Ethic' in M Loughlin and N Walker (eds), *The Paradox of Constitutionalism* (Oxford, Oxford University Press, 2008) 313.
Chalmers, D, 'The European Redistributive State and a European Law of Struggle' (2012) 18 *European Law Journal* 667.
Chalmers, D, 'Crisis Reconfiguration of the European Constitutional State' in D Chalmers, M Jachtenfuchs and C Joerges (eds), *The End of the Eurocrats' Dream: Adjusting to European Diversity* (Cambridge, Cambridge University Press, 2016).
Chalmers, D, Jachtenfuchs, M and Joerges, C (eds), *The End of the Eurocrats' Dream: Adjusting to European Diversity* (Cambridge, Cambridge University Press, 2016).
Chirac, J (Président de la République), 'Message' in *Livre Centenaire*, https://livre.fnac.com/a1508696/Jean-Louis-Halperin-Livre-du-centenaire-Le-Code-civil-1804–1904.
Cluzel-Métayer, L, 'The Judicial Review of the Automated Administrative Act' [2020] *European Review of Digital Administration & Law* 101.
Coing, H, *Zur Geschichte der Privatrechtsystems* (Frankfurt am Main, Suhrkamp, 1962).
Collins, H, 'The Impact of Human Rights on Contract Law in Europe' (2001) University of Cambridge Legal Studies Research Papers Series 8.
Collins, H, *The European Civil Code: The Way Forward* (Cambridge, Cambridge University Press, 2007).

Comandé, G, 'Comparative Remarks' in G Brüggemeier, A Colombi Ciacchi and G Comandé (eds), *Fundamental Rights and Private Law in the European Union*, vol I, *A Comparative Overview* (Cambridge, Cambridge University Press, 2010) 754.

Comparato, G, *Nationalism and Private Law in Europe* (Oxford, Hart Publishing, 2014).

Coppel, J, 'Rights, Duties and the End of Marshall' (1994) 57 *MLR* 859.

Cornu, G, *Introduction, les personnes, les biens*, 10th edn (Paris, Éditions Montchrestien, 2001).

Cosack, K in H Planitz (ed), *Die Rechtwissenschaft der Gegenwart in Selbstdarstellungen*, vol I (Leipzig, F Meiner, 1923–25) 16.

Cover, RM, 'The Supreme Court, 1982 Term – Foreword: Nomos and Narrative (1983) 97 *Harvard Law Review* 4.

Craig, P and de Búrca, G, *EU Law. Text, Cases and Materials*, 6th edn (Oxford, Oxford University Press, 2015).

Craig, P and de Búrca, G, *EU Law. Text, Cases and Materials*, 4th edn (Oxford, Oxford University Press, 2007).

Craswell, R, 'Property Rules and Liability Rules in Unconscionability and Related Doctrines' (1993) 60 *University of Chicago Law Review* 1.

Christodoulis, E, *The Redress of Law: Globalisation, Constitutionalism and Market Capture* (Cambridge, Cambridge University Press, 2021).

Cutler, AC, 'The Judicialization of Private Transnational Power and Authority' (2018) 25 *Indiana Journal of Global Legal Studies* 61.

Dani, M et al, 'It's the Political Economy …' (2021) 19 *International Journal of Constitutional Law* 309.

Davies, G, 'Freedom of Contract and the Horizontal Effect of Free Movement Law' in D Leczykiewicz and S Weatherill (eds), *The Involvement of EU Law in Private Law Relationships* (Oxford, Hart Publishing, 2013) 53.

Davies, A, 'One Step Forward, Two Steps Back? The *Viking* and *Laval* Cases in the ECJ' (2008) 37 *Industrial Law Journal* 126.

Deakin, S, 'Regulatory Competition after Laval' (2007) 10 *Cambridge Yearbook of European Legal Studies* 581.

de Búrca, G, 'The European Courts and the Security Council: Between Dédoublement Fonctionnel and Balancing of Values: Three Replies to Pasquale De Sena and Maria Chiara Vitucci' (2009) 20 *European Journal of International Law* 853.

Dedek, H (ed), *Cosmopolitan Jurisprudence Essays in Memory of H Patrick Glenn* (Cambridge, Cambridge University Press, 2021).

Delmas-Marty, M (ed), *Critique de l'Integration Normative* (Paris, PUF).

de Man, P, *The Resistance to Theory* (Minneapolis, MN, University of Minnesota Press, 1986).

Demogue, R, *Les notions fundamentales du droit privé: essai critique pour servir d'introduction à l'étude des obligations* (Paris, Rosseau, 1911).

Demolombe, C, *Cours de Code Napoléon* (1854–82).

Donahue, C, 'Private Law without the State and During its Formation' in N Jansen and R Michaels (eds), *Beyond the State: Rethinking Private Law* (Tübingen, Mohr Siebeck, 2008) 121.

Drahos, P (ed), *Regulatory Theory: Foundations and Applications* (Canberra, Australian National University Press, 2017).

Dunand, J-P, 'Entre tradition et innovation. Analyse historique du concept de code' in J-P Dunand and B Winiger (eds), *Le Code Civil Francais dans le droit europeen* (Brussels, Bruylant, 2005) 3.

Duranton, M, *Cours de droit français suivant le Code civil*, 3rd edn (1834).

Dürig, G, 'Der Grundgrechtssarz von der Menschenwuerde – Entwurf eines praktikablen Wertsystems der Grundrechte aus Article 1 Abs. 1 in Verbindung mit Article 19 Abs. II des Grundgesetzes' [1956] *AöR* 117.

Durovic, M and Tridimas, T (eds), *New Directions in European Private Law* (Oxford, Hart Publishing, 2021).

Duve, T, 'Preface – Symposium: Legal History and Comparative Law' (2018) 66 *American Journal of Comparative Law* 723.

Eidenmüller, H, *Effizienz als Rechtsprinzip. Möglichkeiten und Grenzen der ökonomischen Analyse des Rechts*, 3rd edn (Tübingen, Mohr Siebeck, 2005).

Eidenmüller, H, 'Recht als Produkt' (2009) 64 *Juristenzeitung* 641.

Eidenmüller, H, 'What Can Be Wrong with an Option? An Optional Common European Sales Law as a Regulatory Tool' (2013) 50 *CML Rev* 69.

Eidenmüller, H, Faust, F, Grigoleit, H, Jansen, N, Wagner, G and Zimmermann, R, 'The Common Frame of Reference for European Private Law - Policy Choices and Codification Problems' (2008) 28 *OJLS* 659, 665.

Eidenmüller, H, Faust, F, Grigoleit, H, Jansen, N, Wagner, G and Zimmermann, R, 'Der Gemeinsame Referenzrahmen für das Europäische Privatrecht - Wertungsfragen and Kodifikationsprobleme' (2008) 63 *Juristenzeitung* 529.

Eidenmüller, H, Jansen, N, Kieninger, E, Wagner, G and Zimmermann, R, 'Der Vorschlag für eine Verordnung über ein Gemeinsames Europäisches Kaufrecht' [2012] *Juristenzeitung* 269.

Eriksen, EO, and Fossum, JE 'Europe at a Crossroads: Government or Transnational Governance?' in C Joerges, I Sand and G Teubner (eds) *Transnational Governance and Constitutionalism* (Hart Publishing, Oxford, 2004) 115–146.

Esser, J, *Vorverständniss und Methodenwhal in der Rechtsfindung* (1970, 1972).

Everson, M, 'The Legacy of the Market Citizen' in J Shaw and G More (eds), *New Legal Dynamics of the European Union* (Oxford, Clarendon Press, 1995) 73–89.

Everson, M, 'The Limits of the "Conflicts Approach": Law in Time of Political Turmoil' (2011) 2 *Transnational Legal Theory* 271.

Ewald, F, 'Rapport philosophique: une politique du droit' in *Le Code Civil 1804–2004 Livre du Bicentenaire* (Paris, Dalloz, 2004) 76.

Ewald, W, 'Comparative Jurisprudence (I): What Was It Like to Try a Rat?' (1995) 143 *University of Pennsylvania Law Review* 1889.

Fauvarque-Cosson, B, 'Faut-il un Code Civil Européen?' (2002) 3 *Revue Trimestrielle de Droit Civil* 463, 480.

Fauvarque-Cosson, B, 'Vers un droit commun européen de la vente' (2012) 188 *Recueil Dalloz* 34.

Ferreri, S and DiMatteo, LA, 'Terminology Matters: Dangers of Superficial Transplantation' (2019) 37 *Boston University International Law Journal* 35.

Fleischer, H, 'Kautelarpraxis und Privatrecht: Grundfragen und gesellschaftsrechtliche Illustrationen' (2018) 82(2) *Rabels Zeitschrift* 239.

Fletcher, G, 'Three Nearly Sacred Books in Western Law' (2001–02) 54 *Arkansas Law Review* 1.

Friedmann, W, Henkin, L and Lissitzyn, O (eds), *Transnational Law in a Changing Society. Essays in Honor of Philip C Jessup* (New York, Columbia University Press, 1972).

Fromont, M, 'Les droit fondamentauz dans l'ordre juridique de la République Fédérale d'Allemagne' in *Recueil d'études en l'honneur de Ch Eisenmann* (Paris, Cujas, 1975) 55.

Gadamer, HG, *Waheheit und Method. Grundzüge einer philosophischen Hermeneutik* (Tübingen, Mohr Siebeck, 1960).

Gadamer, HG, *Gesammelte Werke* (10 vols, 1985–97).

Gaja, G, 'Judgment of June 8, 1984, Corte cost., Italy' (1984) 21 *CML Rev* 764.

Galgano, F, '*Lex mercatoria*' in *Enciclopedia del diritto V* (Milan, Treccani, 2001) 721.

Gambaro, A, 'Codici e diritto giurisprudenziale' in Cappellini, P and Sordi, B (eds), *Codici. Una riflessione di fine millennio* (Milan, Giuffrè, 2002) 507.

Gandolfi, G, 'Per un Codice Europeo dei Contratti' (1991) 45 *Rivista Trimestrale di Diritto e Procedura Civile* 781.

Gény, F, 'La Technique législative dans la codification civile moderne (a propos du centeraire du code civil)' in *Le Code Civil Livre du centenaire* (Paris, Dalloz, 1904) 989.

Gény, F, *Méthode d'interprétation et sources en droit privé positif. Essai Critique*, 2nd edn (Paris, LGD, 1919).

Ghestin, F, *Traité de droit civil. Introduction générale* (Paris, Librairie Générale de Droit et de Jurisprudence, 1994).

Gilmore, G, 'Legal Realism: Its Cause and Cure' (1961) 70 *Yale Law Journal* 1037.

Giubboni, S, *Social Rights and Market Freedom in the European Constitution. A Labour Law Perspective* (Cambridge, Cambridge University Press, 2006).
Glanert, S, 'Method' in PG Monateri (ed), *Methods of Comparative Law* (Cheltenham, Edward Elgar, 2012) 61.
Glanert, S and Girard, F (eds), *Law's Hermeneutic: Other Investigations* (London, Routledge, 2017).
Glenn, HP, *Legal Traditions in the World: Sustainable Diversity in Law*, 4th edn (Oxford, Oxford University Press, 2010).
Glenn, HP, 'Persuasive Authority' (1987) 32 *McGill Law Journal* 261, 263.
Glenn, HP, *The Cosmopolitan State* (Oxford, Oxford University Press, 2013).
Glenn, HP, 'Against Method?' in M Adams and D Heirbaut (eds), *The Method and Culture of Comparative Law: Essays in Honour of Mark Van Hoecke* (Oxford, Hart Publishing, 2014).
Goksor, R, 'Jurisprudence on Protection of Weaker Parties in European Contract Law from a Swedish and Nordic Perspective' (2006) 6 *Chicago-Kent Journal of International & Comparative Law* 184.
Gomez, F and Ganuza, JJ, 'The Economics of Private Law Harmonised Law-making: Mechanisms, Modes and Standards' in R Brownsword, H Micklitz, L Niglia and S Weatherill (eds), *The Foundations of European Private Law* (Oxford, Hart Publishing, 2011), 115.
Gomez, F and Ganuza, JJ, 'The Economics of Harmonising Private Law through Optional Rules in Pluralism' in L Niglia, *Pluralism and European Private Law* (Oxford, Hart Publishing, 2013) 181.
Gordley, J, 'The Myths of the French Civil Code' (1994) 42 *American Journal of Comparative Law* 459.
Gordon, PE and McCormick, J (eds), *Weimar Thought: A Contested Legacy* (Princeton, Princeton University Press, 2013).
Gorla Voce, G, 'Giurisprudenza' in C Mortati and S Pugliatti (eds), *Enciclopedia del Diritto*, vol XIX (Milan, Giuffrè, 1970) 490.
Greer, S, '"Balancing" and the European Court of Human Rights: A Contribution to the Habermas–Alexy Debate' (2004) 63 *CLJ* 412.
Grossi, P, *Assolutismo Giuridico e Diritto Privato* (Milan, Giuffrè, 1998).
Grossi, P, *Universalismo e particolarismo nel diritto* (Naples, Editoriale Scientifica, 2011).
Grundmann, S, *Die Auslegung des Gemeinschaftsrechts durch den Europäischen Gerichtshof: Zugleich eine rechtsvergleichhende Studie zur Auslegung im Völkerrecht und im Gemeinschaftsrecht* (Konstanz, Hartung-Gorre Verlag, 1996).
Grundmann, S, 'Richtlinienkonforme Auslegung im Bereich des Privatrechts – insbesondere: der Kanon der nationalen Auslegungsmethoden als Grenze?' [1996] *Zeitschrift für Europäisches Privatrecht* 399.
Grundmann, S, *Europäisches Schuldvertragsrecht: Das europäische Recht der Unternehmensgeschäfte* (Berlin, de Gruyter, 1999).
Grundmann, S, 'The Optional European Code on the Basis of the Acquis Communautaire – Starting Points and Trends' (2004) 10 *European Law Journal* 698, 710.
Grundmann, S, 'CESL, Legal Nationalism or a Plea for Appropriate Governance' (2012) 8 *European Review of Contract Law* 241.
Grundmann, S, Micklitz, H and Renner, M, *New Private Law Theory in New Private Law Theory: A Pluralist Approach* (Cambridge, Cambridge University Press, 2021).
Grundmann, S, 'Pluralistische Privatrechtstheorie. Prolegomena zu einer pluralistisch gesellschaftswissenschaftlichen Rechtstheorie als normativem Desiderat ("normativer Pluralismus")' (2022) 86 *Rabels Zeitschrift* 364.
Gurvitch, G, *L'idée du droit social. Notion et Système du droit social. Histoire doctrinale depuis le 17 siècle jusqu'à la fin du 19 siècle* (Aalen, Scientiz Verlag, 1972, first published 1932).
Habermas, J, *Between Facts and Norms: Contribution to a Discourse Theory of Law and Democracy* (W Rehg trs, Cambridge, MA, MIT Press, 1996).
Habermas, J, 'Reply to Symposium Participants' in M Rosenfeld and A Arato (eds), *Habermas on Law and Democracy* (Berkeley, CA, University of California Press, 1998) 381–452.
Haferkamp, HP, 'Bürgerliches Gesetzbuch (BGB)' in J Basedow, K Hopt and R Zimmermann (eds), *Max Planck Encyclopedia* (Oxford, Oxford University Press, 2012), 120.

Halberstam, D, 'Systems Pluralism and Institutional Pluralism in Constitutional Law: National, Supranational, and Global Governance' in M Avbelj and J Komarék (eds), *Constitutional Pluralism in the European Union and Beyond* (Oxford, Hart Publishing, 2012).

Halpérin, J-L, *L'Impossible Code civil* (Paris, Presses Universitaires de France, 1992).

Halpérin, J-L, 'Le regard de l'historien' in *Le Code civil 1804–2004 Livre du Bicentenaire* (Dalloz, Paris, 2004) 43.

Halpérin, J-L, *The French Civil Code* (T Weir trs, London, UCL Press, 2006).

Hattenbauer, H (ed), *Thibaut und Savigny. Ihre Programmatichen Schriften*, 2nd edn (Munich, Verlag Franz Vahlen, 2002).

Hartmann, N, *Il problema dell'essere spirituale* (Florence, La Nuova Italia, 1971).

Heiddeger, M, *Die Frage nach dem Ding*, 3rd edn (Tübingen, Mohr Siebeck, 1987).

Heiddeger, M, *Collected Works, vol 63, Ontology – the Hermeneutics of Facticity* (John van Buren trs, Bloomington, Indiana University Press, 1999, first published in 1988; 1923 lectures).

Heiderhoff, B, *Europäisches Privatrecht* (Heidelberg, CF Mueller Verlag, 2012).

Heinrichs, H, 'Umsetzung der EG-Richtilinie ber mißbräuchliche Klauseln in Verbraucherverträchen durch Auslegung' [1995] *Neue Juristische Wochenschrift.*

Heinrichs, H, 'Die Entwicklung des Rechts der Allgemeinen Geschaftsbedingungen im Jahre 1998' [1999] *Neue Juristische Wochenschrift* 1596.

Hellwege, P, 'Understanding Usage in International Contract Law Harmonization' (2018) 66 *American Journal of Comparative Law* 127.

Herresthal, C, 'Die richtlinienkonforme und die verfassungskonforme Auslegung, Privatrecht' [2014] *Jus* 289.

Herzog, T, *A Short History of European Law: The Last Two and a Half Millennia* (Cambridge, Ma, Harvard University Press, 2019).

Hesselink, M, *The New European Private Law* (The Hague, Kluwer Law International, 2002).

Hesselink, M, 'The European Commission's Action Plan: Towards a More Coherent European Contract Law?' (2004) 12 *European Review of Private Law* 397.

Hesselink, M, *CFR and Social Justice: A Short Study for the European Parliament on the Values Underlying the Draft Common Frame of Reference for European Private Law: What Roles for Fairness and Social Justice?* (Munich, Sellier, 2008).

Hesselink, M, 'An Optional Instrument on EU Contract Law: Could it Increase Legal Certainty and Foster Cross-Border Trade?' (European Parliament Policy Department, 2010) PE 425.642.

Hesselink, M, 'A Toolbox for Judges' (2011) 17 *European Law Journal* 441.

Hesselink, M, 'If You Don't Like Our Principles We Have Others' in R Brownsword, H Micklitz, L Niglia and S Weatherill (eds), *The Foundations of European Private Law* (Oxford, Hart Publishing, 2011) 59.

Hesselink, M, 'Private Law, Regulation, and Justice' (2016) 22 *European Law Journal* 681.

Hesselink, M, *Justifying Contract* (Oxford, Oxford University Press, 2021).

Hesselink, MW, 'The General Principles of Civil Law: Their Nature, Roles and Legitimacy' in D Leczykiewicz and S Weatheril (eds), *The Involvement of EU Law in Private Law Relationships* (Oxford, Hart Publishing, 2013) 131–80.

Hien, J and Joerges, C (eds), *Responses of European Economic Cultures to Europe's Crisis Politics: The Example of German–Italian Discrepancies* (Florence, European University Institute, 2018).

Hondius, E, 'Review of Niglia "The Transformation of Contract in Europe"' (2004) 6 *European Review of Private Law* 855.

Irti, N, *L'etá della decodificazione*, 4th edn (Milan, Giuffrè, 1999).

Irti, N, 'L'etá della decodificazione' in *Diritto e Societá* (1978) 613.

Jansen, N, *The Making of Legal Authority: Non-legislative Codifications in Historical and Comparative Perspective* (Oxford, Oxford University Press, 2010).

Jansen, N, 'Legal Pluralism in Europe: National Laws, European Legislation, and Non-legislative Codifications' in L Niglia (ed), *Pluralism and European Private Law* (Oxford, Hart Publishing, 2013).

Jansen, N and Michaels, R, 'Private Law and the State' (2007) 71 *Rabels Zeitschrift* 395.

Jansen, N and Zimmermann, R, 'Recasting the *Acquis Communautaire*? A Critical Evaluation of the Principles of the Existing EC Contract Law' [2008] *MLR* 505.

Jansen, N and Zimmermann, R (eds), *Commentaries on European Contract Laws* (Oxford, Oxford University Press, 2018).
Jessup, PC, *Transnational Law* (New Haven, CT, Yale University Press, 1956).
Joerges, C, 'The Europeanization of Private Law as a Rationalization Process and as a Contest of Disciplines: An Analysis of the Directive on Unfair Terms in Consumer Contracts' (1995) 3 *European Review of Private Law* 175.
Joerges, C, 'The Impact of European Integration on Private law: Reductionist Perceptions' [1997] *European Law Journal* 374.
Joerges, C, 'Europe as Großraum?' in C Joerges and NS Ghaleigh (eds), *Darker Legacies of Law in Europe* (Oxford, Hart Publishing, 2003).
Joerges, C, 'On the Legitimacy of Europeanising Private Law: Considerations on a Justice-Making Law for the EU Multi-level System' (2003) 7(3) *Electronic Journal of Comparative Law.*
Joerges C, 'A New Type of Conflicts of Law as the Legal Paradigm of the Postnational Constellation' in C Joerges and J Falke (eds), *Karl Polanyi, Globalisation and the Potential of Law in Transnational Markets* (Oxford, Hart Publishing, 2011) 465 et seq.
Joerges, C, 'Integration through Law and the Crisis of Law in Europe's Emergency' in D Chalmers, M Jachtenfuchs and C Joerges (eds), *The End of the Eurocrats' Dream: Adjusting to European Diversity* (Cambridge, Cambridge University Press, 2016).
Joerges, C and J Falke (eds), *Karl Polanyi, Globalisation and the Potential of Law in Transnational Markets* (Oxford, Hart Publishing, 2011).
Joerges, C, 'Europe as Großraum?' in C Joerges and NS Ghaleigh (eds), *Darker Legacies of Law in Europe* (Oxford, Hart Publishing, 2003) 167.
Joerges, C and NS Ghaleigh (eds), *Darker Legacies of Law in Europe* (Oxford, Hart Publishing, 2003).
Josserand, L, 'La reconstruction d'un droit de classe' [1937] Dalloz *Chron* 1.
Kadens, E, 'The Myth of the Customary Law Merchant' (2012) 90 *Texas Law Review* 1153.
Kennedy, D, 'Comment on Rudolf Wietholter's "Materialization and Proceduralization in Modern Law" and "Proceduralization of the Category of Law"' in C Joerges and D Trubek (eds), *Critical Legal Thought: An American-German Debate* (Baden-Baden, Nomos Verlagsgesellschaft, 1988).
Kennedy, D, 'Thoughts on Coherence, Social Values and National Tradition in Private Law' in M Hesselink (ed), *The Politics of a European Civil Code* (The Hague, Kluwer Law International, 2006).
Kennedy, D, 'Three Globalizations of Law and Legal Thought: 1850–2000' in DM Trubek and A Santos (eds), *The New Law and Economic Development: A Critical Appraisal* (Cambridge, Cambridge University Press, 2006) 19.
Kennedy D (ed), *Legal Reasoning. Collected Essays* (Aurora, CO, The Davies Group, Publishers, 2008).
Kennedy, D, 'A Transnational Genealogy of Proportionality in Private Law' in R Brownsword, H Micklitz, L Niglia and S Weatherill (eds), *The Foundations of European Private Law* (Oxford, Hart Publishing, 2011) 185.
Kennedy, D, 'Legal Formalism' in NJ Smelser (ed), *Encyclopedia of the Social &. Behavioral Sciences* (Amsterdam, Center for Advanced Study in the Behavioral Sciences, 2001) 13, 8634–38.
Kerber, W and Grundmann, S, 'An Optional European Contract Law Code: Advantages and Disadvantages' (2006) 21 *European Journal of Law and Economics* 215.
Kjaer, PF, 'The Structural Transformation of Embeddedness' in C Joerges and J Falke (eds), *Karl Polanyi, Globalisation and the Potential of Law in Transnational Markets* (Oxford, Hart Publishing, 2011) 85.
Kjaer, PF, *The Law of political economy. Transformation in the Function of Law* (Cambridge, Cambridge University Press, 2020).
Koskenniemi, M, '*The Politics of International Law* (Oxford, Hart Publishing, 2011).
Koskenniemi, M, 'Hegemonic Regimes' in MA Young (ed), *Regime Interaction in International Law: Facing Fragmentation* (New York, Cambridge University Press, 2012) 305.
Koskenniemi, M, 'Sovereignty, Property and Empire: Early Modern English Contexts' (2017) 18 *Theoretical Inquiries in Law* 355.
Koskenniemi, M, 'The Fate of Public International Law: Between Technique and Politics' (2007) 70 *MLR* 1.
Kötz, H, 'Taking Civil Codes Less Seriously' (1987) 50 *MLR* 1.

Kumm, M, 'Who is Afraid of the Total Constitution? Constitutional Rights as Principles and the Constitutionalization of Private Law' (2006) 7 *German Law Journal* 341.

Ladeur, KH, '"We, the European People …" – Relâche?' [2008] *European Law Journal* 14.

Ladeur, KH, 'The State in International Law' in C Joerges and J Falke (eds), *Karl Polanyi, Globalisation and the Potential of Law in Transnational Markets* (Oxford, Hart Publishing, 2011).

Larnaude, F, 'Le Code Civil et la nécessité de sa Revision' in *Le Code civil 1804–1904 Livre du Centenaire* (Paris, Dalloz, 2004) 901.

Larouche, F and Chirico, P (eds), *Economic Analysis of the DCFR: The Work of the Economic Impact Group within CoPECL* (Munich, Sellier, 2010).

Lasser, M, 'Judicial (Self-)Portraits: Judicial Discourses in the French Legal System' (1995) 104 *Yale Law Journal* 1325.

La Torre, M, 'The Poverty of Global Constitutionalism' in L Niglia (ed), *Pluralism and European Private Law* (Oxford, Hart Publishing, 2013) 53.

Laurent, F, *Principes de droit civil français* (1869–78).

Leczykiewicz, D and Weatherill, S (eds), *The Involvement of EU Law in Private Law Relationships* (Oxford, Oxford University Press, 2013).

Legrand, P, 'Kischel's Comparative Law: Fortschrift ohne Fortschrift' [2020] *Journal of Contract Law* 292.

Legrand, P, 'Against a European Civil Code' (1997) 60 *MLR* 44.

Legrand, P, 'Jameses at Play: A Tractation on the Comparison of Laws' (2017) 65 (suppl 1) *American Journal of Comparative Law* 1.

Lenaerts, K, 'Constitutionalism and the Many Faces of Federalism' (1990) 38 *American Journal of Comparative Law* 205.

Lenaerts, K, 'Limits on Limitations: The Essence of Fundamental Rights in the EU' (2019) 20 *German Law Journal* 779.

Lenaerts, K and Gutierrez-Fons, J, 'The Constitutional Allocation of Powers and General Principles of EU Law' [2010] *CML Rev* 1629.

Letto-Vanamo, P, 'Fragmentation and Coherence of Law – A Historical Approach' in P Letto-Vanamo and J Smits (eds), *Coherence and Fragmentation in European Private Law* (Munich, Sellier Europa Publisher, 2012) 151.

Lequette, Y, 'Quelques remarques à propos du projet de code civil européen de M von Bar' [2002] *Dalloz Chron* 2202.

Likosky, MB (ed), *Privatising Development. Transnational Law, Infrastructure and Human Rights* (The Hague, Brill, 2005).

Lindhal, H, 'Authority and the Globalisation of Inclusion and Exclusion: Conceptual and Normative Considerations' (2019) 29 *Duke Journal of Comparative & International Law* 437.

Luhmann, N, *Theory of Society*, vol 1 (R Barett trs, Stanford, Stanford University Press, 2012).

Lukács, G, *History and Class Consciousness* (R Livingstone trs, Cambridge, MA, MIT Press, 1971).

Lurger, B, 'A Radical View of Pluralism?' in L Niglia (ed), *Pluralism and European Private Law* (Oxford, Hart Publishing, 2013) 173.

Madison, J, 'Letter to Jeremy Bentham, London of 8 May 1816 (Washington)' in P Schoefield and J Harris (eds), *Jeremy Bentham, 'Legislator of the World': Writings on Codification, Law, and Education* (Oxford, Clarendon Press, 1998) 36.

Mak, V, *Legal Pluralism in European Private Law* (Oxford, Oxford University Press, 2020).

Markesinis, B, 'Why a Code Is Not the Best Way to Advance the Cause of European Legal Unity' (1998) 5 *European Review of Public Law* 519.

Mattei, U, 'Hard Code Now!' (2002) 2(1) *Global Jurist Frontiers* 1535.

Mattei, U, 'A Theory of Imperial Law: A Study on US Hegemony and the Latin Resistance' (2003) 3(2) *Global Jurist*.

Menéndez, A, 'The Crisis of Law and the European Crises: From the Social and Democratic Rechtsstaat to the Consolidating State of (Pseudo-)Technocratic Governance' (2017) 44 *Journal of Law & Society* 56.

Menendez, A, 'Hermann Heller NOW!' (2015) 21 *European Law Journal* 285.

Mengoni, L, *Diritto e Valori* (Bologna, Il Mulino, 1985).
Mengoni, L, 'L'Europa dei codici o un codice per l'Europa?' (Rome, Centro di Studi e Ricerche di Diritto Comparato e Straniero, 1993).
Mengoni, L, 'Problema e sistema nella controversia sul metodo giuridico' [1976] *Jus* 3.
Mengoni, L, 'Note sul rapporto tra fonti di diritto comunitario e fonti di diritto interno degli Stati membri' in N Lipari (ed), *Diritto Privato Europeo e Categorie Civilistiche* (Napoli, ESI, 1988) 32.
Mengozzi, P, 'The Judicial Protection of Individual Rights and the Principle of Proportionality after Lisbon' in L Niglia (ed), 'Symposium "Balancing in European Law"' (2013–14) 16 *Cambridge Yearbook of European Legal Studies* 335.
Mestmäcker, E-J, *Wirtschaft und Verfassung in der Europäischen Union* (Baden-Baden, Nomos, 2004).
Metzger, A, *Extra legem intra ius: Allegemeine Rechtsgrundsaetze im Europaeischen Privatrecht* (Tübingen, Mohr Siebeck, 2009).
Michaels, R, 'The True Lex Mercatoria: Private Law Beyond the State' (2007) 14 *Indiana Journal of Global Legal Studies* 448.
Michaels, R, 'Of Islands and the Ocean: The Two Rationalities of European Private Law' in R Brownsword, H Micklitz, L Niglia and S Weatherill (eds), *The Foundations of European Private Law* (Oxford, Hart Publishing, 2011) 139.
Michaels, R, 'Code versus Code. Nationalist and Internationalist Images of the Code Civil in the French Resistance to a European Codification' (2012) 8 *European Review of Contract Law* 277.
Michaels, R, 'Legal Medievalism in Lex Mercatoria Scholarship' (2012) 90 *Texas Law Review* 259.
Michaels, R, 'Why We Have No Theory of European Private Law Pluralism' in L Niglia (ed), *Pluralism and European Private Law* (Oxford, Hart Publishing, 2013).
Michaels, R, 'A Symmetry of Asymmetries? A Private-International-Law Reconstruction of Lindahl's Work on Boundaries' (2019) 29 *Duke Journal of Comparative & International Law* 405.
Michaels, R, 'Vorwort zum Symposium: Der Code des Kapitals' (2021) 85 *Rabels Zeitschrift* 852.
Micklitz, H, 'Thoughts on Martijn W Hesselink's, Justifying Contract in Europe, Political Philosophies of European Contract Law' (2022) 2 *European Review of Public Law* 373.
Micklitz, H-W, 'The COVID-19 Threat: An Opportunity to Rethink the European Economic Constitution and European Private Law' (2020) 11 *European Journal of Risk Regulation* 249.
Micklitz, H-W, 'A European Advantage in Legal Scholarship?' in R van Gestel, H-W Micklitz and EL Rubin, *Rethinking Legal Scholarship* (Cambridge, Cambridge University Press, 2017) 262.
Micklitz, H-W, 'The Transformation of Private Law through Competition' (2016) 22 *European Law Journal* 627.
Micklitz, H, 'Monistic Ideology versus Pluralistic Reality – Towards a Normative Design for European Private Law' in L Niglia (ed), *Pluralism and European Private Law* (Oxford, Hart Publishing, 2013).
Micklitz, H, 'The Expulsion of the Concept of Protection from the Consumer Law and the Return of the Social Elements in the Civil Law: A Bittersweet Polemic' (European University Institute, 2012) EUI Working Papers 2012/03.
Micklitz, H, 'The Visible Hand of European Regulatory Private Law' (2009) 28 *Yearbook of European Law* 3.
Micklitz, H-W, 'The Visible Hand of European Regulatory Private Law. The Transformation of European Private Law from Autonomy to Functionalism in Competition and Regulation' (European University Institute, 2008) EUI Working Papers Law 2008/14.
Micklitz, H, *The Politics of Judicial Co-operation in the EU* (Cambridge, Cambridge University Press, 2005).
Micklitz, H, 'The Concept of Competitive Contract Law' (2005) 23 *Penn State International Law Review* 549.
Micklitz, H, and Paterson, D, 'From the Nation State to the Market: The Evolution of EU Private Law' (2012) EUI Working Paper 2012/15.
Micklitz, H and Reich, N, 'The Court and Sleeping Beauty: The Revival of the Unfair Contract Terms Directive' (2014) 51 *CML Rev* 771.
Micklitz, H and Reich, N, *Europäisches Verbraucherrecht* (Baden-Baden, Nomos, 2003).

Mirrow, MC, 'The Power of Codification in Latin America. Simon Bolivar and the Code Napoleon' (2000) 8 *Tulane Journal of International and Comparative Law* 83.
Möllers, C, *The Three Branches* (Oxford, Oxford University Press, 2013).
Möllers, TMJ, 'The Principle of Directive-Compliant Development of the Law and the *Contra Legem* Limit' (2020) 16 *European Review of Contract Law* 465.
Monateri, PG (ed), *Methods of Comparative Law* (Cheltenham, Edward Elgar, 2012).
Monateri, PG, *Dominus Mundi. Political Sublime and the World Order* (Oxford, Hart Publishing, 2018).
Montholon, CT, *Récits de la Captivité de l'Empereur Napoléon à Sainte-Hélène I* (Paris, Paulin, 1847).
Mortari, VP, 'Codice (Storia)' in *Enciclopedia del Diritto* (Milan, Giuffrè, 1970) 227.
Muir Watt, H, 'Private International Law Beyond the Schism' (2011) 2 *Transnational Legal Theory* 347.
Muratori, L, 'Dei Difetti della Giurisprudenza. Trattato', *Venetiis presso* Giambattista Pasquali, 1742.
Nicolò, R, 'Codice Civile' in F Calasso (ed), *Enciclopedia del Diritto*, vol VII (Milan, Giuffrè, 1960), 240.
Nieuwendhuis, H, 'Fundamental Rights Talk. An Enrichment of Legal Discourse in Private Law' in T Barkhuysen and S Lindenbergh (eds), *Constitutionalisation of Private Law* (Leiden, Martinus Nijhoff, 2006) 1.
Niglia, L, 'The Europeanisation of Private Law through Adjudication' (on file with author, 1995).
Niglia, L, 'Diritto giurisprudenziale e direttive comunitarie in materia di diritto privato: note critiche' [1998] *Rivista critica di diritto privato* 459.
Niglia, L, 'Ai confini tra diritto privato e legislazione comunitaria. La teorica dell'obbligo interpretativo' (2001) 1 *Rivista Trimestrale di Diritto e Procedura Civile* 65.
Niglia, L, 'The Non-Europeanization of Private Law' (2001) 4 *European Review of Private Law* 575.
Niglia, L, *The Transformation of Contract in Europe* (The Hague, Kluwer Law International, 2003).
Niglia, L, 'Standard Form Contracts in Europe and North America – One Hundred Years of Unfair Terms?' in C Rickett and T Telfer (eds), *International Perspectives on Consumers' Access to Justice* (Cambridge, Cambridge University Press, 2003b) 101.
Niglia, L, '"The Rules Dilemma" – The Court of Justice and the Dilemma of the Regulation of Standard Form Contracts in Europe' (2006) 13 *Columbia Journal of European Law* 124.
Niglia, L, 'Taking Comparative Law Seriously – Europe's Private Law and the Poverty of the Orthodoxy (Instalment One)' (2006) 54 *American Journal of Comparative Law* 401.
Niglia, L, 'Beyond Enchantment: The Possibility of a New European Private Law (Instalment Two)' (2009) 28 *Yearbook of European Law* 60.
Niglia, L, 'Of Harmonisation and Fragmentation – The Problem of Legal Transplants and the Europeanisation of Private Law (Instalment Three)' (2010) 2 *Maastricht Journal of European and Comparative Law* 116.
Niglia, L, 'Form and Substance in European Constitutional Law: The Social Character of Indirect Effect' (2010) 16 *European Law Journal* 439.
Niglia, L, *Trilogy on European Private Law (2006–2010).*
Niglia, L, *Trilogy on European Constitutional Law (2010–2016).*
Niglia, L, 'Review of *The Cambridge Companion of European Union Law*' (2011) 36 *European Law Review* 760.
Niglia, L, 'The Political Foundations of European Private Law: Editorial Introduction' in R Brownsword, H Micklitz, L Niglia and S Weatherill (eds), *The Foundations of European Private Law* (Oxford, Hart Publishing, 2011) 177.
Niglia, L, 'Of Jurisdictional Balancing' in R Brownsword, H Micklitz, L Niglia and S Weatherill (eds), *The Foundations of European Private Law* (Oxford, Hart Publishing, 2011) 309.
Niglia, L, 'Of Constitutionality and Private Consumer Law in Europe' (2012) 4 *Journal of European Consumer and Market Law* 223.
Niglia, L, 'The Question Concerning the Common Frame of Reference' (2012) 18 *European Law Journal* 736.
Niglia, L (ed), *Pluralism and European Private Law* (Oxford, Hart Publishing, 2013).
Niglia, L, 'Pluralism in a New Key: Between Plurality and Normativity' in L Niglia (ed), *Pluralism and European Private Law* (Oxford, Hart Publishing, 2013) 9.

Niglia, L, 'The Double Life of Pluralism in Europe' in L Niglia (ed), *Pluralism and European Private Law* (Oxford, Hart Publishing, 2013) 249.
Niglia, L (ed), 'Symposium "Balancing in European Law"' (2013–14) 16 *Cambridge Yearbook of European Legal Studies* 333.
Niglia, L, 'Taking Private Law Rights Seriously – Of Balancing and the Jurisprudence of the Court of Justice of the European Union' in L Niglia (ed), 'Symposium "Balancing in European Law"' (2013–14) 16 *Cambridge Yearbook of European Legal Studies* 394.
Niglia, L, 'Law or Economics – Some Thoughts on Transnational Private Law' in K Purnhgen et al (eds), *Varieties of European Economic Law and Regulation* 93 (Berlin, Springer, 2014).
Niglia, L, *The Struggle for European Private Law. A Critique of Codification* (Oxford, Hart Publishing, 2015).
Niglia, L, 'Eclipse of the Constitution' (2016) 22 *European Law Journal* 132.
Niglia, L 'On the "Rationalities" of European Private Law – Between the Internal Market and Law's Discourse' (2016) 22 *European Law Journal* 566.
Niglia, L, 'A "European" Tort Law? Comparative Thoughts on an "Essentially Contested" Private Law Institution' in P Gilliker (ed), *Research Handbook on European Tort Law* (Cheltenham, Edward Elgar, 2017) 321.
Niglia, L, 'Europe and "Crisis" (First Part)' (2018) 3 *European Papers – A Journal on Law and Integration* 601.
Niglia, L, 'Tra Europa e diritto privato. La questione del bilanciamento secondo il diritto civile comparato' (2018) 1 *EDP* 159.
L Niglia, 'Between "Institutionalizing Reason" and Private Law. A Comparative Map of Influences' in M La Torre, L Niglia and M Susi (eds), *The Quest for Rights* (Cheltenham, Edward Elgar, 2019).
Niglia, L, 'The New Transformation of Europe. Arcana Imperii' (2020) 68 *American Journal of Comparative Law* 151.
Niglia, L, 'Comparative Jurisprudence' (unpublished manuscript on file with author, 2022).
Niglia, L, 'Conforming Interpretation' [2022] *European Review of Private Law*.
Niglia, L, 'The European Judicial Saga on Law and Political Economy' '2022' (unpublished manuscript on file with author, 2022).
Niglia, L, 'Public v Private' (unpublished manuscript on file with author, 2022).
Niglia, L, 'Constitutional Europe' (unpublished manuscript on file with author, 2022).
Nipperdey, HC, 'Grundrechte und Privatrecht. Eine Universitätrede' in HC Nipperdey (ed), *Festschrift für Eric Molitor* (Munich, Beck, 1962), 17.
Noerr, KW, *Die Republik der Wirtschaft. Recht, Wirtschaft und Staat in der geschichte Westdeutschlands*, Teil I (Tübingen, Mohr Siebeck, 1999).
Novitz, T, 'A Human Rights Analysis of the Viking and Laval Judgments' (2007) 10 *Cambridge Yearbook of European Legal Studies* 541.
O'Hara, EA and Ribstein, LE, *The Law Market* (Oxford, Oxford University Press, 2009).
Oestmann, P, *Rechtsvielfalt vor Gericht. Rechtsanwendung und Partikluarrecht im Alten Reich* (Frankfurt, Klostermann, 2002).
Oestmann, P (ed), *Gewohnheit. Gebot. Gesetz. Normativität in Geschichte und Gegenwart* (Tübingen, Mohr Siebeck, 2011).
Offe, C, 'Europe Entrapped' (2013) 19(5) *European Law Journal* 95.
Orford, A, 'In Praise of Description' (2012) 25 *Leiden Journal of International Law* 609.
Pastore, B, 'Pluralismi giuridici e trasformazioni del diritto contemporaneo' [2021] *Quaderni Fiorentini* 399.
Patti, S, *Diritto Privato e Codificatione europea* (Milan, Giuffrè, 2007).
Perner, S, *Grundfreiheiten, Grundrechte-Charta und Privatrecht* (Tübingen, Mohr Siebeck, 2013).
Pernice, I and Mayer, F, 'De la constitution composée de l'Europe' [2000] *Revue trimestrelle de droit européen* 623.
Pernice, I and Mayer, F, 'Multilevel Constitutionalism in the European Union' (2002) 27 *European Law Review* 511.

Polanyi, K, *The Great Transformation* (New York, Farrar & Rinehart, 1944).
Portalis, J-E-M, 'Discours préliminaire sur le Code Civil' in *Discours, rapports et travaux inédits sur le Code Civil* (Paris, Joubert, 1844).
Puchta, GF, *Das Gewohnheitsrecht* (Erlangen, Palm, vol I, 1828; vol II 1837).
Raiser, L, *Das Recht der Allgemeinen Geschaftsbedingungen* (Bad Homburg, Gentner, 1961).
Raiser, L, *Die Aufgabe des Privatrechts* (Kronberg/Ts, Athenaeum, 1977).
Ranieri, F, *Das Europäische Privatrecht des 19. und 29. Jahrunderts. Studien zur Rechtsgeschichte und Rechtsvergleichung* (Berlin, Dunker und Humblot, 2007).
Realmonte, F, *Il Problema del Rapporto di Causalità nel Risarcimento del Danno* (Milan, Giuffrè, 1967).
Reich, N, 'Von der Minimal- zur Voll- zur "Halbharmonisierung"' [2010] *Zeitschrift fur Europaisches Privatrecht* 7.
Reich, N, 'Balancing in Private Law and the Imperatives of the Public Interest' in R Brownsword, H Micklitz, L Niglia and S Weatherill (eds), *The Foundations of European Private Law* (Oxford, Hart Publishing, 2011) 221.
Reich, N, 'Pluralism and Private Law in the Union' in L Niglia (ed), *Pluralism and European Private Law* (Oxford, Hart Publishing, 2013) 73.
Reimann, MW, 'The Historical School against Codification: Savigny, Carter, and the Defeat of the New York Civil Code' (1989) 37 *American Journal of Comparative Law* 95.
Reimann, MW, 'Product Liability in a Global Context: The Hollow Victory of the European Model' (2003) 2 *European Review of Private Law* 128.
Reimann, MW, 'Comparative Law and Private International Law' in M Reimann and R Zimmermann (eds), *The Oxford Handbook of Comparative Law*, 2nd edn (Oxford, Oxford University Press, 2008) 1375.
Reimann, M, 'The American Advantage in Global Lawyering' (2014) 78 *Rabels Zeitschrift* 1–36.
Reimann, M, 'The European Advantage in Global Lawyering' (2018) 82 *Rabels Zeitschrift* 885.
Reimann, MW, Hathaway, JC, Dickinson, TL and Samuels, JH, *Transnational Law. Cases and Materials* (St Paul, MN, West, 2013).
Remien, O, Herrler, S and Limmer, P (eds), *Gemeinsames Europäisches Kaufrecht für die EU?* (Munich, CH Beck, 2012).
Rémy, P, 'Regards sur le code' in *Le Code Civil 1804–2004 Livre du Bicentenaire* (Paris, Dalloz, 2004) 99.
Riles, A, 'The Anti-Network' [2009] *American Journal of Comparative Law* 612.
Rodotà, S, 'Ideologie e tecniche della riforma del diritto civile' (1967) *Rivista del Diritto Commerciale* I, 84.
Rodotà, S, 'Il Codice civile e il processo costituente europeo' in V Roppo (ed), *A European Civil Code? Perspectives and Problems* (Milan, Giuffrè, 2005) 183.
Rosas, A, 'Balancing Fundamental Rights in EU Law' in L Niglia (ed), 'Symposium "Balancing in European Law"' (2013–14) 16 *Cambridge Yearbook of European Legal Studies* 348.
Roth, H, 'EG-Richtlinien und Buegerliches Recht' [1999] *Juristen Zeitung* 529.
Ruffert, M, *Vorrang der Verfassung und Eigenständigkeit des Privatrechts* (Tübingen, Mohr Siebeck, 2001).
Rupp, CS, 'Gestaltungsspielraum für die Kautelarpraxis im Sachenrecht? – Beispiele aus dem Wohnungseigentumsrecht' (2018) 82(2) *Rabels Zeitschrift* 315.
Rutgers, J, 'An Optional Instrument and Social Dumping' [2006] *European Review of Contract Law* 199.
Sacco, R, 'Legal Formants' (1991) 39 *American Journal of Comparative Law* 1.
Sacco, R, 'Rapport de Synthése' in Association Henri Capitant des amis de la culture juridique française, *La circulation du smodèle juridique français* (Paris, Journées franco-italiennes/Litec, 1994).
Sacco, R and De Nova, G, *Il Contratto* (Turin, UTET, 1993).
Saleilles, R, *Essai d'une théorie générale de l'obligation* (Paris, Librairie Cotillon, 1890).
Saleilles, R, *De la déclaration de volonté: Contribution à l'étude de l'acte juridique dans le Code civil allemand* (Paris, F Pichon, 1901).
Saleilles, R, *Étude sur la théorie générale de l'obligation d'après le premier Code civil pour l'Empire Allemand*, 3rd edn (Paris, LGD, 1914, first published 1889).

Saleilles, R, *De la personnalité juridique: Histoire et théorie* (Paris, 1910).
Saleilles, R, 'Préface' in F Gény (ed), *Méthode d'interprétation et sources en droit privé positif. Essai Critique* (Paris, LGD, 1919).
Samuel, G, 'Is Legal Neo-Formalism Nothing but Pastiche?' [2020] *Journal of Contract Law* 347.
Samuel, G, *Law of Obligations* (Cheltenham, Edward Elgar, 2010)
Samuel, G, *An Introduction to Comparative Law and Method* (Hart Publishing, 2014).
Samuel, G, *Rethinking Legal Reasoning* (Cheltenham, Edward Elgar, 2018).
Savatier, R, *Les Métamorphoses économiques et sociales du droit privé d'aujourd'hui*, 2nd edn (Paris, Dalloz, 1959).
Schleiermacher, F, *Zur Philosophie* (1938).
Schmid, CU, 'The Instrumentalist Conception of the Acquis Communautaire in Consumer Law and its Implications on a European Contract Law Code' (2005) 1 *European Review of Contract Law* 211.
Schmid, CU, 'The ECJ as a Constitutional and a Private Law Court', ZERP-DO 4/2006.
Schmid, CU, *Die Instrumentalisierung des Privatrechts durch die Europäische Union. Privatrecht und Privatrechtskonzeptionen in der Entwicklung der Europäischen Integrationsverfassung* (Baden-Baden, Nomos, 2010).
Schmidt, K, '*Lex mercatoria*: Allheilmittel? Rätsel? Chimäre?' in J Murakami et al (eds), *Globalisierung und Recht* (Berlin, de Gruyter, 2007) 153.
Sciarra, S, '*Viking* and *Laval*: Collective Labour Rights and Market Freedoms in the Enlarged EU' (2007–08) 10 *Cambridge Yearbook of European Legal Studies* 563.
Sciarra, S, *L'Europa e il Lavoro. Solidarieta' e Conflitto in Tempi di Crisi* (Rome, Laterza, 2013).
Slaughter, AM, 'A Typology of Transjudicial Communication' (1994–95) 29 *University of Richmond Law Review* 99.
Schlechtriem, P, *Restitution und Bereicherungsaugleich in Europa: Eine Rechtsvergleichende Darstellung* (Tübingen, Mohr Siebeck, vol I, 2001; vol II, 2001).
Schulte-Nölke, H, Zoll, F, Jansen N and Schulze R (eds), *Der Entwurf für ein optionales europäisches Kaufrecht* (Munich, Sellier, 2012).
Sclopis, F, *Storia della legislazione italiana, III, Dall'epoca della rivoluzione francese [1789] a quella delle riforme italiane [1847], parte prima* (Turin, 1864).
Shapiro, M, 'Comparative Law and Comparative Politics' (1980) 53 *Southern California Law Review* 537.
Smits, J, 'A Radical View on Pluralism' in L Niglia (ed), *Pluralism and European Private Law* (Oxford, Hart Publishing, 2013) 161.
Smits, J, 'Party Choice and the Common European Sales Law, or: How to Prevent the CESL from Becoming a Lemon on the Law Market' (2012) 50 *CML Rev* 51.
Smits, J, 'Private Law and Fundamental Rights: A Sceptical View' in T Barkhuysen and S Lindenbergh (eds), *Constitutionalisation of Private Law* (Leiden, Martinus Nijhoff, 2006).
Snyder, F, 'The Effectiveness of European Community Law: Institutions, Processes, Tools and Techniques' (1993) 56 *MLR* 19.
Snyder, FG, *The EU, The WTO and China. Legal Pluralism and International Trade Regulation* (Oxford, Hart Publishing, 2010).
Snyder, FG, 'Better Regulation in EU Law: Variations on a Theme' in N Rubio and F Peraldi-Leneuf (eds), *La fabrication du droit de l'Union europénne dans le context du Mieux Légiférer: D modèle ã la réalité* (Aix-en-Provence, Presses de l'Université Aix-Marseille, 2017).
Solari, G, *Individualismo e Diritto Privato* (Turin, Giappichelli, 1959).
Solari, G, *Filosofia del Diritto Privato. Volume II. Storicismo e Diritto Privato* (Turin, Giappichelli, 1971, first published 1940).
Somek, A, *Individualism: An Essay on the Authority of the European Union* (Oxford, Oxford University Press, 2008).
Stein, E, 'International Integration and Democracy: No Love at First Sight' (2001) 95 *American Journal of International Law* 489.
Stein, E, 'The European Coal and Steel Community: The Beginning of Its Judicial Process' (1955) 55 *Columbia Law Review* 985.

Storme, ME, 'The Foundations of Private Law in a Multi-level Structure: Balancing, Distribution of Law-making Power and Other Constitutional Issues' in R Brownsword, H Micklitz, L Niglia and S Weatherill (eds), *The* Foundations *of European Private Law* (Oxford, Hart Publishing, 2011) 379.

Study Group on Social Justice in European Private Law, 'Social Justice in European Contract Law: A Manifesto' (2004) 10 *European Law Journal* 653.

Supiot, A, *Homo Juridicus. Essai sur la Fonction Anthropologique du Droit* (Paris, Editions du Seuil, 2005).

Supiot, A, 'The Public–Private Relations in the Context of Today's Refeudalization' (2013) 11 *International Journal of Constitutional Law* 129, 141.

Tarello, G, *Storia della Cultura Giuridica Moderna. Assolutismo e Codificazione del Diritto* (Bologna, Il Mulino, 1976).

Tavilla, E (ed), *Giuseppe Luosi, giurista italiano ed europeo. Traduzioni, tradizioni e tradimenti della codificazione. A 200 anni dalla traduzione in italiano del Code Napoléon (1806–2006)*, Atti del Convegno Internazionale di Studi, Mirandola-Modena, 19–20 October 2006 (Carpi, APM Edizioni, 2009) 337.

Teubner, G. *Juridification: Concepts, Aspects, Limits, Solutions in Juridification of Social Spheres: A Comparative Analysis of the Area of Labour, Corporate Anti-Trust and Social Welfare Law* (Boston, MA, Walter De Gruyter, 1987).

Teubner, G, 'Legal Irritants: Good Faith in British Law or How Unifying Law Ends Up in New Divergencies' (1998) 61 *MLR* 1, 11.

Teubner, G, 'Societal Constitutionalism: Alternatives to State-Centred Constitutional Theory?' in C Joerges, I-J Sand and G Teubner (eds), *Transnational Governance and Constitutionalism* (Oxford, Hart Publishing, 2004) 3–28.

Teubner, G, *Constitutional Fragments. Societal Constitutionalism and Globalization* (Oxford, Oxford University Press, 2012).

Teubner, G, 'The Constitution of Non-monetary Surplus Value' [2020] *Social and Legal Theory* 1.

Thibaut, AFJ, *Über die Notwendigkeit eines allgemeinen bürgerlichen Rechts für Deutschland* (Heidelberg, Mohr und Zimmer, 1814), reprinted in H Hattenbauer, *Thibaut und Savigny. Ihre Programmatisches Schriften* (Munich, Verlag Franz Vahlen, 1973).

Tridimas, T, 'Fundamental Rights, General Principles of EU Law, and the Charter' in L Niglia (ed), 'Symposium "Balancing in European Law"' (2013–14) 16 *Cambridge Yearbook of European Legal Studies* 362.

Tridimas, T, *The General Principles of EU Law* (Oxford, Oxford University Press, 2007).

Ungari, P, *L'eta' della codificazione. Lotta per la codificazione e scuole di giurisprudenza nel Risorgimento* (Naples, Edizioni Scientifiche Italiane, 1967).

Van Caenegem, RC, *Judges, Legislators and Professors: Chapters in European Legal History* (Cambridge, Cambridge University Press, 1987).

Van Caenegem, RC, *A Historical Introduction to Private Law* (DEL Johnston trs, Cambridge, Cambridge University Press, 1992).

van Dam, C, *European Tort Law* (Oxford, Oxford University Press, 2006).

Van Gerven, W, 'The ECJ Case law as a Means of Unification of Private Law?' in AS Hartkamp et al (eds), *Towards a European Civil Code*, 2nd edn (The Hague, Kluwer Law International, 1998) 91.

Van Gerven, W, 'Codifying European Private Law: Top Down and Bottom Up' in S Grundmann and J Stuyck (eds), *An Academic Green Paper on European Contract Law* (The Hague, Kluwer Law International, 2002), 405.

Van Gerven, W, 'European Private Law: Unification, Harmonisation or Coordination?' in R Brownsword, H Micklitz, L Niglia and S Weatherill (eds), *The Foundations of European Private Law* (Oxford, Hart Publishing, 2011) 337.

Varga, C, *Codification as a Socio-historical Phenomenon* (Budapest, Akadémiai Kiadó, 1991).

Varga, C, 'The Contemporaneity of Lukács' Ideas with Modern Social Theoretical Thought' (2013) 99 *Archiv fuer Rechts- und Sozialphilosophie* 42.

Vauchez, A and de Witte, B (eds), *Lawyering Europe: European Law as a Transnational Social Field* (Oxford, Hart Publishing, 2013).

Vetter, J, 'Kautelarpraxis und M&A-Verträge' (2018) 82(2) *Rabels Zeitschrift* 267.
Vogel, L, 'Re-codification civile et renouvellement des sources internes' in *Livre Bicentenaire* 159. Le Code civil 1804–2004 – Livre du Bicentenaire Dalloz 2004.
Vesting, T, 'Constitutionalism or Legal Theory' in C Joerges et al (eds), *Transnational Governance and Constitutionalism* (Oxford, Hart Publishing, 2004).
Von Bar, C, *The Common European Law of Torts* (Oxford, Oxford University Press, vol I, 1998; vol II, 2000).
Von Bar, C, 'A CFR for European Private Law – Academic Efforts and Political Realities' (2008) 23 *Tulane European and Civil Law Forum* 37.
Von Bar, C and Clive, E (eds), *Principles, Definitions and Model Rules of European Private Law. Draft Common Frame of Reference* (Oxford, Oxford University Press, 2009).
Von Bar, C et al (eds), *Principles, Definitions and Model Rules of European Private Law: The Draft Common Frame of Reference* (Munich, Sellier, interim outline edition, 2008; outline edition, 2009).
von Savigny, FC, *Vom Beruf unserer Zeit für Gesetzgebung und Rechtswissenschaft* (Heidelberg, Mohr und Zimmer, 1814); translated as *Of the Vocation of Our Age for Legislation and Jurisprudence* (A Hayward trs, London, Littlewood & Co, 1831).
von Savigny, FC, *System des heutigen römischen Rechts* (Berlin, Scientia-Verlag, 1840–49).
Wagner, G and Eidenmueller, HGM, 'Down by Algorithms? Siphoning Rents, Exploiting Biases and Shaping Preferences – The Dark Side of Personalized Transactions (March 30, 2018)' [2019] *University of Chicago Law Review* 581 and Oxford Legal Studies Research Paper No 20/2018.
Walker, N, 'The Idea of Constitutional Pluralism' (2002) 65 *MLR* 317.
Walker, N, 'The Anti-political Polity' (2010) 73 *MLR* 141.
Walker, N, *Intimations of Global Law* (Cambridge, Cambridge University Press, 2015).
Watson, A, *The Making of the Civil Law* (Cambridge, MA, Harvard University Press, 1981).
Weatherill, S, 'The Constitutional Competence of the EU to Deliver Social Justice' (2006) 2 *European Review of Contract Law* 136.
Weatherill, S, 'Competence and European Private Law' in C Twigg-Flesner (ed), *The Cambridge Companion to European Union Private Law* (Cambridge, Cambridge University Press, 2010).
Weatherill, S, 'Viking Line and Laval: The EU Internal Market Perspective' in J Prassl and M Freedland (eds), *EU Law in the Member States: Viking, Laval, and Beyond* (Oxford, Hart Publishing, 2014) 23–40.
Weatherill, S (ed), *Better Regulation* (Oxford, Hart Publishing, 2020).
Weatherill, S, 'The Multi-level Structure of Private Law: Introduction' in R Brownsword, H Micklitz, L Niglia and S Weatherill (eds), *The Foundations of European Private Law* (Oxford, Hart Publishing, 2011) 319.
Weber, M, *Rechtssoziologie* (J Winckelmann ed, Neuwied, Luchthand, 1960) 249.
Weber, M, *Economy and Society* (G Roth and C Wittich ed, E Fischoff et al trs, Berkeley, University of California Press, 1968) I, 53.
Weber, M, 'Die Drei Typen der legitimen Herrschaft' in M Weber, *Gesalmmelte Aufsäetze zur Wissenschaftslehre*, 7th edn (J Wincklemann ed, Tübingen, JCB Mohr, 1988) 475–88.
Weiler, JHH, *Il sistema comunitario europeo* (Bologne, Il Mulino, 1985).
Weiler, JHH, 'The Transformation of Europe' (1991) 100 *Yale Law Journal* 2405.
Weiler, JHH, *To Be a European Citizen: Eros and Civilization* (Toronto, Toronto University Press, 1998).
Weiler, JHH, *The Constitution of Europe; 'Do the New Clothes Have an Emperor?' and Other Essays on European Integration* (Cambridge, Cambridge University Press, 1999).
Weir, T, *An Introduction to Tort Law* (Oxford, Oxford University Press, 2006).
Wenckstern, M, 'Kautelarpraxis und Erbrecht' (2018) 82(2) *Rabels Zeitschrift* 299.
Wendel, M, 'Paradoxes of Ultra-Vires Review: A Critical Review of the PSPP Decision and Its Initial Reception' (2020) 21 *German Law Journal* 979.
Whitman, JQ, 'A Simple Story' (2006) 4 *Rechtsgeschichte* 206.
Wieacker, F, *Das Sozialmodell der klassischen Privatrechtsgesetzbuecher und die Entwicklung der modernen Gesellschaft* (Karlsruhe, CF Mueller, 1953).

Wieacker, F, 'Aufstieg, Blüte und Krisis der Kodifikationsidee' in *Festschrift für Gustav Boehmer* (Bonn, Röhrscheid, 1954) 34.
Wieacker, F, *A History of Private Law in Europe* (Oxford, Clarendon Press, 1995).
Wilhelmsson, T, 'Varieties of Welfarism in European Contract Law' (2004) 10 *European Law Journal* 712.
Wurmnest, W, 'Kautelarpraxis und Allgemeine Geschäftsbedingungen' (2018) 82 *Rabels Zeitschrift* 346.
Wüstendörfer, H, 'Die deutsche Rechtswissenschaft am Wendepunkt' (1913) 110 *Archiv für die civilistische Praxis* 224.
Zagrebelsky, G, 'La giustizia costituzionale nel 2003' *Giur. Cost.* 2004.
Zenati-Castaing, F, 'L'avenir de la codification' (2011) 63 *Revue Internationale de Droit Comparé* 355.
Zimmermann, R, 'Codification: History and Present Significance of an Idea' (1995) 3 *European Review of Private Law* 95.
Zimmermann, R, *Roman Law, Contemporary Law, European Law: The Civilian Tradition Today* (Oxford, Oxford University Press, 2001).
Zimmermann, R, 'The Present State of European Private Law' (2009) 57 *American Journal of Comparative Law* 479.
Zimmermann, R, 'Codification: The Civilian Experience Reconsidered on the Eve of a Common European Sales Law' (2012) 8 *European Review of Contract Law* 367.
Zuleeg, M, *Auslegung europäischen Privatrechts und angeglichenen Rechts* (Baden-Baden, Nomos, 1999).
Zumbansen, P, 'Transnational Law, With and Beyond Jessup' (2020) TLI Think! Paper 23/2020.
Zumbansen, P (ed), *The Many Lives of Transnational Law. Critical Engagements with Jessup's Bold Proposal* (Cambridge, Cambridge University Press, 2020).
Zweigert, KE and Kötz, H, *An Introduction to Comparative Law* (T Weir trs, Oxford, Clarendon Press, 1998).

INDEX

Introductory Note

References such as '178–79' indicate (not necessarily continuous) discussion of a topic across a range of pages. Wherever possible in the case of topics with many references, these have either been divided into sub-topics or only the most significant discussions of the topic are listed. Because the entire work is about (in alphabetical order) comparative law, constitutional law, European private law, European Union law, private law, the use of these terms (and certain others which occur constantly throughout the book) as an entry point has been restricted. Information will be found under the corresponding detailed topics.

www.ingramcontent.com/pod-product-compliance
Ingram Content Group UK Ltd.
Pitfield, Milton Keynes, MK11 3LW, UK
UKHW020817290926
15470UKWH00003B/1218

9 781509 925254